GREIL MARCUS

The Dustbin of History

Harvard University Press   Cambridge, Massachusetts 1995

Library of Congress Cataloging-in-Publication Data

Marcus, Greil.
  The dustbin of history / Greil Marcus.
    p.   cm.
  Includes bibliographical references and index.
  ISBN 0-674-21857-4 (alk. paper)
  1. Popular culture—United States—History—20th century.
2. Arts, Modern—20th century—United States. 3. Arts, American.
4. Popular culture—History—20th century. 5. Arts, Modern—20th
century. 6. History, Modern—20th century. I. Title.
E169.04.M365 1995
973.9—dc20

95-8876

For my father,
who with family stories,
legends of the New Deal,
and shelves of mysterious books
first opened this book for me

Contents

Settlements

The Dustbin of History

Sketch

There's a story that's bothered me for a long time—a tale from a newspaper clipping I've hoarded for over a decade, though its background goes more than twenty years further into the past. In the early 1960s, a Louisiana misanthrope named John Kennedy Toole wrote a sprawling comic rant he called *A Confederacy of Dunces*. The hero of the book was one Ignatius Reilly, a joyous paranoid who goes to the movies solely to be outraged; a scholar of Boethius for whom the whole of the modern world is a travesty confirming his mission as holy fool and gnostic prophet; an overweight, unsightly gasbag (literally, unfortunately) who stalks the streets of New Orleans with a sword and a shield, dreaming of leading "many protest marches complete with the traditional banners and posters, but these would say, 'End the Middle Class,' 'The Middle Class Must Go.' I am not above tossing a small Molotov cocktail or two, either."

The book's title came from Swift: "When a true genius appears in the world, you may know him by this sign, that the dunces are all in confederacy against him." Unable to interest a publisher, Toole killed himself in 1969; he was thirty-two. Through the persistence of his mother, Thelma D. Toole, who enlisted the aid of Walker Percy, a box of manuscript ("a badly smeared, barely readable carbon," Percy said) was turned into a book and published in 1980 by Louisiana State University Press. It became a best seller and won the Pulitzer Prize.

Four years later, on 15 January 1984, *San Francisco Examiner* staff writers Charles C. Hardy and John Jacobs filed this report on the looming New Hampshire presidential primary:

Hanover, N.H.—One would think that the Democratic National Convention was being held this week at the old Hanover Inn here at Dartmouth College rather than six months from now in San Francisco.

On the eve of today's televised debate on public television between the eight major Democratic presidential candidates, this elegant old inn was buzzing with ramrod-straight Secret Service agents, hordes of media workers with multicolored identification tags around their necks and, here and there, a certified presidential candidate.

As the candidates talked to a crowd of reporters in a large room with antique chests, sedate sofas and brass chandeliers, a lonely, well-dressed man paced outside the hotel carrying a yellow sign that read: "Why Won't the Democrats Let Toole Debate? What Are They Afraid Of?"

The man holding the sign, John Kennedy Toole, a 39-year-old New Yorker, said he is running for president to call attention to the 2 million homeless in this country "who are out in the cold."

"The criterion for being part of this debate," he told the only reporter in sight, "seems to be national media coverage. Nowhere in the Constitution does it say that."

"No one will talk to me. I'd much rather do that than stand out here holding this sign in the cold, you understand."

If this was not the John Kennedy Toole who wrote *A Confederacy of Dunces* (as evidence, the man's by-then pedantically correct use of "criterion" was scarier than the fact that as *Dunces* ended Ignatius Reilly lit out for New York with his Jewish girlfriend), then it was someone who had read the book and, honoring its author by taking his name, had decided to act it out. Or

so it seemed to me in 1984, or so I hoped. Though the pieces in
this book were published as everyday critical work over the course
of nearly two decades, from 1975 to 1993, it was this story that
crystallized the suspicion and worry that lie behind each of them.
The worry is that our sense of history, as it takes shape in everyday
culture, is cramped, impoverished, and debilitating; that the commonplace assumption that history exists only in the past is a
mystification powerfully resistant to any critical investigations that
might reveal this assumption to be a fraud, or a jail. The suspicion
is that we are living out history, making it and unmaking it—for-
getting it, denying it—all of the time, in far more ways than we
have really learned. "Culture is elusive," Robert Cantwell writes
in *Ethnomimesis,* beginning a passage that I might have begun
with the word "history":

It passes secretly, often silently, telepathically, between a parent and a
child who does not even realize she has been looking on or listening
until years later, when she somehow discovers what she has learned and
can now do herself; it ripens, unintended, often unconsciously, in
dreams, suddenly and unexpectedly to reveal itself in an expression or a
turn of phrase, in a way of relating to one's children or one's spouse, or,
at another level, in our musical or pictorial preferences, in the narratives
we construct about ourselves and others or to which we turn for understanding. It may arise by accident, from a half-remembered memory,
from fingers or hands idling with instruments and tools. Or it may simply
persist, with a peculiar life of its own, in a circuitous transit over several
centuries, from courtly to commercial to domestic culture and back
again.

Later in the book, Cantwell says the same thing in different
language:

Where orders of meaning have vanished entirely, and the sign erupts in
its incandescence onto the cultural surface, we begin history anew and

call our epoch by new names; the more deeply hidden the old order of meaning, the more powerful and persistent is our passion to interpret the isolate material sign—a turbulent, urgent desire to remember what we know we know.

Which is another way of saying something else Cantwell says: "We are all doctors and fortune tellers."

> You are pitiful isolated individuals; you are bankrupts; your role is played out. Go where you belong from now on—into the dustbin of history!
>
> —Trotsky to the Mensheviks, at the Second All-Russian Congress of the Soviets, 25 October 1917

"The dustbin of history" is one of our terms for finality, for putting history behind us, where it seems to belong. There it was as Trotsky spoke on the stage of world history, our present-day ironies curling around him like an invisible snake. There it was in Hanover, New Hampshire, materializing right before your eyes if you were reading a certain story in a certain moment: no thing of the past or even for it, but a trap, a death sentence, or maybe a goal, a promised land, that can be found at any time. It can suck you in; perhaps it can be escaped. Leon Trotsky consigned the Mensheviks to the dustbin of history in 1917, and there they remain, with his shade now keeping their company. John Kennedy Toole consigned himself to the dustbin of history in 1969, and in 1980 was rescued from it—yet he wrote the sort of book that, no matter how or when it is encountered, no matter how many prizes and encomiums it might carry on its cover, speaks only from the dustbin of history.

Probably because a sense of time-marches-on only freezes history, or freezes people out of it, the pieces here are not in any chronological order. They are about the way history is cheapened and restricted; about those people, acts, and events that are casually left out of history or forcefully excluded from it, and about the way much of history finds its voice or bides its time in art works. These concerns are motives; as motives they are arguments; as arguments I hope they are, as a whole, a group of stories. There are some common characters. There are a lot of Germans here, both because in the first half of the twentieth century Germans probably made more history than any other people, and because in the second half of the century they looked so fervently to culture not only as a substitute for history, as a means of escaping from it, but also as a field for making history, for changing their and anyone else's sense of what history is. There are a lot of cowboys, both because the postwar Germans loved cowboys and because an American sense of the past and of action remains bound up in primitive, nineteenth-century wishes and fears. There are a lot of losers, people removed from history as soon as they flatter themselves they can make it. Today, in 1995, six years on from 1989, it is of course necessary to identify Chai Ling, one of the first voices heard in these pages, as a student leader at Tiananmen Square; it was necessary to do so in 1989. I don't know how many years will pass before it will be necessary to identify Tiananmen Square; plenty of people, all over the world, for all kinds of reasons, are working hard to ensure that it is not very many.

"The cultural standards governing emotion . . . have influenced me since childhood (*Gone with the Wind*, *Phèdre* or the songs of Edith Piaf are just as decisive as the Oedipus complex)," says the narrator of Annie Ernaux's *Simple Passion*, and it was in culture—movies, songs, novels, spy thrillers, paintings, TV shows—that I heard a lot of dustbin talk. It was the talk of people waiting, speeches delivered in exile, manifestoes of limitless possibility and desire: "demon-strations," as the San Francisco collagist Jess once put it, "of the hermetic critique lockt up in Art." "How much history can be communicated by pressure on a guitar string?" Robert Palmer asked in *Deep Blues*, and the answer is, more than we will ever know. His question, could I live up to it, would be the epigraph on a great number of the pieces here: how much history can be communicated by John Wayne pressing on a character? Palmer's question revised, or gutted—how much can be transcended by the relief from history so often granted art—could work as an epigraph for the piece on Susan Sontag, or that on Robert Altman's *Nashville* and E. L. Doctorow's *Ragtime*. In their work, it seemed to me, culture replaces history—history as such is its own dustbin, and very nearly everyone is in it.

My tending toward culture, rather than conventionally structured incidents of politics or economics, makes the question of distortion constant here—along with the belief that distortion is not the same as dishonesty. The process of criticism is to me fundamentally mysterious. Often I cannot remember, or even exactly reconstruct, how I came to produce certain arguments—but that, I think, is a result of attempting to trust the artifact, the object of scrutiny. I take it on faith (until proven wrong, or until I run into my own limits) that a historical event or a cultural artifact that has sparked the enthusiasm, discomfort, or confusion of the critic will, if pressed hard enough, or merely in certain uncertain ways, give up untold and nearly infinite secrets. My method, if there is one, is to try to treat historical events as cultural happenstances and cultural happenstances as historical events—or to let the terms of one fade into those of the other.

It is easy enough to say why such an approach is foolish: one can be fooled. This does not seem to me, in our time, the greatest risk. Perhaps the most pernicious strain of contemporary criticism says one thing before it says anything else, says it to whatever historical event or cultural happenstance is supposedly at issue: *You can't fool me*. I think criticism, or a critical engagement with history, has a good deal to do with a willingness to be fooled: to take an idea too far, to bet too much on too small an object or occasion, to be caught up and even swept away. What I am always looking for, as in the story from the *San Francisco Examiner*—in the weird mix of a real-life author acting out the role of his own fictional character courtesy of a second real person confronting a conventionally structured political incident—is an objective platform for a subjective revision of our relations to the past, the present, and the future. Often the hard evidence is inadequate or close to altogether lacking for the stories we want to tell, or that we want to hear. Such an absence of hard facts makes faithfulness to those facts that are extant of nearly absolute importance, while at the same time leading us to invent, imagine, or experiment with versions of history, of events and their actors, that go well beyond or completely past real facts.

This is not a balancing act, but an imbalancing act. Some schools of history, Eric Hobsbawm said in 1993 with undisguised exasperation, assert "that all 'facts' claiming objective existence are simply intellectual constructions. In short, there is no clear difference between fact and fiction. But there is," he said,

and for historians, even for the most militantly antipositivist ones among us, the ability to distinguish between the two is absolutely essential. We cannot invent our facts. Either Elvis Presley is dead or he isn't. The question can be answered unambiguously on the basis of evidence, insofar as reliable evidence is available, which is sometimes the case. Either the present Turkish government, which denies the attempted genocide of the Armenians in 1915, is right or it is not.

The echoes of Hobsbawm's last sentence (picking up, like a dumpster-diver in our dustbin, Hitler's famous dismissal of possible reactions to the planned extermination of the Jews, "Who today remembers the Armenians?") are all through this book, sometimes as an insistence on hard facts, but sometimes as an insistence on the role of radical fantasies—or a willingness to be fooled—in any living sense of history. That is where the pieces on Nazi-hunting thrillers come into play, along with those on *The Manchurian Candidate* and Bob Dylan's song "Blind Willie McTell." Many of our most ambitious critical works, while making claims on objective truth, are precisely radical fantasies, placing the appropriate bets for the appropriate stakes: wagering everything on the hunch that the world is not as it seems. That is how I have tried to come to terms with Camille Paglia's insistence that the real gravitational pull of our history is pagan, not Judeo-Christian, or David Rosenberg and Harold Bloom's attempt to retrieve a hidden, original Bible, or Alexander Marshack's reconstruction of the Upper Paleolithic in Western Europe. In other hands, the same impulse to reveal what seems to lie beneath the surfaces of ordinary history turns lurid, as some abandon any pretense to truth in order to seek it, or anyway dramatize it, without the fetters of manners or rules. This is a gnostic strain of history, which Roberto Calasso, in *The Ruin of Kasch,* describes in terms little different from those Robert Cantwell applies to ordinary cultural transmission: as "largely made up of *'intersignes'* (as Massignon calls them), unusual warnings, coincidences (as historians call them, to avoid them), erratic forms, buried relics, physiognomic marks, constellations latent in the sky of thought." Far more than a willingness to be fooled, this is the work of gamblers anteing up with counterfeit money, the respectable word "hidden" overtaken by the disreputable word "occult." In these pages that strain breaks the surface again and again, whether in the form of the Nazis' secret victory in the Second World War as lined out in Thomas Gifford's *The Wind Chill Factor,* the Masonic symbols issuing prophecies in Bruce Conner's collages, or Umberto Eco earnestly rubbing the magic lamp of his *Foucault's Pendulum,* claiming he does so only to prove there is no genie inside. The distinction between fact and fiction is necessary, but that is not all it is; it may be as useful as a precondition for fiction based in history, or conniving to change it.

Such a suspicion opens up in two directions. There is a sense of history as a story—a story that, by definition, did not have to turn out as it did. There are those moments in history when possibilities quickly lost to us, if we acknowledge only the official record, once loomed up; there are those moments when, as we reconstruct a place and time, things that truly did happen, that have irrevocably shaped us, nevertheless seem like impossibilities, or miracles, too unlikely, too accidental, too erratic or coincidental, to carry any real history with them. Tiananmen Square is an example of the first kind of moment; Deborah Chessler's work in the creation of rhythm and blues is an example of the second kind. I hope some of the stories here take in both, because those kinds of moments represent, I think, the true borders of history, as we make it, or unmake it—borders well beyond those within which what we call history is usually situated. All in all, this book means to be about how we situate ourselves in history: how we understand ourselves as creatures of the past and makers of our own present, and our own future—and, by implication, of our own pasts.

Maps

The Dustbin of History in a World Made Fresh

Workmen are dragging bronze statues on dollies. This is the dustbin of history: Stalin is here, his marble nose broken off, along with other depedestaled heroes such as Dzerzhinsky, Molotov, Kalinin, Sverdlov, all freshly ripped down, all eating grass.

—Alan Jolis, in "Coup de Grace," on the aftermath of the attempted coup in the Soviet Union, *Vogue*, November 1991

We've heard a good deal about the dustbin of history over the last few years—events seem to draw writers and readers naturally to the metaphor, so irresistibly that it rewrites the past, serving as a screen headline over fables that, we must sometimes remind ourselves, we once believed. Here, from a 27 November 1989 UPI dispatch, one headed "NO WORDS ARE TOO GREAT TO DESCRIBE CEAUȘESCU," is a favorite example:

Warsaw—When it comes to describing newly re-elected Romanian President Nicolae Ceaușescu, a rose by any other name would smell as sweet.

So, for those outside Romania who found themselves at a loss for words during the Romanian party congress last week, Polish television offered a list of names frequently used to describe the iron-fisted orthodox Marxist ruler.

In modest terms, Ceauşescu may be described as "the first worker in the country," "the nation's spokesman," "the architect of the country," "the great hero," "reliable leader" and "father and friend of young people."

Metaphorically speaking, he may be called "the sweet kiss of the land," "the new polar star," "the lighthouse," "a man like a fir tree," "the sacred oak of Romania's glory," "the mountain that protects the country" or "a well of living water."

Here are some other versions of the dustbin of history:

"Today is June 8, 1989. It is now 4 PM. I am Chai Ling, Commander-in-Chief in Tiananmen Square. I am still alive."

—From a clandestine tape recording, as reported in the *Guardian*, 26 June 1989

Interviewer: "What do you remember most vividly?"

Reporter, just returned from Beijing: "The students singing as they were being shot. And a student, a girl, who said to me, 'What can they do to us? We have our whole future ahead of us, and we've seen it.'"

—BBC news report, 19 June 1989

BIG RALLY IN BULGARIA AGAINST GOVERNMENT

Sofia—In the biggest public display of opposition to Communist rule ever staged in Bulgaria, tens of thousands of protestors crowded in front of the main cathedral yesterday, shouting for the government's resignation and an end to the one-party state. . . . At one point, protestors held their hands high in a V and kept time to the Beatles song "All You Need Is Love." The rally ended with people linking arms and singing "We Are the World," the pop song written to generate funds for Ethiopian famine relief.

—Tyler Marshall, *Los Angeles Times*, 15 January 1990, as carried in the *San Francisco Chronicle*

SOVIET POLICE BULLDOZE TENT CITY NEAR KREMLIN

Moscow—Police with bulldozers yesterday razed a tent city that had sprung up near the Kremlin in a gesture of disillusionment with Soviet life.

The three dozen residents were rounded up by Interior Ministry police before bulldozers moved in and flattened their makeshift plastic and cardboard dwellings, witnesses said.

"The city was a political protest by the simple people," said Svetlana Sedyk, who lived in the shanty town for three months to further her bid to emigrate. "This was the first and last such protest. There will never be another."

. . . Most of the camp's full-time residents, including pensioners, war veterans and former mental patients, were arrested. Some will be sent to mental hospitals, and others will be freed after investigation, a police officer said.

. . . Some of the signs that adorned the tents and shacks denounced the Communist Party; others told of losing homes and jobs because the protestors dared to criticize their bosses. One sign, framed by a rusting chain and weighted by rocks, read: "Prisoner of the 20th Century."

—Reuters, 31 January 1990, as carried in the *San Francisco Chronicle*

Alan Jolis again, a week after the collapse of the Soviet coup:

I run into a tiny group of barricade boys: the once owners of the street are now disenfranchised, stranded, smoking cigarettes.

A well-dressed man tells them, "It's all over, go back to work." . . . Obviously fighting for freedom is far easier than building democracy, and after seventy-four years of enforced silence, Muscovites are so eager to talk, no one stops to listen. "You boys were all drunk when you fought the tanks!" "No, it was cold; we needed to keep warm." Threats are spit out. Everyone takes turns contradicting themselves. In this borscht of contrary nonsense, it is clear that they love the public debate. They are eating liberty; they are swallowing it down; they are spitting it up like babies' vomit. They are laughing, drinking; they are free, free, freeish. And there's such a sense of total despair, of having lived through such madness, that now with the light at the end of the tunnel looming ever larger, their hope and longing so intense, the hopelessness so deep, the answered prayer so unbelievable, the fear so entrenched, that they prefer to laugh.

A scholar dives into the dustbin:

We are once amore—once amor, once à mort, thank heaven!—in a world made fresh for fundamental metaphors; where it makes all the difference, the difference between Life and Death, whether one goes with Empedocles or with Heraclitus; a difference dawning on me with new light in this year of 1990. Only in this year of 1990, exhilarated by the Dionysian manifestations of new life in Eastern Europe—replaying or redeploying, this time to more general acclaim, the Dionysian manifestations in Western Europe in 1968—soon, very soon, says the chorus in Euripides' *Bacchae,* the whole world will join the dance.

   —Norman O. Brown, "Dionysus in 1990," from *Apocalypse and/or Metamorphosis,* 1991

And, diving into the bin, the scholar falls right through the hole in the bottom. "I didn't understand any of it, but it stirred me," the French film star Miou-Miou said in 1989, recalling her life as a teenage upholstery machine operator in Paris, when, out of nowhere it seemed, France was stopped in its tracks by a wildcat general strike of ten million students and workers: that unnameable thing, "the events," the not-a-revolution, that "May '68." "Ordinary people like me," Miou-Miou says, "started thinking that maybe somehow our lives might somehow change."

   "People who had never found their voice before now spoke, acted in ways that would have been inconceivable a month earlier," it says in *1968: A Student Generation in Revolt,* a 1988 oral history edited by Ronald Fraser. "So when my own school came out on strike, oh, it was so marvelous!" remembered Claire Auzias, then a high school student in Lyons. "I went to speak at a general assembly in the school playground. I wasn't afraid of anything, I was carried forward by the moment. After May '68 I've never again been able to speak at a public meeting. But then I could answer every argument, talk back to anybody." "In that month of talking you learnt more than in the whole of your five years of studying," said René Bourrigaud, in 1968 a student in Angers. "Learnt because you could talk to anyone and everyone. It was really another world—a dream world perhaps—but that's what I'll always remember: the need and the right for everyone to speak." "It was fantastic," said Henri Weber, a student at the Sorbonne. "Everything we did immediately belonged to History."

No—everything you did was immediately written out of history. Now your words sound childish. Listen to yourself and to your fellows: "fantastic," "marvelous," "a dream world"—but even the comrades history denies you already sound strange, speaking from some netherworld: "I am still alive." History is written as we speak, its borders are mapped long before any of us open our mouths, and written history, which makes the common knowledge out of which our newspapers report the events of the day, creates its own refugees, displaced persons, men and women without a country, cast out of time, the living dead: are you still alive, really? Is there a special circle of historical hell where the likes of Miou-Miou, Claire Auzias, René Bourrigaud, and Henri Weber meet the anonymous barricade boys, the Beatles and the Bulgarians who sang their song, Chai Ling and the Prisoner of the 20th Century—some place where, all together, they listen to a great scholar attempt to rouse them, once again, with words they can no longer understand?

There are events that are real but that dissolve when one tries to attach them to the monuments—wars, elections, public works projects, universities, laws, prisons—out of which we make our history. There are people who act and speak but whose gestures and words do not translate out of their moments—and this exclusion, the sweep of the broom of this dustbin, is a movement that in its way is far more violent than any toppling of statues. It is an embarrassment, listening to these stories and these cries, these utopian cheers and laments, because the utopian is measured always by its failure, and failure, in our historiography, is shame. "Those weeks of fraternity and active solidarity," Cornelius Castoriadis wrote of May '68 almost twenty years later, "when one spoke to anybody and everybody without fear of being taken for a fool"—but to speak of such things after the fact is to speak precisely as a fool. "The conservative majority was ashamed and dared not appear in public," Castoriadis says—but shame is history's gift to those who lose, to those who lose because they ask too much of history.

In fact there is no special gathering place, not even in a historical hell, for the denizens of history's true dustbin; it is a wasteland in which all are distant from each other, because this is a territory, unlike history, without any borders at all—without any means to a narrative, a language with which to tell a story. "Taut images from this wild scenario will now always be present," McKenzie Wark wrote of Tiananmen Square in 1990, in "Vectors of Memory . . . Seeds of Fire." "This remarkable series of events will be recorded in a much longer, subterranean history. . . . this event will relay into the future the whole hidden culture of revolt and resistance." But what is that subterranean history? It is, today, little more than a jumble of rumors about the past, of cult pamphlets and anarchist bookstores where Proudhon meets Joachimite heretics who then turn into Nazis. "It is extraordinary how moments in time can feel completely discontinuous," Wark writes of the Tiananmen aftermath. "It probably all makes sense now. It didn't then, that's for sure. Beware of the smooth surface of history, looking backwards, making everything make sense. It made no sense at the time, like a random series of jump cuts. Indeed, like all insurrections, this one stood outside of time for a moment, hoping to catch hold of a different current, hoping to rise above the flux, hoping whoever or whatever edits history plumps for the right cut."

Lovely words, interspersed with the notion, which the writer seems unable to suppress in spite of himself, that this was just a movie. It scans like one, like an entertainment. But the discontinuities enforced by the dustbin are lived, not watched. One more report from the dustbin:

FIRST STUDENT DEMONSTRATION SINCE BEIJING CRACKDOWN

Beijing—In the first known revival of student protests since the army crushed a pro-democracy movement last month, about 300 Beijing University students gathered Sunday night at a campus courtyard and sang Communist songs after being told their sympathies had endangered their job prospects, students said. . . . One said, "We are forced to endure hours of political study every day, telling us that the soldiers killing our classmates was a glorious victory. Sarcasm is our only means of dissent."

—*San Francisco Chronicle*, 26 July 1989

Listen to the language used here—not just the way a massacre has become a "crackdown," but the weird, uncanny devolution of a great, heroic, horrific event into shadows and specters, as only weeks after the killing one speaks of a "revival," the "first known," the dispatch trickling out from the memory hole as it closes up. This is worse than the ephemerality enforced on the memories of Claire Auzias and René Bourrigaud or on the odd stories out of Eastern Europe, but it is not different.

In 1963, in *On Revolution*, Hannah Arendt wrote that "the failure of post-revolutionary thought to remember the revolutionary spirit and to understand it conceptually was preceded by the failure of the revolution to provide it with a lasting institution." That institution, she thought, might be the revolutionary councils that had appeared spontaneously in the course of so many modern revolutions—but that was one more utopian echo, a dream of a politics freed from the social question, from the management of necessity, from hunger, or its terror. This institution of a spirit could be viable only so long as the energy of dissolution and transformation could, in an entirely positive sense, dominate every aspect of ordinary life.

The question of "the revolutionary spirit" remains, though—and Arendt defined it best on the terms René Char set out in his poetry about the "treasure" he discovered in the French Resistance: "The treasure, he thought, was that he had '*found* himself,' that he no longer suspected himself of 'insincerity,' that he needed no mask and no make-believe to appear, that wherever he went he appeared as he was to others and to himself, that he could afford 'to go naked.'" Today there are dozens upon thousands of people who, only moments ago, lived just this life, but who, because this is a story outside of history, thrown out like a ranting drunk eighty-sixed from a bar, can barely credit even their own memories, people who are cut off from each other, and isolated even from their own selves, by the shame of stories they cannot tell and that no one would believe if they could. And yet if one reads in a certain frame of mind, the leavings of those stories stir with a truly strange power. Suddenly they are not ephemeral, not extraneous to real history, but plainly, obviously, the true story the events of the past years have been straining toward all along. And there is a kind of institution appropriate to this spirit: recordings, in the form of books, films, songs, and even comic strips, that treat this story as a central drama, so that the shame of appearing in public is lifted from those who once were, or once will be, unafraid to speak in public, and draped again, if only for an instant, on those who rule.

Common Knowledge, Spring 1992

History Lesson

When I woke up this morning, to celebrate I put on my favorite record: the Sex Pistols. But when "Holidays in the Sun" came on, it struck me—someday, when I have a child, and I want to tell my son or daughter about my favorite record, I'm going to have to explain what the Berlin Wall was.

—A friend on the occasion of his thirty-eighth birthday, 6 January 1990

When Sam Cooke sang "Wonderful World" in 1960, the first line, "Don't know much about history," was just a catch-phrase. As Paul Simon and James Taylor imagined him years later, sitting in school, his mind wandering, the singer didn't "know much about the Middle Ages" ("Look at the pictures, I just turn the pages"); he knew he loved the girl he was singing about, and that was all that mattered. But the ironies of culture, preserving a tune that wasn't meant to last, have given the music a weight it was never meant to carry—a weight it supports very easily. The sunny melody, which Cooke didn't so much follow as muse over, has long since turned the song into an elegy for the singer—who died too young, shot to death at thirty-three in 1964, in the Hacienda Motel in Los Angeles, in circumstances which have never been satisfactorily explained. The melody now carries a sense of the singer's absence, of the fact that he will never fulfill the promises of the song—which have been definitively passed on to the listener. History is bunk, the song starts out saying; taking in disappearance and an unsolved mystery, it has become a kind of history itself.

This is not how history is usually presented in everyday culture: as a complex and unsettled story that draws you in. Turn the television to almost any station and you'll soon catch the ruling mode, as someone in a sitcom or drama or commercial snaps off one version or another of "It's history." This cant phrase, in all its myriad variations, has worked its way through our talk for more than a decade now—like a language-germ, a neologism that won't go away, that holds its place in culture by poisoning the language around it—and what the phrase means is the opposite of what it says. It means there is no such thing as history, a past of burden and legacy. Once something (a love affair broken off, a fired baseball manager, a war, Jimmy Carter) is "history," it's *over,* and it is understood that it never existed at all. We swat it away like a fly—along with the possibility that, in history, nothing is ever truly over.

The result is a kind of euphoria, a weightless sense of freedom. It's a feeling chronicled all too precisely in *The German Comedy: Scenes of Life after the Wall,* a collection of essays by the (formerly West) German novelist Peter Schneider. In earlier books and essays Schneider had assumed the Wall was permanent, and tried to understand it less as a thing than as a symbol, a looking glass that no matter the intentions of its makers told Easterners they were ugly and Westerners they were beautiful. "I wonder what would happen if a messenger arrived on horseback, direct from the Kremlin, to order the demolition of the Wall," Schneider once wrote, as if such an event could never happen. History fooled him: the event took place, the Wall was a thing, it could be taken down and it was. Now even capitalizing the word seems strange.

Gone—it's history. Working to anchor the cloud of history as it floats off, Schneider fixes on his new old country as a never-never land: the wall may be gone but a thousand invisible looking glasses have been raised in its place, and everyone happily walks through them a hundred times a day. *The German Comedy* is a search for a dislocation that, against all official promises that the Germans always were and always will be one people, must be there, somewhere. If the wall was a part of history—a force that for a generation, for twenty-eight years, shaped and disfigured millions of lives—can it and all its works vanish overnight, as if they had never been? It seems so—and thus Schneider fights almost desperately against the apparent fact of disappearance. He fights for history, as if to say, if we were never there, we cannot be here.

Among the many stories Schneider retrieves from the rubble of the wall, one is especially disconcerting—a German version of the American classic "MAN BITES DOG." After the dissolution of the wall, several thousand East German dogs, once used to patrol the borderline, were, so to speak, left unemployed. People "feared the worst," Schneider reports: "wild and dangerous packs of homeless animals prowling the suddenly accessible streets of West Berlin." Soon enough, though, the dogs were adopted by open-hearted Westerners—and, weirdly, the dogs continued the story most people no longer wanted to hear. They insisted on the reality of a history that was no longer real. The newly Westernized dogs were quickly acculturated to new sorts of food, and they learned to take commands in new dialects. But, Schneider says,

whenever they accompany their new Western masters on walks near where the Wall once stood, they are suddenly deaf to every call and run their programmed beat without veering right or left. The Wall itself has disappeared so completely that even native Berliners can't always say exactly where it used to stand. Only the Wall-dogs move as if tethered to an unseen leash, with absolute certainty, following the old border along its wild zigzags through the city—just as though they were looking for, or maybe missing, something . . .

But perhaps this story is only a legend—like the Wall itself.

This is history as disappearance. It's as if parts of history, because they don't fit the story a people wants to tell itself, can survive only as haunts and fairy tales, accessible only as specters and spooks.

You could do worse. History is a kind of legend, and we do understand, or sense, buried stories, those haunts and specters, without quite knowing how or why. A bet on that premise is *City of Quartz: Excavating the Future in Los Angeles,* a leftist critique by long-time Angeleno journalist Mike Davis. He focuses on Los Angeles as a creation of racism (really Aryanism) and on capitalism as aristocratic racketeering. Digging up the bodies of the city's interred, martyred facts, Davis goes for what's been written out of history—for what, like the wall only dogs can hear, exerts its force-field nonetheless.

City of Quartz is serious, measured, outraged, flinty, ironic, fast-moving. As it happened, though, I was reading the book when HBO was running its made-for-cable *Cast a Deadly Spell,* and the book collapsed into the movie. *City of Quartz* is an attempt to correct the L.A. legend of sun and freedom; *Cast a Deadly Spell* was a counter-legend. At least for as long as the film ran, its cheap power reduced Davis's attack to mere righteousness.

Cast a Deadly Spell combined a plot cobbled together from the works of ghosts 'n' demons novelist H. P. Lovecraft with the milieu and dialogue Raymond Chandler made for Philip Marlowe. Fred Ward played detective H. Philip Lovecraft—the most deadpan version of Chandler's hero in screen history. You got the feeling a truck could have run over his face and his expression wouldn't change. The setting was Los Angeles, just after World War II, "when"—and this was the twist—"everyone used magic."

Witches are licensed by the city; cops light cigarettes by snapping their fingers ("It saves time," one says to Ward, embarrassed, as if he's been caught drinking on the job). Goblins brought back by GIs as souvenirs from the Pacific Theater run loose; gargoyles on mansions come to life and do their masters' bidding; virgins conjure up unicorns (it's explained that only virgins can). Developers import zombies from Haiti for the massive postwar home-construction projects (they come in crates, like refrigerators, with a six-month guarantee; after that they keel over and disintegrate). The story is immediately crazy and instantly recognizable. Los Angeles has been the focal point for the occult in the United States for more than a century, and for all that time the occult has been more than anything else a short cut, an edge on the other guy, a way of getting what you want, an impulse that combines capitalist hustle with a religious fervor that transcends all ethics.

Ward's H. Philip Lovecraft is the last honest man—the only private eye in town who won't use magic. For that reason alone he's approached by a millionaire client who means to call up ancient monsters from the bowels of the earth and bring about the end of the world. Ward alone can be trusted to retrieve a stolen, all-powerful Satanic book without fiddling with it himself.

Needless to say, the plot grows ever more absurd and convoluted—and, just below its B-movie surface, ever more compelling, more *likely*. As I watched, it seemed as if all of Raymond Chandler, all the books and all the films, had been compressed into a story Chandler had always known was there, but could never get up the nerve to tell with a straight face.

Now, one of the stories Mike Davis tells in *City of Quartz* has to do with the penetration of the California Institute of Technology—and the whole nascent southern California military intelligence industry—by Satanists. Davis follows the path of the British warlock Aleister Crowley, who in the 1930s founded a Los Angeles branch of his Ordo Templi Orientis, a secret society that traced its origins to the medieval Knights Templar. Davis then moves on to one John Parsons. From a wealthy family, Parsons was a Cal Tech genius and a founder of the Jet Propulsion Laboratory; in 1939 he took over as head of Crowley's temple and, at Crowley's direction, turned it toward "sex magick." Soon enough, in the genteel town of Pasadena, where black people were not allowed on the streets after dark, naked pregnant women were jumping through circles of fire.

Not long after, Parsons met L. Ron Hubbard, then a science fiction writer and later—not coincidentally, given Parsons's influence—the founder of Scientology. Together Parsons and Hubbard "embarked on a vast diabolical experiment," Davis writes. Their goal was "to call up a true 'whore of Babylon' so that she and Parsons might procreate a literal Antichrist in Pasadena." They finally found her, and—

And, in essence, you have the plot of *Cast a Deadly Spell*, and maybe a clue to its undertow. On the page, even contextualized with skill and passion, Davis's story slips the bounds of history and loses its voice; what is supposed to be ominous is funny instead. And only funny: it becomes clear that Davis's attempt to link the military and the occult in the secret history of Los Angeles is specious, jerry-built, and altogether incidental to the creation of the postwar world. The more carefully you read, the less significant it all seems. Yet *Cast a Deadly Spell*, dressed up in its impossible clothes, tells a much looser, broader story—and leaves you with the fearsome sense that Los Angeles is, by its nature, a place of sorcerers, who can do anything. It is, in its way, if not better history than *City of Quartz*, an opening into more history.

Disappearance; mystery; then bunk. Last Columbus Day, anticipating the Quincentennial of the great voyage of discovery, the papers were full of articles on the multiculturalist debate over whether the day ought to be celebrated, over whether the devastation wrought by the European invasion of the world the names of which are lost to us might be better marked by a Day of Mourning. There were even attempts to deny the import of what plainly was, by measure of the irreversible changes it set off all over the planet, the most cataclysmic event in human history: contact between two worlds that for all practical purposes were unknown to each other.

It's tempting to see the denial of Columbus Day as a reverse image of the denial of the Berlin Wall by Germans happy to pretend it never existed. Here, history is no more than detritus to be shaped with transitory meanings according to the transitory power of one group or another. The idea that history might have its own directions, its own magnetisms, its own sense of time—that it's a force to be understood rather than a set of facts to be manipulated—is missed. History will be what we say it is, the newspapers implied—if only we could agree.

The legend we use for history is more resistant than that—and that is why the most contrived, nonsensical counter-legend can cast a spell the most scrupulous analysis may never match. The legend we use for history is a master-narrative, a narrative that cannot be easily interrupted, revised, or seized, but can only, in certain moments, be replaced. The insertion into that master-narrative—which in America is a tale of equality, individualism, virtue, and success—of the so-called contributions of people previously excluded from that narrative (African Americans, women, Asian Americans, and so on) will not necessarily change the narrative in any way. Such insertions may only initiate those once excluded by the master-narrative into its untruth.

Any society's master-narrative is by definition an untruth. It is an interested construction rather than a literal, all-seeing account of what really happened (as if such a thing were possible)—and this may actually be its justification. Cultural awakening comes not when one learns the contours of the master-narrative, but when one realizes—thanks to a teacher, a book, or the disruptions of an unpredicted historical event—that what one has always been told is incomplete, backward, false, a lie. There is nothing more liberating; there is nothing that leads more surely to the need to question whatever is presented as fixed, certain, inevitable. And it makes sense that the means to such a liberation are not always where one has been taught to look for them.

Threepenny Review, Summer 1992

The Mask of Dimitrios

Nothing is absolutely dead; every meaning will have its homecoming festival.

—Mikhail Bakhtin

One of the most telling comments on Eric Ambler's 1930s spy novels—"political thrillers," in Julian Symons's phrase—comes from Ambler himself. "Before the War, I was very much an anti-fascist writer," he told Symons in 1989, on the occasion of his eightieth birthday, "and after August 1939 and the Nazi-Soviet pact, I'd really lost my subject matter. I was of the Thirties, and long after the tears had been wiped away there was still a sense of loss, a loss of belief." But this is not the most telling comment I know; that came from a friend of mine, who was transported some time ago by Ambler's thirties tales, and who then tried to read Ambler's later books, such 1950s and 1960s work as *State of Siege* and *The Light of Day:* "After the war, he must have lost his sense of dread."

The two judgments are not congruent. Ambler's words imply the hope of a fellow-traveler (as Ambler more or less names his thirties self in his autobiography, *Here Lies*—though the punning, preposthumous title tells you with how much salt to take anything it says). His words imply not only hope but, as Ambler says, belief: belief in the Communist project of a New World, a New Man. Even more than belief, the words distantly suggest a sort of relish in the prospect of world conflict. "I was of the Thirties"—the echoes in those words cannot be enclosed by the politics of their author. Listen and you may hear the wish, shared by some on the left with some on the right, for a cleansing, wiping away the cabals of profit and domination that edge around the corners of Ambler's prewar books, those combines of plutocrats and hired killers that carry such blandly sinister names: Pan-Eurasian Petroleum, the Eurasian Credit Trust. Europe's rush toward disaster, dissolution, and a carnage to make the Great War seem like a rehearsal, Europe's hidden wish for an *end* to the story everyone knew—this is the master-story lurking behind every plot twist in Ambler's best books, in *Background to Danger* (1937), *Cause for Alarm* (1938), and *A Coffin for Dimitrios* (1939, titled *The Mask of Dimitrios* in Great Britain). My friend's words speak of a terror, a fright, that supersedes any project, any moral yearning for a new world; that is what Ambler's old books communicate today, precisely to the degree that they communicate barely anything of hope or belief. Reading now, as in Ambler's books characters almost suicidally out of their depth struggle to do the right thing while all around them Europe closes ranks like Poe's shrinking closet, you'd think Ambler would have found his subject in the great betrayal of the Hitler-Stalin pact, not lost it.

They are, in their unrelievedly entertaining way, very close to being nihilist books: fables about the nihilism of the notion that anyone can escape from history. The protagonist is never a professional spy, merely an ordinary Englishman. He's someone without politics or convictions caught up in a crossfire of conspiracies well beyond his frame of reference, a man trapped in a backwater of European violence, his only weapon a memory of the certainty that freedom is simply a matter of privacy and peace of mind, of a day's pay and being left alone. As the books end, the Englishman goes home, returns to the banality of his everyday affairs, a banality that, after the horrors that have touched him—meaninglessly, it seems; by accident; he breathes in their unreality, exhales real life—feels like paradise.

He goes to sleep, but history—no Marxist grid, just the steady accumulation of events he never suspected had anything to do with him—doesn't sleep. History has other plans, and as for one man lucky enough to be alive after all that Ambler has put him through, one man lucky enough to have, for the moment, escaped history's embrace, history is no lover. It could care less. At the end of *A Coffin for Dimitrios,* Charles Latimer, the book's protagonist and even its hero, mild-mannered English-country-house detective-story writer (in the movie version played by Peter Lorre almost as a precursor of Woody Allen), is released from the story. He travels away in a first-class rail cabin: "He needed, and badly, a motive, a neat way of committing a murder and an entertaining crew of suspects. . . . His last book had been a trifle heavy. He must inject a little more humor into this one. As for the motive, money was always, of course, the soundest basis. A pity that Wills and life insurance were so outmoded. Supposing a man murdered an old lady so that his wife should have a private income. It might be worth thinking about. The scene. . . . The train ran into a tunnel." But the darkness of that last, corny image is what Ambler was writing about—or anyway that is what a reader feels today. In other words, to read Ambler's first books now, separated from us by more than half a century—to go back to the 1930s, with all of Ambler's echoes of long-forgotten, perhaps always obscure incidents in the politics of Italy, Romania, Turkey, Bulgaria, Macedonia, of assassinations, cover-ups, crushed revolts, massacres, dead twenties revolutionaries and vibrant thirties fascists—is to know Ambler's sense of dread. Dread is not the same as fear: the shared generational fear, say, of 1950s American children listening in their beds as airplanes passed over their homes. Dread has a moral dimension, best caught in Norman Mailer's insistence, in the midst of the Vietnam War, one of many postwar wars Ambler never really wrote about, that the worst truth about any society could be found in an "unearned freedom from dread."

Any of Ambler's prewar books* could have been titled *Why England Slept*, as John F. Kennedy's first book was: *Because you slept, millions must die.* But what Ambler was saying in these books was not exactly political, and not at all about the promises of the Communist International or the Popular Front. There was a way in which Ambler did believe that a life based in the quiet, compromised, uncommitted yeses and noes of the ordinary Englishman, not tending his own garden but merely looking to earn the money to buy one, was better than a life sparked by the absolutes of other places: places like Central Europe or the Balkans, where Ambler's stories unfold.

The Balkans were where the First War began what, in the 1930s, Ambler was sure Central Europe would finish. As he wrote, Central Europe was at the center of world history, the place where the abyss would take shape, where it would take its anti-shape: the place Ambler's Englishmen would flee, and the place where, a few years later, they would be sent back. Listen to him:

The Turkish troops descended upon the non-Turkish quarters and began systematically to kill. Dragged from their houses and hiding places, men, women and children were butchered in the street which soon became

---

*Though the description is off: the war to come is present in all of them, even in Ambler's first, *The Dark Frontier*, a 1936 satire of the spy stories of the time, or in the relatively trivial *Epitaph for a Spy*, 1939, left unpublished in the United States until 1952 and then recast as a postwar tale without much loss. *Journey into Fear*, published in 1940, after the war in Europe had begun, is nevertheless governed less by the events already underway than by the foreboding of the earlier books.

littered with mutilated bodies. The wooden halls of the churches, packed with refugees, were drenched with benzine and fired. The occupants who were not burnt alive were bayoneted as they tried to escape. . . . By the time dawn broke on the fifteenth of September, over one hundred and twenty thousand persons had perished; but somewhere amidst that horror had been Dimitrios, alive.

Ambler is describing what happened in Smyrna, in 1922, when the Turkish army overcame a retreat of Greek forces. "How was it that *you* survived?" those who emerged from Nazi extermination camps would ask each other twenty-three years later; that, a few years before the ovens were lit, is the question Ambler asks of his character Dimitrios, the pan-European fiend who is at once a squalid miscreant and an exemplar of the venality that has seized his continent and will soon consume it. Listen again, this time in *Background to Danger,* to a British traveling salesman, telling one of Ambler's who-me protagonists—and this who-me is a sophisticated foreign correspondent—what Europe is all about:

Fifteen years I've been trailing about this blasted Continent now, and I've hated every moment of it. . . . They say the British are all stuck up about foreigners, that we're all men and women just the same, that they've got a lot of good points that we haven't. It's all lies, and when you've been away from home as long as I have, you'll know it, too. They're not like us, not at all. People come over here for a fortnight's holiday and see a lot of pretty *châlets* and *châteaux* and *Schlösser* and say what a fine place it is to live in. They don't know what they're talking about. They only see the top coat. They don't see the real differences. They don't see behind the scenes. They don't see them when their blood's up.

The salesman takes a breath:

I've seen them all right. I was in sunny Italy when the Fascisti went for the Freemasons in twenty-five. Florence it was. Night after night with shooting and beating and screams, until you felt like vomiting. I was in

Vienna in thirty-four when they turned the guns on the municipal flats with the women and children inside them. A lot of the men they strung up afterwards had to be lifted on to the gallows because of their wounds. I saw the Paris riots with the *garde mobile* shooting down the crowd like flies and everyone howling *"mort aux vaches"* like lunatics. I saw the Nazis in Frankfurt kick a man to death in his front garden. After the first he never made a sound. I was arrested that night because I'd seen it, but they had to let me go.

Nice chaps, aren't they? Picturesque . . .

Even in the novel, Ambler sidles away from the salesman; in his autobiography he says it was just something he overheard one day, a bit he thought might work in a book. But the charge in the writing is its own proof of what he meant to say.

As an exemplar of his times, Dimitrios fades into the history so carefully recounted in the other books, and in his own. Master of masks—common thug, assassin, spy, heroin smuggler, or international banker—Dimitrios has no face. Though the killings demanded by Ambler's plots are kept to a minimum, there are countless faceless corpses between the lines: the books communicate terror because they are driven by it. Zaleshoff, the Soviet secret agent who in *Background to Danger* and *Cause for Alarm* functions as a sort of Jim to the who-me Englishman's Huck, is a recognizable romantic hero: he knows what to do at any moment, his resolve never flags because his faith is certain. The New World, the New Man, is always on the horizon. But finally Zaleshoff is irrelevant. He relieves nothing of the intrigues he tries to shape. He is free from terror because he believes in history, but none of Ambler's protagonists can believe in what he believes, or in anything else—and, today, the reader knows that a man like Zaleshoff, so full of humor and spunk, would almost certainly have been shot by Stalin, his own spymaster.

Ambler presents a Europe, on the verge of making world history, that is savage, barbaric, a swamp of internecine killing, breaking into pieces but soon to write the world-historical script we have acted out ever since, up to this fortuitous moment—fortuitous, at any rate, for the reading of Ambler's prewar spy novels. Today in Central and Eastern Europe, Ambler's ground and a backwater of history ever since the story that began with the Nazi-Soviet pact robbed him of his subject, all is dissolution, country after country seizing upon the word *democracy* as a way out of the history they were not permitted to make, the anti-history they could only endure. But nothing is certain in this here and now: old nationalisms, ancient tribal loyalties, suppressed religions, murdered rebels, and dead tyrants are reappearing in the wake of the collapse of conspiracies that in the thirties, in Ambler's books, fall short of the realization he quietly promised would come soon enough.

All things seem possible on this terrain, damned for so long: all horrors, and also paradise. What does Ambler think, as he gazes out upon the map he drew so vividly in his youth? You could say that, now, after the oppositions of the Cold War period, the spy novel that so facilely pitted an obvious us against an obvious them will have to go; that a new spy novel will once again have to take up the individual, on no side, the person who knows nothing, cares less, and gets caught anyway. You could say that in a new spy novel, there must once again be a world to win, this time without capital letters: a new world, with new men and women, everything up for grabs. But if, today, you read Ambler as, at the same time, you read the newspapers, you may feel the sense of dread that wrote his books—a sensation that, today, may not be so completely present anywhere else. It is, after all, a sensation—an idea—that is easy to shrug off, though history wears it like a rotting suit of clothes, under the top coat that, as Eric Ambler once wrote, is all we see.

Threepenny Review, January 1990

Myth and Misquotation

This is not a position I ever imagined occupying. In 1964 I was, I think, the first student in the annals of the sophomore history honors seminar to get a C in that course. After that, I pretty much spent my time in English and Political Science.

In that same year, though, an event took place that I want to turn to today. That was the Free Speech Movement: a few students, then several thousand students, insisting the limits the University administration had placed on their advocacy of social change were wrong. This event had far-reaching consequences, though not even the most far-seeing of those who were part of the event could have imagined the most concrete, perhaps the most important.

Today, thanks to the commercial hook of media anniversaries, there are plenty of books in the stores highlighting the Free Speech Movement as the spark for the decade of protest called "the sixties"—but this may just be gush. More vitally, the Free Speech Movement was very likely the crucial factor in Ronald Reagan's election as governor of California in 1966—and thus,

Originally the address at the commencement ceremonies of the Department of History, University of California at Berkeley, 20 May 1988.

if one follows the line, his election as president of the United States fourteen years after that. In 1980, Ronald Reagan, calling for "national renewal" and setting himself against the chaos of the previous two decades as the embodiment of traditional values, was still running against the Free Speech Movement. Edwin Meese, who as an assistant district attorney of Alameda County led the prosecution of Free Speech Movement demonstrators, who ensured that sentences would be stiff (in some cases, as much as six months for occupying a campus building),* is today attorney general of the United States; it was that prosecution which brought him to the attention of Ronald Reagan. It was often said, in 1964, that those who took part in a revolt against their own institutions would some day be running them; it hasn't worked out that way.

It's a commonplace that history is written by the powerful; it's more to the point to say that power writes history. Events that do not change shape into power, or that occur outside the normal circuits in which power is exchanged, outside the normal circuits of legitimacy, of the institutional distribution and control of social goods—such events, in certain ways, do not make history at all. They are resistant to history, because history does not know how to account for them; history resists them in turn, because it can get away with it. Such evanescent, off-the-record events are what Walter Benjamin was talking about when he spoke of the articulation of real history as the attempt to "seize hold of a memory as it flashes up in a moment of danger." But because such moments do not turn into history, they lose their shape, and turn into stupid self-parodies, legends, nonsense—old stories, told by cranks.

I'm talking about words on a page—the words some of you

---

*In 1993, quoting this passage in his book *The Free Speech Movement*, David Goines, who served time, noted that "actually, the worst anybody got was 120 days, which was still pretty damn stiff considering that first-offense trespassing usually got something like a $25 fine at the outside."

will be putting on pages. Now, no decent historian would think of quoting one of Ronald Reagan's inaugural addresses merely by referring to a newspaper account, an oral anecdote, a vague memory. Any decent historian would go to the archives, get the documents, copy them out, get it right. During the Free Speech Movement, though, a speech was given that became famous, became a sort of touchstone of its time and place: the speech FSM spokesman Mario Savio gave on the steps of Sproul Hall on 2 December 1964, just before the occupation that led to the finale of the drama. In the years that followed, down to this day, this speech has been quoted again and again—and in the scores of books and articles I've read, with one exception, once no more than a year had passed, it was never quoted accurately.

The words Mario Savio spoke were not, as a theory of social change, brilliant. They were full of contradictions. They do not stand up under analysis, which in any case they have never received. But Savio's words were poetic, part of a particular moment of danger—they helped define that moment, even partly created it. The speaker's cadence was part of whatever meaning his words had; the rhythm was part of the meaning. So was the strain, the catch, almost the whine, in Savio's voice—something his words, presented accurately on a page, can contain. This is what he said:

There is a time, when the operation of the machine becomes so odious, makes you so sick at heart, that you can't take part; you can't even tacitly take part, and you've got to put your bodies upon the gears and upon the wheels, upon the levers, upon all the apparatus and you've got to make it stop. And you've got to indicate to the people who run it, to the people who own it, that unless you're free, the machine will be prevented from working at all.

Well, we could pause and think about those words: about their odd politeness, about Savio's use of the word "indicate," about his fundamental acceptance of things as they are—there is no suggestion of destroying the machine. The cadence of the lines could, perhaps, tell us something about that time and place. But what interests me today is both the poetry of the words and the transformation of that poetry into a certain historical fact: that is, once past the year 1964, these words, for all the hundreds of times they have been quoted, printed, published, have almost never appeared as they were spoken. Almost no one has gotten them right. Almost no one has bothered to get them right. No one had to.

Over the years, following these words through the essays and books in which they appeared, I played a sort of game. What obnoxious bit of false punctuation, what transposition of once carefully chosen words—or of words perhaps not carefully chosen at all, but simply seized out of the moment, generated by the moment—would take place? Here's a quote: "There comes a time when you've got to bend, fold, spindle and mutilate—AND SHUT THE MOTHERFUCKER DOWN!" Unquote. That is a published version of Mario Savio's speech; trees died that it might be published. I heard Savio's speech. If, some day, you read that you graduated in 1989, and, running down the list of graduates, find your name misspelled, you'll understand the displacement I feel, quoting that version.

Why did this violence occur? This violence to history, which, Walter Benjamin to the contrary, is not just a matter of capturing the moment of danger, but also of what Benjamin defined as its opposite, capturing "the way it really was"—because how do you shape the moment of danger without a sense, as absolutely clear as is humanly possible, of "the way it really was"?

There was no shortage of documents. Savio's speech was recorded, and even issued commercially on a phonograph record; the University library has it. The correct words, with all of their rhythm intact, were part of the impeccably researched, magnificently detailed narrative chronology of the Free Speech Movement included in the basic anthology on the event, a book published by a major New York house. It's in any good library.

Savio's words were not quoted accurately—given the importance of cadence, rhythm, poetry, they were not quoted at all—because they were not part of the circuit of significance. Not in 1964, and not today. Nor is anything else about the sort of moment they spoke for. Those words did not change into power, and so they did not make history.

The sort of history they spoke for is the history told by cranks. As a pop music critic, I've had fun diving into the role of a crank: lonely protector of the true text. It's a ridiculous role—and it's amazing how much work it offers.

Probably the most famous statement in the history of rock 'n' roll is a line spoken by a woman named Marion Keisker, who in the early 1950s was the co-manager of Sun Records in Memphis, Tennessee. She was quoting her boss, Sam Phillips, as she remembered him speaking in 1952 or 1953, when he made his living recording black blues singers: "If I could find a white man with the Negro sound and the Negro feel," she said Sam Phillips said, "I could make a billion dollars." A year or so later, she and Phillips discovered Elvis Presley.

This statement is subject to all the uncertainties of oral history. Today, Sam Phillips denies he ever said any such thing—"it makes it sound like I only cared about money," he says. Marion Keisker herself says she said Phillips said "a million," not "a billion." The interview with Keisker was taped, and you can examine it at the library at Memphis State University—still, this too is outside the circuit of significance. That is why Albert Goldman, the most widely read biographer of Elvis Presley, could, for his own purposes, alter the statement, still attributing it to Sam Phillips and still placing it within quotation marks: "If I could find a white boy who sang like a nigger, I could make a billion dollars."

These obnoxious, libelous words were published in 1981. It

was no matter that, from all evidence, Sam Phillips never used the word "nigger," in any way, in any context—from all evidence, he wasn't that kind of person. The new version has entered into history: in this book, in that book, in utterly respectable books, some of them by eminent professors, one of them published by Oxford University Press. I was sent galley proofs of that book; I wrote the publisher, pointing out the error, doing what I could to say it was serious. The publisher wrote back, and explained that the author was sure the Goldman version was correct because it was "more vulgar," and in the history of popular culture, "vulgarity is always closer to the truth."

Another crank story: in 1969 I was part of the team at *Rolling Stone* magazine preparing a report on the Rolling Stones' free concert at Altamont—the race track just over the hills toward Tracy, the place you see on TV these days with the wind generators. At the end of their epochal 1969 tour, the Rolling Stones, feeling small after the Woodstock festival, at which they had declined to appear, decided to mount a festival of their own. Three hundred thousand people showed up. But something was off on that day from the start. There was violence in the air. The Hell's Angels had been hired to guard the stage. There was violence all day—the people in the crowd were mean, selfish. Everyone waited for the last act.

The last act was the cold-blooded murder of Meredith Hunter, a black Berkeley teenager, by the Hell's Angels. He got too close to the stage; the Hell's Angels chased him away from it; one caught him, and stabbed him, stabbed him again; then the teenager pulled a gun. He was running away from the stage at the time. The Hell's Angels chased him back toward the stage, caught him, and beat him to death. The gun was never fired.

This is what actually happened. It really isn't important that, in the next day's papers, one could read that the teenager had approached the stage, pulled a gun, aimed it at Mick Jagger—in some accounts, even fired the gun—and was only then attacked. That's the next day's papers. That isn't history, and it doesn't pretend to be. What was important was the context. In *Rolling Stone,* as in the next day's papers, we reported that the killing had taken place as the Rolling Stones played "Sympathy for the Devil." We had a bad tape of the show—of course there was no announcement on the tape, "The murder has taken place." But in truth it sounded as if it had: because it was poetically appropriate. A murder at a Rolling Stones concert as they played "Sympathy for the Devil"—what could be more perfect?

We found out, not long after, that we were wrong: the killing had happened during a different, less poetically appealing song (not that less appealing—it was "Under My Thumb"). There was no doubt—movie footage captured it. In the movie *Gimme Shelter,* millions saw it. So we set the record straight, right away—we ran a correction, and not just a line, but a story, since it seemed important.

Neither the correction nor the movie ever had any effect. Every time Altamont was mentioned, so was the killing that had taken place during "Sympathy for the Devil." We became somewhat obsessed; we ran a lot of corrections. The error never went away. We got tired of it. Seven years after the fact that no longer existed, we joked about running a cover story, some famous photo from Altamont, and a simple headline: NOT "SYMPATHY FOR THE DEVIL," "UNDER MY THUMB." But this was an error that could not be corrected. "Even if it didn't happen," the editor finally said, "it did."

What he meant was this: when an event takes place outside the strictures of power, it is swallowed by the imperatives of history, which are partly the imperatives of myth. History is a story: we want a story that makes sense, is poetically whole, that fits what we already think we already know. This is what happens when a historian, after a hundred hours in the microfilm room, decides to omit a reported incident that contradicts her thesis, because no one will ever care that she omitted it. She is not exactly lying: she knows the omission will shape real truth. This is what happens when a historian, after five years crisscrossing foreign countries in search of witnesses, finally gains an interview with his most important subject, and then, when the long-sought subject turns out dull, bland, and plainly dishonest, elides a few phrases, reads between the lines, and, without exactly meaning to, invents a quote. Of course this is far less likely to happen when the history in question is attached to power—when one knows it would be checked. But if one is pursuing a different story, a story that is not about power—and there is no real crime, because it is always the truth, the unspoken, the unreported truth, the *necessary* truth, that is being recorded—one is safe. This is the temptation of history—who hasn't felt it? It's one of the glories of history, the way you can make it right.

Today, it is a fact that at Altamont a murder, or anyway killing—there was a trial, and the defendant was found not guilty—took place during "Sympathy for the Devil," even though, at the trial, whatever it was that happened certifiably took place during "Under My Thumb." More documents—and irrelevant. Who, writing about Altamont, feels a responsibility to the event? Sam Phillips said whatever he said—and even though his statement, or Marion Keisker's account of it, is a foundation stone of worldwide popular culture, we now have an obscene perversion of what he did or didn't say embedded in some of the more widely read and respectably published books on our culture.

As for Mario Savio's words—certainly they define a moment of danger, in all of its weakness, all of its passion. They would, that is, if anyone had bothered to get them right. As they actually appear they define nothing.

Imagine that today Mario Savio is the attorney general of the United States. There would be little question of the misquotation of words he had uttered twenty-some years before; those words would be seen to have had consequences, they would be taken as a clue to his successes and failures, his perspicacity and his blindness, and rightly so. He would be accountable to the words he once said—and rightly so.

History is finally a matter of accountability: a good historian can bring all of us up on trial. We are all accountable to what we have seen and done, to what shaped us, to what made our place and time. In a good history, we are not permitted to get it wrong, so far as it can be known what is right. A good historian will challenge *us* when we forget, when *we* elide, and we invent: the historian will have the documents, and we will have to face them. I was wrong, we will say, shamed by the evidence, and explain why; no matter what, we will say, I was right, and we will explain that too, if we can.

Threepenny Review, Fall 1988

Postscript

It ought to have been no surprise that in a talk on the way in which errors can poison history I would find myself hoist, or at the least jerked, by my own petard. After its appearance in *Threepenny Review, Harper's* published a slightly edited version, under the title "History outside of History," in its December 1988 issue. That provoked the following exchange with my friend Stanley Booth, author of *Dance with the Devil: The Rolling Stones and Their Times. Harper's* published an edited version of Booth's first letter, and my reply; his second letter was not published.

December 21, 1988

Dear Sirs,

In "History Outside of History," Greil Marcus, while calling for high standards in writing about the past, makes a number of statements that seem to one who witnessed the events in question, factual errors, not to say—in his words—"an obscene perversion."

He says, "the Rolling Stones, feeling small after the Woodstock festival . . . decided to have a festival of their own." But the Stones had already, more than a month before Woodstock, given a festival in Hyde Park, its audience estimated at two hundred and fifty to five hundred thousand. Having then made a successful tour of the United States—the first since their drug arrests and Brian Jones' death—the Stones, who knew that the Beatles were history and that they themselves were just starting, felt anything but small. Hubris, not an inferiority complex, was a factor at Altamont.

Marcus refers to "the cold-blooded murder of Meredith Hunter," then calls it "anyway a killing." I saw the attack on Hunter and what preceded it. I believe he died not because of his proximity to the stage but because he stood with his white date too close to a Hell's Angel and made the fatal error of pulling a gun when the Angel pushed him away, not so much to keep Hunter from the stage as to distance himself from the sight of potential miscegenation. However that may be, nobody stabbed Hunter until he pulled the gun. I saw it happen. Hearing now, nearly twenty years later, yet another entirely original version, or perversion, of what I observed—and in such a context—followed by the words "That is what happened," blows, as we used to say in the 'sixties, what's left of my mind.

"History is finally a matter of accountability," Marcus preaches, but in spite of the solipsistic irony of his conclusion that history is also whatever you think it is (not that his point is invalid), what this good man and well-meaning writer has demonstrated here is the accuracy of Henry Ford's observation: "History is bunk."

Yours sincerely,

Stanley Booth

In reply: My friend Stanley Booth is surely right that Meredith Hunter was attacked because of his white girlfriend. As to the circumstances of the killing itself, my description was based on the testimony, first published in *Rolling Stone* and later repeated in court, of an eyewitness who stood next to Hunter near the stage, followed his flight into the crowd, and attended him as he died. This account is the most detailed and convincing of the many contradictory reports I have encountered, and it still seems most credible.

February 17, 1989

Dear Sirs,

Not to flog this poor old horse *ad nauseam,* but—that Greil Marcus, who did not see Meredith Hunter's killing, bases his account of it on the report of the Alameda County Grand Jury's hearing concerning Hunter's death is not surprising. What seems odd is Marcus's choosing to believe only the testimony of the one man in a crowd of at least 300,000 who said that Hunter was stabbed before he pulled a gun. The other major witnesses before the Grand Jury, among them Hunter's date, Patty Bredehoft, described the action as I observed it and Al Maysles' camera captured it—with Hunter being stabbed directly he had pulled his pistol. God knows it matters not to Hunter at this date, but in the context—the ethics of writing history—Marcus might have concluded with "that is what one man said" rather than the grandiose "That is what happened."

Yours sincerely,

Stanley Booth

Territories

A Single Revelation

We were sitting on the top deck of the riverboat *Mark Twain,* waiting for it to put out into the Mississippi . . ."

Then a steam whistle blew a signal . . . it was as though a whole nation had set its lips to a giant flute—a long-drawn-out screech so bestial and brutal, but at the same time, what with the billowing clouds of black smoke and the vastness of the Mississippi, so proud, so grandiose, that, embarrassed and yet bodily shaken, I could only look off to one side. So overpowering was that signal that, splintered by fear, I lived a dream of America that up until then I had only heard about. It was a moment of expertly organized resurrection, in which the things around me ceased to be unrelated, and people and landscape, the living and the dead, took their places in a single painful and theatrical revelation of history. Theatrically flowed the Mississippi, theatrically the tourists moved from deck to deck, while an old man's deep, far-carrying voice told the story of the great riverboats over the loudspeaker: the new era of travel and commerce they had initiated, steamboat races, black slaves loading firewood by the light of the moon, boiler explosions; and finally, how the railroads had taken the place of the riverboats. Sick as I was of loudspeaker voices on tours, I could have listened to that dramatic voice forever.

The voice here is that of Peter Handke; the passage is from his novel *Short Letter, Long Farewell*. Like *The Great Gatsby*—which Handke, with great self-deprecating humor, invokes as he begins his story—this is an attempt to discover what traps America has set for those who believe in its promises; in a deeper, more persistent way it is an attempt to discover what promises America still has the power to keep.

The book begins in Providence, Rhode Island, as the narrator, like Handke a young Austrian, receives a letter from his wife, who has left him: a warning not to follow her, though she tells him where she is. He sets off for New York, then traces her to Philadelphia. Outside Philadelphia he rejoins an old lover and travels with her and her daughter through the Midwest and into Missouri; threatening messages arrive from his wife, then a fake bomb. He leaves for the Southwest; his wife follows him and has him beaten up. He flies to the Northwest; there, at the edge of the Pacific, his confrontation with his wife takes place. Then together they take the bus to Los Angeles to meet John Ford, who explains where they've been.

It's in the middle of his journey that the narrator, alone, goes to see Ford's *Young Mr. Lincoln* and, feeling the life in the picture, understands that he must see Ford himself, must play Dorothy to Ford's Wizard. And yet in this intense little book Ford is a symbol only until we meet him, and the trip the narrator and his wife make across the country is a symbol only because such a trip must be a symbol, not because Handke ever forces it to be one. I didn't even notice, until I finished the tale and sat back to think about it, that the narrator had retraced the path of American history, had himself reached, settled, abandoned, and pursued every retreating frontier until, at the frontier's end, he had no choice but to settle his affairs. Like the narrator, until his vision on the riverboat I didn't understand that whatever he was fleeing—his wife, himself—he had put much more of himself into searching out a wholeness so complete, expansive, and out of reach that only a place as big, dangerous, and contradictory as America could even hint at it.

For if Handke doesn't impose symbolism on America, he means to comprehend the symbolism America has inevitably imposed upon his story. "What we see in the landscape isn't nature," a woman tells Handke's narrator, "but the deeds of the men who took possession of America, and at the same time a call to be worthy of such deeds. We were brought up to look at nature with a moral awe. Every view of a canyon might just as well have a sentence from the Constitution under it." A page later, the man sees that only the sort of vision offered by the *Mark Twain* can contain such a paradox: one is estranged from nature and yet forced to make a moral connection to it. Only such a paradox, and such a vision, can bring up the dreamed unities that might rescue the narrator from the confines of his own history, from his narcissism—can detach him, for a moment, from what he has taken to be his fate.

Rolling Stone, 5 May 1977

Götterdämmerung after Twenty-One Years

Thanks to a birth date falling between V-E and V-J days, I absorbed a fair amount of World War II folklore, and grew up with more or less conventional, popular-culture ideas about Nazis. They were bogeymen (albeit more personal bogeymen for me than for my friends, because I was Jewish and my friends weren't). Thinking about what the Nazis had done to the Jews was scary, but it was scary in the way thinking about kidnappers was scary: I couldn't sleep, but I knew my father would never let anyone do that to me. Sometimes I tried to think hard about atrocities, about crimes I knew were as tangible as streets and houses, but I couldn't do it. I drew a line between the world of the war in which I had been conceived and the world into which I had been born. Fantasies—not all of them self-produced—replaced flesh and blood. As the movies I would later see defined the men my parents' generation had fought—cold, blond, thin-lipped automatons with riding crops—Nazis were merely the most effective component of a mythology that I, like other children, sometimes liked to scare myself with. They stood in for Grimms' fairy tales. Nazis had another function: since

I was raised in a strongly liberal household where one learned not to hate people because they belonged to a certain national or racial group, Nazis were the single commonality onto which one could project fantasies of hatred without the slightest feeling of guilt. Like other children, I found a guilt-free object of hatred useful.

Little of this changed—which is to say, deepened—over the years, though I developed an interest in movies and TV programs that depicted Nazi horrors, or just Nazi horribleness. Partly this had to do with a forbidden fascination with evil, but there was, as a safety valve, the certainty that that evil had been wiped out. If there was any sort of unconscious or half-conscious process of masochistic gratification at work, it too seemed altogether safe—though when, years later, I read George Steiner's comment that a long immersion in the literature of Nazi brutality made him feel like he was reading pornography, I knew what he meant.

Evil had its compensations. The absolute evil of the Nazis made our side, my side, at least as it had been in the past, seem absolutely good—regardless of any knowledge I might have picked up to the contrary—and I liked that. I still like it; today I have no immunity at all to the political sentimentality of World War II anti-Nazi movies like *Casablanca* or *Passage to Marseille,* let alone to that of stronger stuff like *Odette,* a film about a British secret agent captured and tortured by the Gestapo, or *The World at War* TV series, which I have seen at least half a dozen times. In that sentimentality, of course, is a link to the fairy tale sensibility—with a happy ending guaranteed to follow the worst of stories—that I started with.

Because Nazism was a fairy tale and a sentimental melodrama, both cleanly cut off by history, the trial of Adolf Eichmann—the Nazi war criminal abducted from Argentina in 1960 by Israeli agents and executed in Israel in 1962—had no real effect on me. Like the Japanese soldiers who keep turning up in the Philippines, still refusing to believe the war is over, Eichmann seemed to me a sort of unreasonable anomaly. I knew that many Nazis had found refuge in South America—I had seen *Notorious*, after all—but I thought of them as inhabitants of a time warp, relics, curiosities of history. "Adolf Hitler is alive and well and living in Argentina" did not send chills down the spine of anyone I knew. Eichmann had been in hiding as long as I had been alive, and in those years I had built up a system that proved, emotionally at least, that his life had ended when mine began. Because he was alive, and real, he had no place in that system, and so I cast him out of it.

Even before Eichmann's execution I had been to Germany, with a group of students. We spent a good part of the summer of 1961 in a West German Socialist Party youth camp that had once served as an SS training station; we visited Dachau, where the group leader, whose parents had both been killed in extermination camps, had a heart attack. I liked Germany, but something of Dachau stayed with me—simply, there was a greater horror there, beneath my feet and in front of my eyes, than my system of all-in-the-past could contain. Later, when we went on to Yugoslavia, the group leader warned us against using any of the German we had picked up. "People haven't forgotten what the Germans did here," he said. "You don't want anyone thinking you're German." I remember finding that quaint. At sixteen, I thought people who lived their lives in reference to the past were less than alive.

Years later, I visited Germany with my wife. Things looked different. Everyone knew Germans "didn't want to talk about the war," but there was something ominous in the forgetfulness. West Berlin was too bright and rich, the famous Berlin architecture jokes about the new monuments and memorials too happily ironic. We headed south. The Germans we encountered close up were obnoxious, arrogant, flesh on the bones of stereotypes. My wife decided she wanted to see Dachau; it was on our way. I told her—with a touch of I've-been-around condescension, but also with complete seriousness—that if she knew what it was like to go there she would not want to go. We went, and drove out of Germany that night as if we were being chased.

Still, these were ghosts to lay to rest. By this time—1967, 1968—equations of the Nazi regime with the American government were common, on account of either the Vietnam War or political repression at home, and because of the sentimental fairy tale I carried in my head I accepted some of those equations, or if nothing more did not trouble to dispute them to myself. Nixon, I reasoned, would have been a Nazi, given the chance. And what good was history if it couldn't serve as a metaphor?

About a year ago, I was watching *The World at War* again, and enjoying it as I always had. I got a thrill from the aura of nobility surrounding the struggle against Hitler; seeing *Passage to Marseille* once more, I wondered, for perhaps the hundredth time, what it must have been like to have fought in a war one knew was right, a feeling my own generation had not had, a pleasure I could contemplate only through a film of nostalgia. Then one night I saw a public television documentary about Lebensborn, the Nazi program devoted to the racial purification of the Reich. Women who had worked in baby-breeding institutions now spoke guardedly of Germans making better Germans. It was ludicrous: the most absurd level of Nazi narcissism, even more distant and unreal than a Sgt. Fury comic book. But then the film shifted into an area I knew nothing about.

It showed how, in Poland and other Central European countries, Nazis would assemble villagers and townspeople. As often as not, the men and women would be shot or deported. In some cases, as in Lidice, in Czechoslovakia, the children would be sent off to camps to be experimented on; the knowledge gained might prove useful to the SS doctors running Lebensborn. But occasionally there were a few children who were lucky. They were blond; they matched special SS skull and spinal charts; they were very young. Accordingly, they were taken to Germany to be raised by Germans. Ideally, they would benefit from the experiments performed on their neighbors, or their friends, or their brothers and sisters.

In a few years the war was over. By that time, the kidnapped children had disappeared into the postwar chaos of the Third Reich. Some had no families left; some had come from towns that no longer existed even as places on the map. But the parents of others had survived, and they began to look for their children.

The remainder of the film was devoted to the results of this appalling search. There on the screen were two women, sisters, who, as adults, had somehow been reunited with the remains of their family. In a queer way, their terrible stories paralleled my childhood nightmares of kidnappers and bogeymen, but their stories made me shudder at the conceit of those nightmares: while I was thinking them up, these women were living them out. They spoke nervously about games they had invented, more than thirty years ago, hoping to preserve a memory of their parents; about the secret, terrified attempts they had made to resist the new lives they were offered; about the slow and steady failures of their games and their resistance; about the hideous acceptance that eventually overtook them.

Here were people close to my own age who were just now emerging from Nazism—who had only in the last few years escaped it. As I watched them, my sense of history, of all-in-the-past, began to dissolve, and as the film continued it evaporated. Now one saw reporters trying to interview a woman who had been taken from her family in Central Europe during the war. Like the two sisters she grew up after the war in Germany, in a Lebensborn family; unlike them, she still lived there, and now had a family of her own. Through an organization formed to track down Lebensborn victims, her mother had located her. But the woman refused to have anything to do with her mother. I have a life, she said. It happened a long time ago. I do not remember my mother. The woman who raised me, here, is my mother. I have a life, leave me alone. The film ended with an appeal to the woman by her natural mother, now very old and living alone. Let me see you once before I die, she said. All these years I have dreamed of seeing you again. All that kept me alive was the thought that I might see you again. All these years I have prayed that you were safe. I am happy for you. I want to see my grandchildren. Why don't you answer my letters? I am going to die soon. I want to see you before I die.

One can call such an ending dishonest because it smothers the possibility of a pluralistic response to the event, but there may be no decent plurality of response. I was working as a TV critic when the Lebensborn documentary aired, but though I made pages of notes, I couldn't write about it. A sensibility I had nurtured for nearly three decades had fallen apart—more, in fact, because of the two sisters, who had escaped, than because of the young woman and the old woman, who had not. Identifying with the two sisters was possible; identifying with their Lebensborn sister and her mother was unthinkable.

I tried to forget about the show, and began a new job, writing about books; dozens of them, on every conceivable subject, were soon arriving in the mail. One of the first I picked up was Amnesty International's 1975 *Report on Torture*. Here I read that over the last fifteen years torture had become institutionalized in many parts of the world, not as anything so paltry as a means of securing information or confessions, but as policy, as the essence of terroristic, totalitarian power, as the foundation of politics, the secret behind public life. Most of this I knew, though I did not think about it very much. The last section of the book dealt with Chile after the coup against the Allende government. This passage jumped out:

Reports of direct Nazi influence keep cropping up. The most persistent report concerns Walter Rauff, once head of the SS in Milan. . . . Rauff, convicted at Nuremberg of mass murder—he devised the mobile gas chambers—escaped to Chile. West Germany has failed in its repeated attempts to extradite him . . . rumors are that he is directing Pinochet's prison system, running DINA,* and planning the work camps for children.

In Germany, years after the fact, two women had broken free of their Nazi kidnappers; in Chile, the story was likely beginning again, not in facile metaphor, but in person, in the flesh. I thought of Rauff, patiently biding his time for thirty years. I couldn't begin to think about the stories that might be told in Chile thirty years from now, by those who might spend their childhood in a Nazi's camps. And so, when a publicist for a New York publisher asked me if I liked books about Nazi hunters, I immediately said yes. I had never read one, but since then I have read quite a few.

2

Isser Harel was head of the Israeli secret service at the time of Adolf Eichmann's capture in 1960, an operation he directed; in *The House on Garibaldi Street* he writes of the thoughts he had when he was first informed that Eichmann, missing since the end

*DINA, the secret police apparatus established under Pinochet, is widely suspected of having engineered the Washington, D.C., assassination of Orlando Letelier—under Salvador Allende, Chile's ambassador to the United States, and in exile one of the most effective opponents of the Pinochet regime—and of his American aide Ronni Moffitt; an event that took place, as I write, yesterday. [It was later established in court that the murders of Letelier and Moffitt were the work of the American DINA agent Michael Townley, on orders from Manuel Contreras, head of DINA in Chile.]

of World War II, had been located. "I knew," Harel says, "that his principal function was the extermination of the Jews. . . . This somber chapter in the history of the Jewish people haunted me like a nightmare that had no place in the world of reality—something going so far beyond the known limits of dastardly crime, wanton cruelty and moral hatred that no human being could plumb the depths of its significance." There was a time when language of this sort was used, with effect, in political discourse and in writing history; today it is the language of pulp, of the thriller. ("As compelling as *The Odessa File*," says the publisher's blurb on Harel's nonfiction book.) Specifically, this is the language of the Nazi-hunting thriller—though no good thriller writer would employ a word so full of comic, Snidely Whiplash–associations as "dastardly"—and one recognizes Harel's language as thriller language because it is portentous, overdramatic, and overblown.

That is how it appears. Harel's words seem like thriller writing, and thus discourage analysis of what they say, not necessarily because they actually are overblown, but because those who write history, and who define the boundaries of respectable political discussion, have abandoned this kind of language. One has learned that those who are to be taken seriously on the subject of Nazism do not speak in this manner, and it is only because historians and political analysts have abandoned this language that thriller writers have been able to claim it. One can go further: it is only because historians and political analysts have abandoned this language that it has become necessary for thriller writers to claim it.

It has become necessary, I think, because Harel articulates some first and final truths about Nazism. Harel is saying that there is something in Nazism, in Nazi crime, that defies understanding—that cannot, for those who did not experience Nazi crime firsthand (and perhaps not even for them), be made real;

that cannot be adequately explained by facts or appeals to instrumentalities; that cannot be enclosed by theory—and he is saying
that, for him, it is in this that part of the true horror, the true
evil, of Nazism lies. It "had no place in the world of reality"; it
went "far beyond the known limits." Nazi crime cannot be simply
fitted into the fabric of human history, no matter how bloody
and criminal that history has been, Harel is saying in language
we have been schooled to dismiss. "No human being could
plumb the depths of its significance," except perhaps Sax Rohmer.
The House on Garibaldi Street—"More compelling than *The Mask
of Fu Manchu!*"

With that in mind, consider two recent books on the Nazi
period, Lucy S. Dawidowicz's *The War against the Jews, 1933–
1945,* and John Lukacs's *The Last European War, 1939–1941,* and
then the late Hannah Arendt's 1963 *Eichmann in Jerusalem,* a
report on Eichmann's trial, and also an inquiry into the extermination of the Jews and other racial or ethnic communities. In
neither of the first two books is there a single passage that in any
way resembles Harel's statement in style or meaning. Dawidowicz
avoids Harel's territory because she plainly believes she can explicate Nazi genocide with documentation and analysis, but while
she seems to be laying a road on solid ground, in truth she is
building a bridge over Harel's abyss. She pushes the inexplicable
to the side in favor of facts, goals, numbers, incidents, and results.
George Steiner notes in a review that other historians have found
Dawidowicz's material "almost too irrational, too incredible to
handle"; Dawidowicz's bypassing of this quality reduces the
event, and even to a degree conventionalizes it. If to a nonhisto-
rian like Harel Nazism by definition cannot be fully understood,
to a historian like Dawidowicz by definition nothing can fully
resist understanding. Lukacs, however, does not believe there is
all that much to understand. It is his *intention* to conventionalize
Nazism.

In *The Last European War* Nazism differs from ordinary European politics only by degree and, as it were, by accident. Fashionably, Lukacs reminds the reader again and again that Stalinism was far worse than Nazism—a contention that is, strictly in terms of numbers, questionable, and in the terms Harel raises beside the point. The irrational vanishes. Lukacs claims that the systematic extermination of the Jews, or anybody else, was not an essential element of Nazism, but merely represented the German response to the entry of the United States into the war, which Hitler is said to have blamed on pressure exerted by American Jews—a version of history that merely on the crude but rather primary level of chronology is patently false. The book is not to be taken seriously—but Lukacs's blithe refusal of Harel's confrontation with unthinkable evil is to be taken seriously. *The Last European War* represents that side of contemporary sensibility which has been able to deny any present-day significance to Nazi crime; which yearns, in an age of increasing individual crime and economic uncertainty, for an anticommunist society of order and discipline; which finds Nazism not only fascinating but in some ways attractive.

Thirteen years makes a difference. When Hannah Arendt wrote *Eichmann in Jerusalem,* memories were stronger; there were more witnesses to say no. (And there was Arendt herself, who would not have let Lukacs's book pass without comment.) Like *The Origins of Totalitarianism, Eichmann in Jerusalem* is a passionate book; Arendt's style has nothing in common with Harel's, but she does know his abyss. She does not explain it, because that is not what one does with an abyss; instead, cutting through the restraint one has come to expect from serious writers on Nazism, she locates it. Without in any way removing Nazism from history, she denies it any simple connection to ordinary political or criminal history, or to the history of anti-Semitism up to the Nazi era: the basic *purpose* of the Nazi regime, she writes in a proposition

so divorced from ordinary instrumentalities as to trivialize both
Dawidowicz and Lukacs simultaneously, was ultimately the committing of unheard-of crimes. In *Eichmann in Jerusalem* the
burden of Harel's thoughts—"no place in the world of reality . . .
something going so far beyond the known limits"—thoughts
which helped lead to Eichmann's capture, are, to Arendt, precisely the burden of the history the Nazis made.

It was when the Nazi regime declared that the German people not only
were unwilling to have any Jews in Germany but wished to make the
entire Jewish people disappear from the face of the earth that the new
crime, the crime against humanity—in the sense of a crime "against the
human status," or against the very nature of humankind—appeared . . .
an attack on human diversity as such, that is, upon a characteristic of the
"human status" without which the very words "mankind" or "humanity" would be devoid of meaning.

What the Nazis did, Arendt said, was something new: they
altered the limits of human action. In doing so the Nazis provided
humanity with more than a burden—the need to comprehend
their actions—they also provided a legacy: "It is in the very nature
of things human that every act that has once made its appearance
and has been recorded in the history of mankind stays with
mankind as a potentiality long after its actuality has become a
thing of the past . . . Once a specific crime has appeared for the
first time, its reappearance is more likely than its initial emergence
could ever have been."

It is this sort of uncompromised language, and this sort of
daring, daunting thinking, that has mostly disappeared from respectable work on Nazism—and it is this sort of vision, which
incorporates Harel's vision, or anti-vision, that the thriller writers
have taken up and used as the basis for the contemporary genre
of Nazi-hunting books. The genre is rooted in an acceptance of
Arendt's conviction that something exceptional took place in

Nazi Germany, and it is rooted in the belief that, as Arendt quotes Yosal Rogat's *The Eichmann Trial and the Rule of Law*, "evil violates a natural harmony which only retribution can restore . . . a wronged collectivity owes a duty to the moral order to punish the criminal"—the belief, in Arendt's own words, as she imagined "the only reason" that could justify Eichmann's execution, that "just as you supported and carried out a policy of not wanting to share the earth with the Jewish people and the people of a number of other nations . . . we find that no one, that is, no member of the human race, can be expected to want to share the earth with you."

This is a powerful basis for any genre of fiction. No matter how luridly the theme may be carried out, it raises a moral question that, given the Nazis living and holding economic and political power in South America, the United States, the Arab countries, or present-day Germany, has not been resolved, and in serious fiction has hardly been addressed, because the Nazi-hunting theme is so sensationalistic as to destroy the pretentions of serious fiction in advance. Thus the Nazis belong to the thriller writers, and they have seized on them, these best-selling authors of *The Boys from Brazil*, *The Odessa File*, *Marathon Man*, *The Wind Chill Factor*, and so many more, for many reasons, no doubt most of them less than noble. The most convincing of these authors have chosen to write about Nazi hunting because there is a reality, or an irreducible unreality, in the theme that no one else is facing; because there are true fears surfacing in these thrillers that these days can find a voice nowhere else.

3

The working papers for the then already-burgeoning legion of Nazi-hunting thriller writers were assembled in 1973 by British war correspondent William Stevenson, in his book *The Bormann*

Brotherhood. Stevenson's work was messy, speculative, teasing, and threatening—just right for a genre that sets its plots in the present but posits Nazi survivors as concrete threats to Israel, the United States, democracy, or, as the book covers like to say, "the fate of the world."

Stevenson detailed the efforts of ODESSA, or "The Bormann Brotherhood," an organization believed by some to have been assembled by Hitler's deputy Martin Bormann before the end of the war—though Bormann was officially considered a suicide upon the fall of Germany, his remains have never been positively identified—and administered by him ever since.* This network of safe houses and escape routes, monasteries and Allied intelligence agents, Swiss bank accounts and organized crime fronts, Stevenson argues, got many of the major SS war criminals out of Europe and reestablished lesser-known criminals in the power structures—of business, the police, the military, the diplomatic corps, the intelligence services, the universities, the financial institutions, and the governments—of postwar Egypt, Iraq, Argentina, Chile, Paraguay, the United States, West Germany, and numerous other countries. (It was only eight years ago that the then chancellor of West Germany, Kurt Kiesenger, was exposed by Nazi hunter Beate Klarsfeld as a former aide to Hitler.) Steven-

---

*In 1972, when, as has happened periodically with the Loch Ness Monster, speculation regarding Bormann's possible survival of the war and his current whereabouts reached a fever pitch, tooth and bone fragments that turned up in the course of the excavation of a West Berlin street were declared official Bormann remains by the Federal Republic of Germany. However, according to a 7 December 1994 Moscow dispatch in the *Frankfurter Allgemeine-Zeitung,* "Martin Bormann—Stalins Mann in Berlin?" Bormann died in the Soviet Union. The fall of the USSR, plus the expiration of a fifty-year embargo on certain KGB documents, allowed the former Secret Service agent Boris Tartakowski to publish chapters from a forthcoming memoir in the neo-fascist journal *Fatherland* claiming Bormann had been a KGB agent throughout the war, was spirited out of Germany upon the fall of Berlin in 1945, and lived out the rest of his life in Russia. Tartakowski reported being shown Bormann's grave, in a cemetery for Germans near Moscow's Lefortowo Prison, by a KGB general; the date on the tombstone was 1973.

son focuses especially on Reinhard Gehlen, under Hitler chief of anti-Soviet espionage. In postwar West Germany Gehlen supervised offensive intelligence and worked closely with the CIA. Here he emerges as centrally influencing the establishment of the Cold War and responsible for the infiltration of the CIA and other Western intelligence agencies by war criminals of all sorts, particularly those who first tasted blood as members of Eastern European fascist movements, and who, after the war, could pose convincingly as anticommunists, which, after all—so the reasoning went—they were.

Stevenson's information is often unconvincing; the emotion in his book is not. He speaks with rage and loathing of Klaus Barbie, the unrepentant "Butcher of Lyons," peddling his memoirs in South America; of Josef Mengele, "The Angel of Death," the doctor in charge of experiments at Auschwitz, living easily in Argentina off Nazi money smuggled out of Germany decades ago; of the thousands of free criminals they represent. Stevenson writes with real horror of the corruption of the Allied victory by the Allies' ready acceptance or recruitment of Nazis—and their "de-Nazification"—in the years that followed. The result, he argues, can only be a thinly disguised legitimization of Nazism as little more than a went-too-far version of ordinary history.

The assumptions of this world view are shared—on paper, at least—by almost all writers of Nazi-hunting thrillers, but of the many such books I've read over the last year, only one—Thomas Gifford's *The Wind Chill Factor*—communicates the sense of chaos and dread one would expect such a view of the world to churn up. The power of the novel is in the author's ability to lead his hero, and his reader, into something very close to an acceptance of Nazism, though in *The Wind Chill Factor* it is an acceptance of political power exercised secretly, in the present, all over the West, on a scale far beyond anything a writer like William Stevenson would ever imagine.

Set in 1972, the book begins in a blizzard that has cut off a small northern Minnesota town from the rest of the world. This is where the hero's late grandfather, presented as one of the many prominent Americans who in the 1930s actively supported Hitler, lived; it is where the hero, shamed by his grandfather's politics, grew up. The hero has returned, and there is a stunning scene as he enters his grandfather's house, wanders through the deserted rooms, and comes upon the framed photographs still hanging in the library: his grandfather with Goering, with Hitler, with Eva Braun. Soon the town is under siege. Citizens are killed, public buildings are blown up. Under cover of the storm, the siege is conducted by legatees of the man whose friendship with dead Nazis seemed so safely frozen in the past, by men protected by the wind chill factor, as the temperature drops, and drops, and drops, and nobody can move as a reading of 100° below zero waits in the dark.

As the story moves on, a different sort of cold settles over the book, a quality of horror similar to the wind chill factor only in that it too paralyzes, and mocks the will to act. Finally the hero's task is reduced not to solving the mystery he has stumbled into but to escaping it; he doesn't, and the book is made to ensure that at least for the time it takes to read the tale and sleep it off, you don't either.

As a reader approaches the end, the specter of Nazism as an inevitable and proper system for the ordering of human affairs cries out for acceptance, not because it is proper, but because the weight of its power, as exercised across three hundred pages, has come to seem so ubiquitous, so perfectly disguised, so unsurprising, that when a reader—god knows, when the hero—reaches for the comfort of institutions and friends on whose purposes and motives he has always depended, they dissolve at the touch, and in their place appear precise replicas, but with purposes and motives presumed by most to have perished with the Third Reich. The book creates a complete conspiracy, a conspiracy smiling over the naiveté of those who refuse to believe it is real, because the conspiracy has overthrown reality. Eager for any kind of certainty, the hero listens as the mystery is defined for him:

"I have been in constant touch with Europe all through the years—or, I should say, they've been in touch with me. Sometimes through Washington, the Pentagon, sometimes through your grandfather, but always in close touch. . . . I funneled our agents into key positions in our own government, in Canada, all through Central and South America—all our people. We chose which ones would escape from Germany, which ones would take over the postwar government there and in the other free countries of Europe, which ones would stand in the dock at Nuremberg. Obviously, we didn't want to keep the most famous ones, the symbols, and we didn't want the monsters, the real war criminals. . . . The only one we really failed with, the only one we really wanted and didn't get was Albert Speer. . . . In any case we have made great use of the scientists, the administrators, the intelligence operatives. Gehlen is only the most famous and Allen Dulles wanted him badly, particularly in the years immediately after hostilities ceased, when we knew so little about the Communist apparatus and he knew so much . . .

"What will be difficult for you to understand, of course, John," he said like a gentle schoolmaster, "is that what I am discussing with you is not a mad plot to rule the world—"

"But a perfectly serious, rational, right-minded plan to rule the world," I said.

I felt lightheaded, like giggling. Or crying. I tightened my grip. I was fighting the icicle.

"Not a mad plot, John, but United States policy, a continuing policy, but beneath the surface. Elected officials have seldom been involved or even informed of the movement. We don't need figureheads, you see— all we need are the intelligence people, the operations people, the diplomats, the professors, and a handful of Congressmen at key points, on the proper committees and so on. You see . . ."

Such a situation parallels, with a vast inflation of realities, the beliefs of some private, real-life Nazi hunters, as recounted in *Wanted! The Search for Nazis in America,* a book by former *Village Voice* reporter Howard Blum. After finding years of efforts to expose war criminals subverted by bureaucratic dissembling, the people Blum spoke with have come to believe either that the U.S. Immigration Service is infiltrated by ODESSA, controlled by functionaries American members of ODESSA have bought, or that it is sabotaged by politicians whose crypto-Nazi sympathies ensure they do not even have to be bought, merely pointed in the right direction. *The Wind Chill Factor* wraps up all three possibilities in one, but the point is not that because Nazi war criminals live in safety or hold political power the Reich will rise again; I don't believe that, and I doubt Thomas Gifford does either. But I do believe that nothing is more difficult—if it is possible at all—than to reestablish limits that have been smashed.

I said earlier that there were fears surfacing in Nazi-hunting thrillers that these days could find a voice nowhere else; *The Wind Chill Factor* is frightening because, drawing on the brief contained in books like *The Bormann Brotherhood,* in Simon Wiesenthal's *The Murderers among Us* or Blum's *Wanted!* it gives voice to the fear that, contrary to our day-to-day assumptions, we are living in a world in which it is the principle of the destruction of all limits on human action that has been reestablished, and not the limits themselves. For me, few things have brought home the weight of Nazism, as a fact of history and an idea about action, more than this pulp novel about how easily the world the Nazis made could be fitted within our own. The quality of incomprehensibility that can adhere—I sometimes think, must adhere—to a contemplation of Nazi crime isn't lessened by Gifford's pretense that Nazis control the West, but it is made palpable by the very shock of that pretense, and by the dim echoes of that pretense in contemporary reality. What is then beyond easy definition is not some mere disturbance in the past, or an incident in the history of the Jews, which is how Nazism is more and more commonly seen, but a fantasized subversion of the present, which, once perceived, then makes the past real, and makes real its legacy of broken limits, symbolized by those Nazis who will never be hunted down, upon which the present society rests.

Rolling Stone, 4 November, 18 November, 2 December 1976

You Could Catch It

O n 22 February 1991, a small ad appeared in the *Times Literary Supplement*. Running in French, just below the much larger announcement of a "Search for the Director of the Bancroft Library" at the University of California at Berkeley, the ad read:

> GUY DEBORD
>
> Judging it necessary to disavow the new Editions Lebovici, SEEKS LITERARY AGENT or distinguished independent editor for books that will expose the modernization of the society of the "integrated spectacle." Write to . . .

There was an irony here. The Bancroft Library was the one place in California—perhaps in the United States—where one could still find the now-yellowing photocopies of transcripts of the Sigma project, launched in 1964 by the late novelist, junkie, and self-described "cosmonaut of inner space" Alexander Trocchi. Sigma was meant to revolutionize the planet: to bring together cultural dissidents from all over the West, until their various schemes and finally single voice, seductive and plain, would rise from Sigma's clandestine circulars into a rumor which would turn into a shout that soon enough would leave the discourse of power and money in doubt. And then anything would be possible.

That voice was Guy Debord's. In the mid-fifties, in Paris, he and Trocchi had made common cause. Trocchi joined the Lettrist International, Debord's tiny, closed group of Lollardist writers and artists; from 1954 to 1957 they published a brutal, funny, unyieldingly disruptive little mimeographed newsletter called *Potlatch*, the prototype for Trocchi's Sigma papers. In 1957, Trocchi became a founding member of the Situationist International, a shadowy, pan-European circle of aesthetic revolutionaries, or revolutionary aesthetes—people convinced that by developing a critique in words to match the "critique in acts" they saw erupting all over the globe, they could detonate a new revolution that would leave Communism and capitalism in twin dustbins of history. Across the next decade, through countless splits, exclusions, recruitments, disappearances, the situationists, with Debord always at the center, pursued a carefully composed assault on modern life in all its forms. The attack was noisy, arch, and cool, at once vulgar and aristocratic: in a word, exciting. In the pages of the journal *Internationale situationniste*, published in Paris from 1958 to 1969 in twelve expertly designed numbers, the band worked the rewrite desk, forcing the news of the world to surrender truths it wanted to hide: the truths that, in the situationist revision, linked commodities to suicide, art to blindness, wealth to alienation, riot to poetry, nihilism to happiness.

In late 1967, Debord published *The Society of the Spectacle:* 221 theses on social life as a show that rendered all men and women, even those who staged the play, passive spectators and consumers of their estrangement from their own words, gestures, acts, and desires. It was a severe, Hegelian treatise. But somehow, perhaps simply in the incisive cruelty of its prose ("All that was once directly lived has become mere representation. . . . In a world that has *really* been turned on its head, truth is a moment of falsehood"), the book was also pop: the ideas moved with the same implacable momentum the Rolling Stones would find a year later in "Sympathy for the Devil." *The Society of the Spectacle* was discovered, trumpeted, damned, and celebrated as the signal text of the students and workers' uprising in France in May 1968; discovered in the midst of that unshaped revolt, and especially after it, the book lasted, traveling the world in pirate editions and unauthorized translations. I read it for the first time in 1980, en route to London to talk to the Gang of Four and Lora Logic, punk musicians, and it was as if the story I was after was right in my lap, the complete punk critique of public housing, deathly entertainment, "at home he feels like a tourist," "life ain't gonna show at a retail price," "God save history, God save your mad parade." It was all there, and yet the critique, in Debord's cutting words, was already looking back from a future of stone—the future punk would fail to crack. Debord's critique was as unsatisfied in 1980 as it was in 1967, or as it remains today. "A little Yes and a big No," as George Grosz titled his autobiography. Yes, you can make your own world; no, you won't.

Always, it was the pessimism in Debord's voice—the romance and dispensation of defeat—that kept his little yes alive, and it was his little yes that gave his big no its kick. From the fifties on, friends and enemies alike called Debord absolutist, megalomaniacal, paranoid—all the charges were true, proved by his words, and then dissolved by his words as you read. Through the pages of *Internationale situationniste,* a vast critical ambition, black humor, and the steeliness of a certain reserve drove the progressive chronicle of "the collapse of a world," as if the great day were almost present, issue by issue, as if one needed to wait only for the next number to sight the new dawn. In *The Society of the Spectacle* the collapse was a practical impossibility and a moral necessity, an immovable object and an irresistible force. T. J. Clark, in the late 1960s a member of the Situationist International, spoke much later, in 1985, in his book *The Painting of Modern Life*, of Debord's "chiliastic serenity"; as the situationists liked to say, "the real revolutionary knows how to wait."

There is great weight in the accumulation of theses in *The Society of the Spectacle*, and also a quickening. One feels the weight of the world as it is as one reads, but also the world straining, breaking, ready, as in the English Civil War, to turn upside down. But of course there is also everyday life—the ordinary exchange of appearances and humiliations, time wasted and time spent. In Debord's case this meant Editions Lebovici—before the unsolved murder in 1984 of its owner, the film producer Gérard Lebovici, the house was named Champ Libre. From the early 1970s, after the Situationist International broke up, Debord had guided its list as an elegant voice in the wilderness. Then in 1991 Lebovici's widow made to sell the company and Debord left, taking his books with him, threatening to have all stock on hand destroyed. The house crumbled amid charges of deceit and betrayal, and so Debord cried out, in his little advertisement, from a greater wilderness. He had always held himself out of the light, dodging celebrity if not fame, never appearing on radio or television, declining all interviews, refusing any medium but his own; now his refusal left him isolated before history as well as commerce, before those readers he had, over the years, gathered from all over the world. He spoke in the only voice left to him, the voice of a crank, promising the "books that will expose the . . ." precisely as in the small ad that for years has run in every issue of the *Nation:*

> SCHOLARLY BOOKLET PROVES
> JESUS NEVER EXISTED!
> Conclusive proof Flavius Josephus created
> fictional Jesus, authored Gospels. AMAZING
> but ABSOLUTELY INCONTROVERTIBLE! Send $5
> to . . .

As it happened, in the exchange of appearances and humiliations, this wilderness opened onto a great street. In 1992 Debord contracted with Gallimard, the most prestigious and powerful house in France, both for new titles and the republication of his old ones. Gallimard speedily brought out the third French edition of *La société du spectacle* and reprinted Debord's 1988 *Commentaires sur la société du spectacle.* Which brought them to *Panegyric,* Debord's last book with Editions Lebovici, published as *Panégyrique* in 1989, and in 1993 simultaneously reappearing in French and appearing in English for the first time—as cryptic and self-effacing a self-portrait as can be found anywhere.

In his *Le Monde* review of the Lebovici edition of *Panegyric,* Philippe Sollers jumped up and down ("the most original and the most radical thinker of our time"), clapped his hands, waved his arms, and finally all but grabbed passers-by by the throat: "I bought this book of 92 pages for 80 frs, and I read it immediately, right on the street." Anyone can certainly do the same with the English version—big type and big margins don't leave room for too many words on its seventy-nine pages—and even if one knows nearly nothing of Debord, one might be drawn to do so. The tone is seductive, the feeling elegiac, and the book is never what it seems.

"All my life I have seen only troubled times, extreme divisions in society, and immense destruction," Debord begins, dramatically, finishing the sentence with a flat *no:* "I have joined in these troubles." He speaks as "a person who has led an action" and promises "to say what I have done." "I will be compelled to go into some details," he says—but he doesn't. We're told he was born in Paris in 1931 and, by allusion, that he came into his own there in about 1952. He speaks of "the grave responsibility that has often been attributed to me for the origins, or even for the command, of the May 1968 revolt." That's about it for conventional autobiography.

Aside from a single first-name-only reference to Debord's second wife, no comrade, associate, enemy, friend, or lover is ever named directly. Debord's best-known attachment and his most famous book are mentioned—once each, and only in a single broken quotation from a 1972 *Nouvel Observateur:* "The author of *Society of the Spectacle* has always appeared as the discreet but indisputable head . . . at the center of the changing constellation of brilliant conspirators of the Situationist International, a kind of cold chess player, rigorously leading . . . the game whose every move he has foreseen." But this panegyric-in-miniature is dismissed as a particularly egregious example of "the police form of knowledge"—even if a reader might suspect it's meant to be read for exactly what it says.

Panegyric is in fact a whole book of quotations, akin to Debord's first book, *Mémoires,* which was published in 1958. In that book—a cryptogram about the long first year of the Lettrist International, beginning in June 1952 and ending in September 1953—Debord simply cut up books and magazines for quotes and pictures; he assembled them into forty-six montages which were overpainted by his situationist comrade Asger Jorn. Save for three epigraphs, not a word carried an author's name; there was no identification of affiliations or traveling companions. Still, compared to *Mémoires, Panegyric* reads like an ordinary book. Most of the quotations are identified. You can tell Debord's words from those of others. Or so it appears, until he warns that "at a critical moment in the trouble of the Fronde, Gondi . . . improvised happily before the Parlement de Paris a beautiful quotation attributed to an ancient author, whose name everyone vainly searched for, but which could be best applied to his own panegyric: *In difficillimis Reipublicae temporibus, urbem non deserui; in prosperis nihil de publico delibavi; in desperatis, nihil timui.* He himself translated it as 'In bad times, I did not abandon the city; in good times, I had no private interests; in desperate times, I feared nothing.'" The warning pays off near the end of the book, when Debord, speaking of "men more knowledgeable than I," launches into yet another long quotation—this time a blind one, because he is quoting himself.

What is going on here is this: having introduced himself as a figure of history, a man of deeds and events, Debord—who ended *Mémoires* with the faintly reproduced words "I wanted to speak the language of my century"—immediately turns himself into a literary construct. I don't mean he is engaging in any sort of structuralist conceit. Rather, when he says his quotations are meant "only to show fully of what stuff this adventure and myself are made," he enters a history of his own making; the noisy megalomania of *Panegyric*'s first-sentence claim to a world stage becomes a quiet conversation with the past. Debord disappears into the shades of a host of writers; as he takes on their shadows, they take on his. It is in this sense that *Panegyric* is almost purely literary, in this sense that one need know or care nothing of the author to be captured by it: Debord is seeking to hijack his era into timelessness, and to pull that off he must be emotionally specific and otherwise hazy. So if again and again one is reminded of Machiavelli, it is not the author of *The Prince*, a man of affairs trying to make something happen, but the author of *The History of Florence;* the man who could write "I love my native city more than my own soul," and who, to write the *Discourses,* dressed himself in the raiments of the ancients, the better to commune with them—and they with him? Debord's story, like Machiavelli's, is a story of loss, defeat, and patience, and so intensely written that after a bit there is little need to ask how, who, why, what for. Often insisting he is more than history ("I wonder if even one other person has dared to behave like me, in this era"; "it could almost be believed . . . that I was the only person to have loved Paris"—compared with this, "No one has twice raised Paris to revolt" is no boast but a modest apology), Debord seeks history's sleep—the sleep of Sleeping Beauty.

The formal divisions in *Panegyric,* then—chapters on ancestors, infamy, military strategy, exile, and alcoholism, for example—don't mean much; a language is being spoken here, there is no account being settled. But one chapter, beginning "In the zone of perdition where my youth went as if to complete its education," is the center of the book—the power center, the place that anchors every quotation, that gives Debord's many lines that fly their wings.

As he did in *Mémoires,* in his second film, *Sur le passage de quelques personnes à travers une assez courte unité de temps* (On the Passage of a Few People through a Rather Brief Moment in Time, 1959), and in his last film, *In girum imus nocte et consumimur igni* (We Dance in a Circle in the Night and Are Consumed by the Fire, 1978), Debord returns once more to the site of the beginning of his entry into "play and public life"—returns again to the first years of the fifties, when, as he said in *In girum,* "There was, then, on the left bank of the river . . . a neighborhood where the negative held court." He returns obsessively, as if he will never get to the bottom of this moment, never succeed in making the milieu give up its secrets. It was a setting, Debord once wrote, where one could feel the world turning; whenever he writes of it, he instantly summons up the fortune and danger of, once, having been in the right place at the right time.

The people there, Debord says in *Panegyric,* were wastrels. What brought them to their stage was "modern poetry. . . . We were a handful who thought that it was necessary to carry out its program in reality"—to drive its stampede toward the dissolution of language straight through all the walls of social life.

An angry queen of France once called to order the most seditious of her subjects: "There is rebellion in imagining that one could rebel."

That is just what happened. Another, earlier contemner of the world, who said that he had been a king in Jerusalem, had touched on the heart of the problem, almost with these very words: the spirit whirls in all directions, and on its circuits the spirit returns. All revolutions go down in history, yet history does not fill up; the rivers of revolution return from whence they came, only to flow again.

To read Guy Debord for the writer he is one must untangle this mix of guff, preening, simplicity, and profundity. One must be able to open oneself to the shocking eloquence of "All revolutions go down in history, yet history does not fill up" ("Toutes les révolutions entrent dans l'histoire, et l'histoire n'en regorge point"—the rhythm may actually be stronger in James Brook's translation). Even if the allusion is clear—to Ecclesiastes 1:6–7: "All the rivers run into the sea; yet the sea is not full"—one must be ready to entertain the notion that Debord's version, at least for our place and time, is better.

This is, of course, not modern poetry, but old-fashioned poetry. The image of history as a magic cauldron that cannot be filled is more than a lot of good historians leave behind; as the image stays in the mind as one reads, if it does, the rest of Debord's little book takes its shape. From year to year, from deeds to exile, from hangover to glorious binge, from calumny to celebration, the cauldron empties, becomes a gong, is struck, and sounds the call of lost youth: "One could feel certain that we would never do any better." It's corny, like so much of Debord's best work; if he is, as *Le Monde* called him in 1988, "The Last of the Mohicans," that is because one of the things he refuses to give up is romanticism. All that really means, though, is that he refuses to pretend the world has satisfied the demands he and others once made on it; quietly, he writes to keep those demands loose in the world, to let the world be judged by them.

Believing, as Sadie Plant writes in *The Most Radical Gesture: The Situationist International in a Postmodern Age*, in "the possibility of a life of playful opportunity in which the satisfaction of desires, the realisation of pleasures, and the creation of chosen situations would be the principal activities"—believing that, as the half-century turned, the time was ripe for everyday life to replace the canvas or the page as the site of experiment and creation—the situationists were cranks, doomed to history's back alleys. Debord's pathetic little ad in the *TLS* was coded in his grandiosity. What was not coded, however, were the actual words by which the situationist project was shaped and pursued—their heat and light—or those which Debord is still writing. It's scary to read the words of cranks; they're like a disease, and you could catch it. But that was the idea then, and that is the idea now.

London Review of Books, 25 March 1993

■ On 30 November 1994, Guy Debord shot himself in his house in Bellevue de la Montagne. He was sixty-two.

Dylan as Historian

B ob Dylan's "Blind Willie McTell" moves in a circle of images—tent meetings of itinerant holiness preachers, antebel-
lum plantations, the slave driver's lash, chain gangs, painted
women, drunken rakes—and it calls up many more. You might
think of Ingmar Bergman's *The Seventh Seal:* the road traveled
early in the film by Max von Sydow's thirteenth-century knight,
back from the Crusades to find God on his own ground. Instead
he finds plague and the Angel of Death; mad monks and a line
of flagellants; torturers and a child witch on a huge pile of sticks
and branches, ready to be burned. The witch is convinced of her
guilt, and the knight accepts her punishment, even though he
understands that it is his homeland, his realm of knowable good
and evil, that's guilty; even if it's a guilt that his world, with curses
laid on it six hundred years later by a filmmaker, will never have
to pay for. But to say all of this, to say any of it, to dive straight
into the world made by "Blind Willie McTell," is to violate the
sense of time that governs the tune—to go into it too fast.

The song dates to 1983. It was a discarded track from *Infidels,*
Dylan's first commercial step away from the born-again Christianity—the shocking apostasy of one born and raised a Jew—that

had ruled his three previous records: *Slow Train Coming, Saved,* and *Shot of Love,* increasingly lifeless works that had all but destroyed a subjective, critical voice with the imposition of a received ideology. Jesus was the answer, the albums said; if you didn't believe it, if you didn't believe answers were the question, you were damned. "How does it feel," the Christian songs seemed to ask, "to be on your own, with no direction home, like a complete unknown," and the songs answered: it feels like perdition. Still, despite its title, *Infidels* seemed secular; it was full of protest songs. War was bad; capitalism was bad; *Infidels* was a hit. Critics approved and the radio played it. Listening now, you can imagine why "Blind Willie McTell" was put aside. It would have dissolved the certainties and rancor of the rest of the music, upended it, given it the lie.

Still too fast. "Blind Willie McTell" begins slowly, with the hesitations, doubts, but finally irreducible willfulness that defines the blues. It is in fact just a rehearsal. An earlier, full-band recording had been dumped; this sounds like an attempt to find the song Dylan must have heard inside the song. Here he hits D-flat on the piano, in the Dorian mode, which communicates like a minor key, somber and fearful. The mode takes him back to the old ballads and country blues that shaped his first music, and back to the invention of Christian music as it's known, to the beginnings of Gregorian chant and the piety loaded into it. There are following steps from guitarist Mark Knopfler, marking time, but this you barely register. What you feel is absence, as if Dylan is for some reason refusing to follow his first note with whatever notes it might imply. Then he hits E-flat, then D-flat again, and the song gets underway.

No knowledge of musical notation or musical history is needed to catch the drama in the moment. The message is clear because it is coded in more than a millennium of musical culture, high and low, vulgar and sanctified: *this is it*. This is the last word.

Who was, who is, Bob Dylan? In the rush of the mid-1960s—
when he made the music that, had it not been made, no one
would be speaking of him now—it was obvious that he was, and
performed as, someone who was always a step ahead of the times.
("I'm only about twenty minutes ahead," Dylan told John Lennon in the mid-sixties, "so I won't get far.") In late 1965, as the
protest politics of the decade were hardening into slogans, he
argued for the substitution of dada over directives on placards
(". . . cards with pictures of the Jack of Diamonds and the Ace
of Spades on them. Pictures of mules, maybe words. . . . 'camera,' 'microphone,' 'loose,' just words—names of some famous
people"). In 1968 he countered the Beatles' super-psychedelic
Sgt. Pepper's Lonely Hearts Club Band with music that sounded
as if it could have been made by a particularly literary and reflec-
tive Hank Williams in 1953, just a year before Elvis Presley cut
his first singles, assuming Hank Williams wasn't already dead. But
today one has no idea who Bob Dylan is. Who is the man who,
nearing his fiftieth birthday, appeared on the Grammys telecast
to receive a Lifetime Achievement Award, and sang "Masters of
War," his twenty-eight-year-old song about arms merchants? He
sang as if to break the spell of the Gulf War, the war you could
have watched live if you'd changed channels from CBS to CNN.
His words were so slurred the song was at first recognizable only
by its melody, the melody now wrung out of the old acoustic
ballad you might have in your mind by a three-piece hipster band
that called up beat coffeehouses and Chicago blues joints, a band
that made no concessions to anyone's sense of time. The equations Dylan now offers can't be factored. He no longer beats the
Jesus drum, but the echoes are there in any interview: his revulsion at wanton women and loose desire, his insistence on someone else's sin. Reading the conversations, the nice career talk
suddenly shaken down, you can almost see the eyes that once

seemed to freeze an epoch in an image go cult blank. But this is not what happens in "Blind Willie McTell."

It's long been obvious that Bob Dylan can no longer be listened to as any sort of avatar; "Blind Willie McTell" makes it clear that his greatest talent is for bringing home the past, giving it flesh—and proving, as the ethnologist H. L. Goodall, Jr., puts it, that "in addition to the lives we lead we also live lives we don't lead." Art is made partly to reveal those lives—to take their lead. And this is what happens in "Blind Willie McTell."

Those slow first notes raise a sign: "Seen the arrow on the doorpost / Saying, 'This land is condemned / All the way from New Orleans / To Jerusalem.'" "From new Or-lee-ans to Jer-u-sa-lem," Dylan sings, drawing out the words until the line they trace seems to circle the globe again and again. The sign sparks a quest, and the only active incident in the song: "I traveled through East Texas / Where many martyrs fell." Everything else in "Blind Willie McTell" is passive, a witnessing: I saw, I heard. Or an imperative, a demand that the listener witness, too: see, hear, *smell*. As one scene after another opens and fades, the senses are alive, but only to transgression. There's no hope of action or change; all is crime and failure, "power and greed." In Revelation, the last book of the New Testament, the Lamb of God opens the seven seals of a book, and terrible visions burst out with every loosening; it's only the seventh seal that can reveal God's final resolution. In "Blind Willie McTell" the first visions are present, brought down to earth and into the everyday, but the seventh seal is missing. There is only a plainly irreligious affirmation, which can't be fitted to the forgiveness or even the knowledge of any sin. I've traveled, the singer says, I've seen, I've heard, but I know nothing. Or almost nothing. I know one thing: "I traveled through East Texas / Where many martyrs fell / And no one can sing the blues like / Blind Willie McTell."

As Dylan sang in 1983, Blind Willie McTell, born in Georgia in 1898, was twenty-four years dead. His work is found on archival albums; he sang sacred songs, dirty songs, story songs, rags, blues, whatever people on the street would pay him to play. Most famously he wrote and sang "Statesboro Blues," a 1971 hit for the Allman Brothers. He played twelve-string guitar—which he first heard played, he said, by Blind Lemon Jefferson, who indeed traveled out from his birthplace in East Texas, though he fell in Chicago, in 1929, according to legend freezing to death on the street. McTell had a light, romancing tone, altogether inappropriate, one might think, for a Bob Dylan song about the resistance of Judgment Day; about the way, as the believer waits for it, Judgment Day recedes.

Perhaps the most entrancing challenge in "Blind Willie McTell" is to hear in its namesake's music what Bob Dylan heard. In Dylan's song, revelation struggles to rise out of every scene the singer witnesses, but only the profane refrain that ends each verse—"No one can sing the blues like . . .," "But nobody can . . .," and, once, startlingly, "I KNOW NO ONE . . ."—can take the witness from one place to another. As revival tents are taken down, folded, stowed, and driven off to the next town, the singer hears only a hoot owl, perhaps imagines it as himself: "The stars above / The barren trees / Was his only audience." He sees a harlot and a dandy, "bootleg whiskey in his hand," and for that line Dylan's voice reaches a pitch of disgust and pain not matched for lines formally describing things far worse: "See them big plantations burning," he sings with an almost laconic nostalgia, "hear the cracking of the whip / Smell that sweet magnolia blooming / See the ghosts of slavery ships."

But those lines need no more disgust. They take you into some immobile past-present that can never be escaped; they make you put your hands into a wound that will never be closed. One hundred and twenty-six years ago, in his second inaugural ad-

dress, Abraham Lincoln imagined that the Civil War might "con-
tinue . . . until every drop of blood drawn by the lash, shall be
paid by another drawn by the sword." But the debt hasn't been
paid, and "Blind Willie McTell"—most of all in the old and
wearied tones of Dylan's voice—says that it can't be. The singer
can't pay it, and neither can Jesus. That the singer has found
something Jesus can't pay for is in some way his truest testament
of faith, his proof that he took his faith to its limits, and found
those limits in the crimes of the world.

One phrase seems to hide silently behind all the lines of the
song: "Vanity of vanities, all is vanity"—Ecclesiastes 1:2. It isn't
surprising, then, that "Blind Willie McTell" quotes the same
source, with "God is in his heaven," or that Dylan changes the
words that follow in the Bible from "And thou upon the earth"
to "And we all want what's his"—turns the words sour, insisting
that we have cut ourselves off from God, seeing in his face only
our own greed and lust for power. But Ecclesiastes is more than
a reference in "Blind Willie McTell"; "Blind Willie McTell" is a
version.

Both the song and the lamentations of Ecclesiastes, "son of
David, king in Jerusalem," are about the absolute rebuke the
world offers every believer—every believer in anything, be it
Yahweh, Jesus, earthly justice, money, love, or simply a world
better than one finds when one looks, when for an instant one
can glimpse not only power and greed but also intimations of
honor and right. "I have seen the task which God hath given to
the sons of men to be exercised therewith," the king said. "He
hath made everything beautiful in its time; also he hath set the
world in their heart, yet so that man cannot find out the work
that God hath done from the beginning even to the end. . . . And
he that increaseth knowledge increaseth sorrow." Perfection has
been laid in the heart as a rebuke to all, because not even the best
are worthy of it. Even the best of humankind sense perfection

first and last as suffering, for it is given to them to feel "the evil work that is done under the sun." "There is nothing new under the sun"; but for the witness every crime is new. Against this, Dylan offers only "Nobody can sing the blues / Like Blind Willie McTell"—but in the constant renewal of the way he sings the phrase, in the infinite reserves of spectral comradeship he seems to find in it, it is, for as long as the song lasts, somehow enough.

Always slowly, with Dylan's piano keeping a tricky, unsettled country time, sometimes flashing up and rattling as if it were Mississippi bluesman Skip James back from the dead to play the keys, "Blind Willie McTell" rides the bones of the melody of "St. James Infirmary," the standard perhaps done best—certainly most delicately, and most harrowingly—by Bobby "Blue" Bland. It's a source Dylan acknowledges in his last verse, as the singer finds himself in the "St. James Hotel"—though perhaps there is a second source. Closer in spirit is an early blues recording by an obscure singer named Richard "Rabbit" Brown (ca. 1880–1937), a man whose most notable brush with common knowledge came in 1962, when he was cited as a favorite in the notes to Bob Dylan's self-titled debut album. Set down in 1927, the year McTell first recorded, Brown's song is called "James Alley Blues," after the New Orleans neighborhood where he lived.

Dylan's recasting, or rereading, of "James Alley Blues," if that is what "Blind Willie McTell" is, breaks down any useful geneal-ogy of what comes from what in American music. The melody is not similar; no analogue of either Brown's weird percussive guitar flappings and gongings, or of his comedy ("'Cause I was born in the country / She thinks I'm easy to rule / She try to hitch me to her wagon, she want to drive me like a mule"), is present. But the spirit is: Brown's preternatural, bottomless strangeness, seem-ingly the voice of another world, right here, where you live, the prosaic dissolved by a faraway ominousness, a sense of the un-canny, an insistence on paradox and curse.

Dylan was singing "James Alley Blues" in 1961, when he taped a poor rendition at a friend's apartment; he may not have listened to it since, but no one who has heard "James Alley Blues" forgets it. As Brown must have with that song, the power of which has very little to do with words, Dylan saw all around his life with "Blind Willie McTell," and as one listens one is given entry to all the lives moving in the song; one is drawn in. The song is rich enough to pull a skeptic close even to Dylan's acceptance of Jesus Christ, for the song is undeniably the fruit of that event, and rich enough to lead one to the sort of sights its singer witnesses, with little more than the song itself as a companion—as, finally, the singer, a solitary, cut off or cut loose from God, has no more than his memories of an old blues singer.

San Francisco Focus, July 1991

Happy Endings

S ome months before the critical tidal wave that lofted Robert Altman's *Nashville* and E. L. Doctorow's *Ragtime* into the promised land, a cartoon by Edward Koren appeared in the *New Yorker*. Pictured was an author, grinning like a madman and pounding away at his typewriter as a chorus line of imagined reviewers cheered him on. "A brilliant achievement," one critic shouted. "Writing at its most illuminating," cried a second. "Gripping." "Explosive." "Long overdue." "True vision." "Plain speech." And finally the prize: "Proclaims the failure of our civilization as a whole."

Koren's cartoon says as much about the drift of present-day discourse as it does about an author's fantasies. As *Ragtime* and *Nashville* prove, a stylish work that proclaims the failure of our civilization—of America, to be precise—has become the artistic equivalent of the sucker punch. It is no matter that *Ragtime* starts out in the early years of the century, or that *Nashville* is set in the present; stories that seek to put an end to a history are a never-ending story.

The book and the movie, in their different ways (Doctorow with solemn or wry irony, Altman with happy-go-lucky swings of a sledgehammer), both proclaim the failure of our civilization, and both have received notices—or obeisances—that add up not to the usual ballyhoo for enjoyable works by respected artists, but to announcements of cultural landmarks. With *Nashville*, the common comparison is to *Citizen Kane*, with *Ragtime*, to *The Great Gatsby*—though *Ragtime* has also been compared to *Citizen Kane*, not to mention *Ulysses*. These works are cited as instant, full-blown metaphors for America itself: mirrors that challenge us to endure, if we can, the twisted visage and empty eyes that stare back. What is perhaps more remarkable—for works so disturbing, dark, and serious, it is nearly unprecedented—both book and movie have been hailed as immediately and totally accessible, enormous fun, and sure-fire hits: "an orgy for movie-lovers," on the one hand, and "impossible to put down," on the other.

All of this—the book, the movie, and their reception—seems particularly suited to the spirit of passivity and fatigue that animates, if one can use that word, the times.

In his most provocative comment on the practice of art in America, Herman Melville wrote that "all men who say *yes*, lie; and all men who say *no*,—why . . . they cross the frontiers into Eternity with nothing but a carpet-bag,—that is to say, the Ego." But there are times when saying no—to one's society, culture, to one's civilization as a whole—is to say yes to one's audience: to take the easy way out, to ask the easy questions and provide the easiest answers, to offer the safest and most shallow satisfactions. Just such a yes is brought forth in both *Ragtime* and *Nashville*—a yes enveloped by a coldness emanating from the artists' all but perfect insulation from their subjects. Altman and Doctorow are never for a moment implicated in the stories they tell, the lessons they draw, or the actions—the failures—of their characters. When Gatsby lost, it's plain, so did Fitzgerald, and, it has turned out over the years, so did everybody else. But speaking like sages—in the most suspicious author's voice there is—Altman and Doctorow remain on high.

They keep their distance—or rather enforce it. They aren't bent on discovering the fate of their characters as they emerge, but on imposing it. Exceptions are either killed off aesthetically when they bid to take over the story, or else killed off plain and simple, to make the author's point. Instead of struggling with the open possibilities all interesting fictional characters hold—facing the real choices artists have to make not merely as to where they will take their characters, but as to where their characters will take them—Doctorow and Altman falsely foreclose openings to make a statement: our by now deadeningly familiar proclaims-the-failure song and dance.

It's interesting that when Altman screenwriter Joan Tewkesbury went off to compose a film script about some characters in the country music mecca, Altman insisted, before there were any characters, that one of them die at the end—and that when Tewkesbury came up with the Loretta Lynn–like country singer Barbara Jean, and disposed of her as a suicide, Altman substituted an assassination, and dropped in the plot thread of a mysterious political campaign moving in parallel with the wanderings of an altogether unbelievable stock mad killer, in order to produce an ending whose meaning no one could possibly escape. It is just as interesting that the characters Doctorow cannot handle in the same mechanistic way—they are, it turns out, his most vital characters, and all of them female—are either dropped (the siren Evelyn Nesbit, abandoned right on the verge of real adventures and open questions), or defined as socially lobotomized mutes and robbed of whatever presence they threaten to display.

"Unlike the stories and novels of Hemingway, Fitzgerald, and Faulkner," Albert Murray writes in "A Clutch of Social Science Fiction Fiction," collected in *The Omni-Americans*, ". . . those of more recent American writers frequently read like interim research reports and position papers. Indeed, what most American fiction seems to represent these days is not so much the writer's actual sense of life as some theory of life to which he is giving functional allegiance." This seems to me the sharpest possible summation of the aesthetic that governs in both *Ragtime* and *Nashville*. Altman, as Robert Mazzocco wrote in a sane piece in the *New York Review of Books,* is the man of the hour because he stands for it: "because he represents a certain failure of nerve. He has a feeling perhaps about the hopelessness or aimlessness of the world . . ."

Altman objectifies this vague feeling into argument by presenting an unmotivated and all but incomprehensible act of murder. It's the most dependable element in his movies. Sometimes, as in *McCabe and Mrs. Miller* and *Thieves like Us,* it works, somehow leaving the viewer as bereft and stranded as the victim's survivors; otherwise, as in *The Long Goodbye* and *Nashville,* it's an insult to his characters as well as his audience. Doctorow uses murder in much the same way, though he lacks Altman's gratuitous vengefulness—everything in Doctorow's writing has a message, nothing is just for pleasure. He proves America is empty by creating empty characters, executing those who won't sit still for his typology or exiling them from the plot. In *Ragtime* he presents a string of historical figures (Evelyn Nesbit, Henry Ford, J. P. Morgan, and so on) interacting fictionally with each other and with a set of ideologically determined representative families: White Upper Middle Class, Black, and Immigrant. After a slew of ironic deaths, the three families merge into one: a dismal parody of the melting pot. So that the point of their representativeness is never lost, none of the family characters ever has a life of his or her own, because that might undermine their function.

As such—as works that represent "not so much the writer's actual sense of life as some theory of life to which he is giving functional allegiance"—*Ragtime* and *Nashville* are aesthetic, moral, and political ready-mades which, in this time of cynicism and abandonment, have elicited a critical response that matches them in grandiosity and intelligence. The bigness of the ideas dissolves their banality. Let us take a look at what has been said.

The purpose of *Nashville, Newsweek* announced in its cover story, is to "expose complacency." It "demonstrates the true lesson of Watergate—the cost of putting the ends before the means." (What this has to do with *Nashville* I have no idea, but it demonstrates that the movie's sensibility is contagious.) Said Pauline Kael (whose notorious pre-release *New Yorker* review stands up better than any other rave—I wanted to agree with it): "*Nashville* is about the insanity of a fundamentalist culture in which practically the whole population has been turned into groupies." Andrew Kopkind in Boston's *Real Paper:* "The real disaster is America, the doom in store for us is not as merciful as Altman's oblivion, but the long nauseating terror of a fall through the existential void. . . . We are the disaster."

This is heady stuff, but Tom Wicker, writing in the *New York Times,* far surpassed it. He came completely unglued. In *Nashville,* he said, we see "the vulgarity, greed, deceit, cruelty, barely contained hysteria, and the frantic lack of root and grace into which American life has been driven by its own heedless vitality. . . . the American mobility culture, with its autos obsolete and crunchable the day they're sold, its fast food parlors, plastic motel rooms, take-out orders [for shame!], transient sex [nice juxtaposition] and junk music . . . where patriotism and sentimentality salve the wounds of progress, and madmen peer mildly from benign eyes . . ."

With *Ragtime* no one has gone quite so berserk, but in the more restrained milieu of book reviewing the reception has been in the same vein. *Time* spoke of the book with awe, as if it were simply too powerful to talk about: "Its lyric tone, fluid structure and vigorous rhythm give it a musical quality that explanation mutes." (There's a lot of muteness running around the book; some of the characters barely talk.) Nevertheless, explanation is provided: "In Doctorow's hands, the nation's fall from grace is no catalogue of sins" (and it isn't, because sins are committed by people, and there are only types here: society is the criminal). *Newsweek* came through with its entire book section. *Ragtime* has "grace and surface vitality, but [lest you think this is just another entertainment] beneath . . . sound[s] the neat, sad waltz of *Gatsby*. Doctorow has found a fresh way to orchestrate the themes of American innocence, energy and inchoate ambition— with the antiphonies of complacency [our old friend], disorder and disillusion." Doris Grumbach, in the *New Republic*, rose to almost *Nashville*an heights of proclaims-the-failurism: "Unerring backward vision" to "a time when it might still have been possible to make peace between classes and races in this country, between children and parents [so much for Freud—one of *Ragtime*'s bugaboos], between the world of simplicity and optimism at the turn of the century and the weary, corrupt decadence with which the century is wearing itself out." (How—or why—do you "make peace" between the beginning of a century and the end of it?) "It implies all that we could ask for in the way of texture, mood, character and despair," George Stade wrote on the front page of the *New York Times Book Review*, as if imitating Edward Koren's cartoon—in effect declaring that despair has become one of the requirements of art.

Now, one can respond by saying you can't blame a book or a movie for the reviews it gets. In these cases I think you can, because it seems to me *Nashville* and *Ragtime* were made to elicit exactly such responses: a common orgy of yes disguised as no. Some of us want the security of knowing our great experiment has been a failure—so that we no longer have to harbor danger- ous, risky ambitions for our politics, our culture, or ourselves, or believe that one has anything to do with another.

It is probably spoiling all the fun to point out that before a work can be convincing as a metaphor for something as big and complex as America—as Altman pronounced *Nashville,* and as reviewers are taking *Ragtime*—before it can function as anything so grand as a portrait of "our fall from grace," a book or a movie must be convincing on the more basic, if seemingly tiresome level of plot, character, motivation, and quotidian detail. One feels out of place noting that the most chilling scene in *Nashville*—the vicious, heartless reaction of the country music crowd to Barbara Jean's onstage breakdown—cannot possibly be a metaphor for anything but the director's cynicism and disinterest in his ostensible subject, since no country audience would respond to the collapse of a singer as well loved as Barbara Jean is supposed to be with anything but compassion and fear. Doctorow's allegory of the crushing of The Black Man is weightless, and costs the reader nothing, because his black man, Coalhouse Walker, Jr. (and that first name—why didn't Doctorow just call him "Dinge"?), is the same stick-figure victim so often met in American fiction: one more pathetic example, again to quote Albert Murray, of the need of white writers to "behave as if the slightest notion of a black compatriot as a storybook hero compels them to equate the strongest Negroes with the most helpless." Given, say, Ishmael Reed's work, especially the myriad indomitable trickster characters in *Mumbo Jumbo*—a novel that begins, historically and in every other way, where *Ragtime* leaves off—Doctorow's creation of Coalhouse Walker should have been treated as a scandal.

But not only must detail be convincing, the artist's ideas must be convincing. *Newsweek,* quoting Altman's summation of *Nashville*—"Country music stars and politicians are alike in this country. Basically they're just involved in popularity contests"—calls such things "extraneous," which is neatly self-defensive; with ideas like this they'd better be extraneous. Altman's statement is remarkable only in that it tells us even less about politics than about country music. Those who think George Wallace, on whom the shadow political candidate in *Nashville* seems modeled, is just engaging in a popularity contest are kidding themselves.

The ideas in *Nashville* are not extraneous to its shape and texture anymore than they are in *Ragtime,* and the ideas in *Ragtime* are just as flat. What is most striking about the book is that it is all surface. I am not a fast reader, but I initially read *Ragtime* in something under four hours. I read it again, and it was work. Once you have read the book there is absolutely nothing more to be gotten from it. It is dead on the page. The writing carries a reader along, but it implies nothing, suggests nothing, never makes you stop and think, never makes you puzzle out motives, because there really are none. It certainly never hits you with the kind of power that leads you to stop reading, compose yourself, and meditate on the ceiling. It's not that you can't put the book down, it's that you don't have to.

Doctorow's barely outlined, imprisoned characters—Father, Mother, Younger Brother, Little Boy, The Black Woman, The Black Man, The Immigrant, His Wife, His Beautiful Daughter—cannot support, let alone redeem, the ironic burden they are forced to carry: the burden of big ideas like the purposelessness of American values, the power of plutocracy, the chaos hidden in the American lust for system and order. But a lot of the ideas in *Ragtime* are just silly. Doctorow has anarchist Emma Goldman, who seems to be the voice of the book's politics, announce that sex symbol Evelyn Nesbit, with whom the masses will be manipulated into identifying—courtesy of yellow journalism, Hollywood, and other odious forms of popular culture—"would in the long run be a greater threat to the workingman's interests than mine owners or steel manufacturers." Such an idea cannot be taken seriously, but it is, for a book that moves along so well, effectively glib. Doris Grumbach thought *Ragtime* spoke to the decadence of our age, and so it does, by imitating it. If such an idea is not the essence of an enfeebled, decadent Marxism, I don't know what is.

I think such facile pronouncements of no-way-out, of our-time-has-passed-or-never-was, of the-failure-of-our-civilization-as-a-whole, are what the fuss is all about. Yet great works, with which *Nashville* and *Ragtime* have been so blithely compared—and *The Great Gatsby* and *Citizen Kane* are indeed the best examples—cannot be forced into such pigeonholes. We may have come to see them as grand metaphors for our culture, each an acting-out of the whole of our historical possibilities; they are also, each time you return to them directly on the page or on the screen, irreducibly about individuals, people you and I are not, except perhaps in the inherited fantasies we share with them, the fantasies that, by now, for us, they have partly shaped.

Village Voice, 4 August 1975

Cowboys and Germans

Wim Wenders's *Emotion Pictures* reads like conversation in a hurry: good conversation, but always with another subject pushing on the one at hand, another thought in the back of your mind crowding out what the person across the table is telling you. A bit more than half of the book is taken up with short pieces on movies and rock 'n' roll that Wenders—born in 1943 in Düsseldorf, and the director of *Summer in the City* (1970), *The Scarlet Letter* (1973), *The American Friend* (1977), *Paris, Texas* (1984), and *Wings of Desire* (1987), among other films—wrote between 1968 and 1971, when he was a film student in Munich: "I was not reflecting *upon* movies," Wenders writes in his preface, "I was reflecting them, period." The rest of the book includes conventionally analytic, less fannish pieces, and ends with "The American Dream," from 1984, a long bad poem ("long bad poem" is the genre; the poem itself has its moments)—but the action is up front, where Wenders's writing moves in fits and starts.

New rock albums are used to frame old films and vice versa ("Films about America should be composed entirely of long and wide shots, as music about America already is"); there's less interest in what narrative might be on the screen or in a song than in trying to catch the sort of moment that can stop a conversation cold and turn it in a new direction. Wenders on an Anthony Mann movie:

After the terrible fist-fight between Gary Cooper and Jack Lord, which takes place in the middle of horses rearing with fear, Lee J. Cobb (gang-leader Doc Tobin in *Man of the West*) says: "I've never seen anything like it in my whole life."
  Other things you've never seen in your whole life:

And then Wenders moves through quick paragraphs on scenes from *North to Alaska, 3.10 to Yuma, Johnny Guitar, The Man Who Shot Liberty Valance*, and more: "Even in a Western in which you don't expect to see anything new anymore," he says of *The Left-Handed Gun*, "an amazing thing can still happen. Paul Newman shoots the sheriff, who is knocked around so violently by the bullet that he loses a boot, which stays standing upright beside the corpse!"*

  In these early pieces Wenders writes casually, as someone who doesn't expect to make writing his life (even though, he says, "I didn't learn much in film school but I learned a lot from writing"). He's in a hurry because he wants to reflect himself back at the screen and break through it—he wants to make his own movies. He's also in a hurry because he's running, running in place: he writes as a foreigner in his own country, a young West German trying to imagine himself as an American, a citizen of the place where all his thrills come from (if rock 'n' roll "wasn't

---

*Or, as Mikhail Gorbachev would put it years later, in an August 1990 interview with Alan Cranston, "The good thing about American crime films is that sometimes 20 people die during that film, and you're not sorry. You're not sorry for any one of them!"

literally a life-saver," he says in "The American Dream," "it did save me *from* another, / more joyless life").

The writing is so full of energy it's impossible to distinguish between connections Wenders gets wrong and those an American would miss altogether. In a piece on John Ford Westerns, as shown dubbed on West German TV, he veers off into *Easy Rider,* its soundtrack, then toward "Wide-shots of California, in colour and Cinemascope. *Retrospective: The Best of Buffalo Springfield. 3614 Jackson Highway* by Cher. *Spiritual Guidance* by Sonny Bono," and the American reader pulls up short and thinks: *Cher, okay, maybe, who knows, but Sonny Bono?* You think—you say to Wenders—*Buddy, you don't have a clue.* But because of what Wenders has been saying about John Ford and the Westerns that followed Ford's ("I miss the friendliness, the care, the thoroughness, the seriousness, the peace, the humanity"), you also think: *Well—Sonny Bono. Here's a record that mattered to someone in Germany, which is also a record I've never heard of. Maybe I ought to listen to it.* Then Wenders turns again, this time to bootleg LPs—*LIVEr Than You'll Ever Be* (the Rolling Stones in Oakland, 1969), or *Great White Wonder* (early Bob Dylan demos and the Basement Tape)—and closes: "There are no bootlegs of John Ford films, but someone ought to start making them." You remember that Wenders has had to watch *My Darling Clementine* and *The Searchers* with German English-dubbers bleeding the life out of Henry Fonda's doubt, John Wayne's madness; you understand that what Wenders is writing about, what he's writing out, is a hunger for culture, which is also a hunger to escape from history.

That hunger drives the book. It begins as a lust for novelty, for simple freedom. Over and over in *Emotion Pictures,* the experience of novelty—"other things you've never seen in your whole life"—opens up into every direction, the preternaturally clear landscape of the Western inviting the viewer into a West of the mind, a personal West. (The most liberating, "the most exciting notion" about Westerns, Wenders says in "The American Dream," was "that these adventurous stories / of pioneers, of the wilderness / happened only a hundred years ago"—a long time ago for a Westerner, only yesterday for a German.)

It becomes clear, though, that Wenders's sensibility comes together as much from a desire for clarity as from a lust for novelty. As *Emotion Pictures* moves on, past a young man's breathless celebrations, a somewhat older man's search for clarity leaves the imaginary West of the movies and is turned back upon Wenders's own landscape. Years after his surrender to the action poetry of Westerns and the pleasure principles of rock 'n' roll, Wenders looks at his first country, confronting Joachim Fest and Christian Herrendoerfer's *Hitler: A Biography*, a 1977 documentary made with Nazi footage and a voice-over narration. The repression Wenders feels watching the movie throws into relief the liberation he felt when he watched Westerns; the Westerns he carries within himself turn that repression into suffocation. Like Wenders, you might think, you can't wait to finish his essay and go see *The Searchers* again. There are free images and there are imprisoned images, Wenders seems to be saying, images made in freedom and images made to imprison, and even if the distinction falls apart as soon as it's made (in what sense is a mystification, that is, the standard heroic Western image, free?), Wenders's tone, his vehemence, remains whole.

As a genius of propaganda, Hitler took control of image making and remade an entire nation in his image. The result, after what bodies were left were buried or burned, was, Wenders writes, "a profound mistrust of the sounds and images about" Germany itself, a place "that has therefore, over the last thirty years, greedily swallowed up all the foreign images it could, as long as they distracted it from itself." But Wenders wants to make images, about America, about Germany, about struggle, pleasure, mystification, everything; in 1977 he has already made a lot of them, a lot of movies. So he digs into the lie of Nazi cinema, which is also the lie of cinema itself, the sensation that what one sees is real, that what one sees is true, that what one sees, no matter how disgusting it might be, is a kind of inviolable truth, superseding any thoughts it might provoke or that might be brought to bear upon it: working with their Nazi footage, Wenders says, "Fest and Herrendoerfer cheerfully open up the stinking can again, proud of their horrible discoveries." Looking for a critical voice, for Fest and Herrendoerfer's position on what they are now offering to the public, Wenders finds only a kind of happiness. He describes the filmmakers' voice-over as they describe the invention of Nazi concentration camps: "this outrageous voice . . . sounds relieved, I swear it,

relieved, "What happened behind the barbed wire was masked by funfairs for the people. . . . The Germans kept themselves to themselves." Embarrassment, anxiety and fear, which were mentioned a moment ago, are no longer the content, but have become the form of the commentary; repression is no longer the film's subject, but has become its method.

There is no real need to explicate what Wenders is saying, though one could easily say, along with him, that any film that says the Germans were embarrassed, anxious, and scared, even though they didn't have a clue, is a lie—any discourse that means to have it both ways is a lie. Reading Wenders, one is less compelled by the issue he's raising than by the voice he found—just as, in his piece on *Hitler,* he is less concerned with the formal narrative of the film than with the voice used to structure it. Wenders's language—"cheerfully opening up the stinking can again"—is violent, extreme, and unfair, but if criticism is about a search for truth (in its smallest, or most protean version, a search for what one truly means to say), then extremist language, violent and unfair, is always called for—but we don't hear it today. We don't hear it applied to musicians pushing anti-Semitism (Public Enemy), racism (Guns N' Roses), or homophobia (3rd Bass), or to filmmakers recycling clichés until cultural death, the murder of good actors, is all you see (*Heart Condition* and *Everybody Wins* are this month's examples); instead critics offer resignation, dispensation, or a spirited defense. To grapple with Wenders's extremism, right now, is to feel free—or a bit more free than perhaps you likely felt before catching his delight at seeing *Man of the West,* his disgust over *Hitler.* You might feel ready to say what you think without leaving out a single, unfair word.

For all that's worth, though, there is a way in which Wenders's giddy yea-saying might be worth more. Throughout his little collection, Wenders hails the old—*Retrospective: The Best of Buffalo Springfield, The Left-Handed Gun*—as if it were still news, or ever was. It's as if he's not only escaping history, or even discovering it, but making it, making it happen. In Wenders's personal West, as perhaps in anyone's, until the tree falls in his forest it has never fallen at all. The difference between Wenders and just anyone is that he has the desire and the ability to bring down the trees, then to make the reader feel as if he or she were there to take part, and then to make a reader think—*Why can't I do that?*

California, April 1990

Cowboy Boots and Germans

S usan Sontag has been a factor in our cultural life for almost two decades. She has helped introduce American and British readers to such Continental modernists as Antonin Artaud, Walter Benjamin, Roland Barthes, and Hans-Jürgen Syberberg; produced her own fiction; made movies; and worked to define and take her stand on essential aesthetic issues. But she is less "our most important critic," as her publisher forgivably has it, trumpeting *A Susan Sontag Reader,* than our most visible and trend-making.

Sontag has achieved a presence on the page because she has made herself felt in the media at large; her provocative public persona reflects back on her work to give it a charge that, as writing, it doesn't really have. Unlike, say, Pauline Kael or Leslie Fiedler, who as better writers and more original thinkers simply make people mad, Sontag has made news.

She caused a stir right from the start, in 1964, with her "Notes on Camp" (included in her *Reader,* as is everything mentioned below, unless noted to the contrary), which made Sontag's then-betters in the New York literary establishment feel decidedly unhip. She caused a hubbub with "How to Love the Cuban

Revolution" (not included); she won countless fans among the New Left literati (and lost forever those who had already concluded she was irredeemably soft on pop) when, in the face of the Vietnam War, she wrote off the entire intellectual tradition to which she had and, since, has devoted her life with the announcement (not included) that "the white race is the cancer of human history"—a phrase that, whatever one who shared Sontag's Caucasian persuasion was supposed to do about it, inarguably had a certain dash. She caused a scandal when, in response to the crushing of Solidarity in Poland, she denounced Communism as "fascism with a human face" (the twinkle in Uncle Joe's eye?), and pilloried American intellectuals for their supposed softness on Stalinism. The Trotskyist intellectuals who had never bought into paradisiac Cuban or North Vietnamese myths in the first place, as had Sontag, were put out.

So Sontag has been a public critic, an engaged critic, willing to speak out, to make a fool of herself, to risk her reputation, and I would not write with such a snotty tone if, when all was said and done, I trusted her writing. But I don't.

Sontag is a cold writer. If as a public figure she is engaged, at her most critically involved she repels the engagement of the reader. "In place of a hermeneutics we need an erotics of art," run the famous last words of her 1964 piece "Against Interpretation" (and how very sixties in ideology and how neatly distanced from the 1960s in style those words are)—but Sontag has written since not as though she had defined a new credo, merely as though she'd gotten off a good line. Everyone has taken pictures, so everyone can be assumed capable of some kind of involvement in a book such as *On Photography* (excerpted in the *Reader*), but no book could be less an erotics and more a hermeneutics of photography. For the erotics of photography as captured in criticism, one can go to any of Michael Lesy's books—*Wisconsin Death Trip* and *Real Life*, his investigations of commercial photography in the 1890s and 1920s, respectively, or even *Time Frames,* his failed study of family snapshots—because there one will find shame, lust, fetish, irrational appetites, and insane demands on manners and rules; there one will gaze upon the familiar and be shocked at what is there. In *On Photography* one will find instead such ultra-hermeneutical sentences as "It is not reality that photographs make immediately accessible, but images." Sontag's formula is classy but false; as Lesy's books, or Kael's, or Fiedler's, prove, there is no contradiction between hermeneutics and eroticism. For that matter, great critics might well be defined by the way they practice an erotic hermeneutics.

Sontag often seems to write to close subjects, not to open them (*Illness as Metaphor,* not included in the *Reader*), to have both the first and the last word (her 1979 essay on Syberberg's *Hitler,* which begins by introducing a film few of her readers could have then seen and ends with the claim, "After seeing *Hitler, a Film from Germany,* there is Syberberg's film—and then there are the other films one admires"). While her style is recognizably her own, an uneasy combination of academic and hip, it is also pedantic, effete, unfriendly—the reverse of the sort of writing that used to be called "virile," an adjective that in a better world would have nothing to do with gender. The opening lines of "The Pornographic Imagination" mean to seem authoritative: "No one should undertake a discussion of pornography before acknowledging the pornograph*ies*—there are at least three—and before pledging to take them on one at a time." It's difficult to read this without gaping, or laughing. It dissolves in fussiness, gracelessness, self-congratulation, evasion—I mean, talk about an "erotics of art"! You can begin a discussion of pornography with the crack of a whip, but not with the wag of a finger.

The last lines of "Fascinating Fascism"—"The color is black, the material is leather, the seduction is beauty, the justification is honesty, the aim is ecstasy, the fantasy is death"—are so often quoted because, for Sontag, they are so radically untypical. As Pauline Kael once said, Sontag "has never had much dramatic sense—it's hard to think of an American writer with *less* dramatic sense." Those last lines from "Fascism," whatever their analytical value, which is minimal at best, have momentum, passion, poetry, force. As a critical device, as a finale, they don't need analytical value; they need do no more than nail the essay that precedes them into the reader's mind. They do that—but what else in Sontag's work does?

"The Romantics thought of great art as a species of heroism," Sontag begins her essay on Syberberg's *Hitler,* and the line pretty well sums up Sontag's sense of culture. Great art equals genius equals heroism, and nothing else in this world—certainly not events, myth, or anyone's or any people's sense of history, none of which can be ascribed to a single genius, a single hero—approaches this trinity. The profoundly dubious nature of the notion of genius as heroism is, save for a bit of historical and cultural contextualizing, left unexamined; as with almost all of Sontag's most important or self-important critical flourishes, the reader is meant to step back before it. A swift, even slick phrase seals the paragraph: a great work "both excites and paralyzes the imagination." Really.

Sontag is not soft on pop. She doesn't understand it, has little or no real interest in it; her famous juxtaposition of Robert Rauschenberg and the Supremes, shockingly cross-cultural in certain backward intellectual circles in the mid-sixties, told a reader nothing about either.* Rather, Sontag is soft on genius, and her celebration of Syberberg's *Hitler* is perhaps the key to her work— or rather, as with any ambitious critic, the key to the self-

---

*"As for equating high and popular culture, she explains: 'I made a few jolly references to things in popular culture that I enjoyed. I said, for instance, one could enjoy both Jasper Johns and the Supremes. It isn't as if I wrote an essay on the Supremes.'" Sontag, profiled in *Time,* 24 October 1988.

constructed arena in which her work takes place, an arena, in this case, where such things as events or one's sense of history, of burden or legacy, prison or gift, are less transcended than excluded altogether.

In "Fascinating Fascism," Sontag takes on Nazi filmmaker Leni Riefenstahl, her postwar rehabilitation, and her 1970s lionization by cineastes, and proves herself a devastating polemist. Sontag accepts Riefenstahl as a sort-of genius (myself, I've never seen it: what did she do that Griffith or Eisenstein hadn't done better?), but because Riefenstahl was and, at the heart of her aesthetics, remains a Nazi, Sontag cannot accept her as a (to-thine-own-self-be) true, free artist. In 1965, in "On Style," Sontag granted Riefenstahl the standard genius's dispensation for *Triumph of the Will* and *Olympiad*—the films "transcend the categories of propaganda or even reportage"; the "'content'" (the idea being itself so dubious the word must appear in scare quotes) is "purely formal." In "Fascism" she cuts through Riefenstahl's canonized films and her 1970s photo essays on doomed but heroic-looking African tribes as perfectly linked, perfectly accomplished constructs of fascist ideology. All well and good: at least for those convinced by Sontag, Riefenstahl is back in the trash can of history, where she belongs. Which brings up the question of Syberberg's *Hitler, a Film from Germany*.

There is a deep acceptance of Hitler in Syberberg's movie. His fundamental argument is that Hitler, the ultimate conceptual artist, perceived and empathized with the essential desires of twentieth-century Western civilization, and therefore constructed a situation in which those desires might be realized, might be transformed into events—or, to read a postwar concept back upon the prewar period, happenings. (As Sontag writes, "one of the film's conceits is that Hitler, who never visited the front and watched the war every night through newsreels, was a kind of moviemaker. Germany, a Film by Hitler.") It is this argument that makes *Hitler* interesting, sickening, scary, a labyrinth of images and ideas, and it is this argument that ultimately leaves the film corrupt. It is, one might realize, the most advanced—the most modernist, the most *arty*—version of the notion that if everyone is guilty, nobody is. Face it, Syberberg says: you wanted a spectacle of horror that went beyond your worst nightmares; you were in revolt against the limits of your unconscious, and just as Freud freed you from those limits in theory, Hitler freed you from them in practice, as you wished him to.

This is only half of what Walter Benjamin meant when in 1936 he wrote, "Fascism attempts to organize the newly created proletarian masses without affecting the property structure which the masses strive to eliminate. Fascism sees its salvation in giving the masses not their right [to change property relations] but instead a chance to express themselves. . . . The logical result of Fascism is the introduction of aesthetics into politics." Syberberg, as it were, keeps the aesthetics and tries to drop, or obscure, the politics—and it is because he is interested in Hitler as an aesthetic figure, as an artist, that he is able to make the obscene statement that Riefenstahl's *Triumph of the Will* is Hitler's "only lasting monument, apart from the newsreels of his war." Tell it to the survivors of Hitler's extermination camps, who have devoted their lives to the creation of a monument that may last even longer than Riefenstahl's movie—human memory.

Syberberg's argument that Hitler acted out a deep, common dream is not what Hannah Arendt meant when she wrote, in *Eichmann in Jerusalem,* that the determinant purpose of the Nazi regime was the execution of altogether novel crimes. As a Jew, Arendt would have understood what Sontag, herself Jewish, seemingly does not, even given Syberberg's claims for Hitler's only lasting monument: that, just as many white Southern politicians do not include black Southerners when they say what "Southerners" want, Syberberg does not include those who were exterminated when he dramatizes the common wish for a

Hitler—and in both cases the absence of certain parties from the frame of reference is implicitly immaterial to the validity of the argument.

To avoid this issue, and to avoid the question of why graphic or even merely specific presentation of Nazi crime is conspicuous in *Hitler* mainly by its absence, Sontag goes back to the tried and true—the transcendence of genius. There is no trash can of history in her treatment of *Hitler* because there is no history. Sontag takes *Hitler* as an efflorescence, an explosion of talent, vision, invention, experiment, and so what is at stake is art for art's sake, not the possibility that artists as historically innocent as Riefenstahl is guilty use art for self-serving purposes. Still, Syberberg's movie is also a celebration of genius, Hitler's genius, and as such it is, no matter how inadvertently, something of a critique of the very notion of genius. But Sontag does not address this question either. You get the feeling that once she has accepted someone in her pantheon, ethics are beside the point, less because true genius supersedes ethics than because true genius is, somehow, inevitably clean—and cleansing. But who knows? To read Sontag on a European genius is to be informed, instructed, perhaps even entertained; it is certainly to be mystified.

Sontag is fundamentally and unnaturally an un-American critic, or at the least a non-American critic. As Tocqueville's *Democracy in America* makes all too plain, in its description of a country that on many levels has not changed, genius is fundamentally and unnaturally un-American; genius both trivializes and humiliates democracy, just as democracy both trivializes and humiliates genius. This is why Pauline Kael's and Leslie Fiedler's best work is characterized not by Sontag's messianic imperiousness but by a back-against-the-wall pugnaciousness, even a defensiveness—by anger, arrogance, doubt, hysteria, seductiveness, humor, revulsion, fear, and a great sense of drama. They are artists of the tension between genius and democracy.

Sontag was raised in Arizona and California, but there is nothing in her voice or her sensibility to betray that fact, save perhaps the cowboy boots she sometimes wears. Her work seems to assume a domain of letters in which everybody, or rather tout le monde, becomes a Parisian sooner or later. Can one imagine an American critic who has made a difference of whom it could be said that his or her place of origin was of no consequence? Emerson? Hawthorne? Matthiessen? Fiedler? Kael? Forget it. It's the radical pluralism of American society, combined with an insensate pressure toward conformity, that defines the United States—and just as there is no echo of Sontag as a Californian in her writing, there is no hint of this contradiction. This might not matter were her audience different—were it not drawn precisely from a community defined by radical pluralism and an insensate pressure toward conformity, a contradiction that may well define our contribution to world culture: our deepest notion of what it means to create, and to be fully human.

But it is to this audience that Sontag offers the example of European genius: this is what it means to be fully human, even if to be fully human one must cease to be American. And this means that no matter how intensely Sontag has made herself felt in American political life, as an intellectual she has produced more than anything else a series of elegant and learned formal introductions ("Hans-Jürgen, have you met America? No? Well, I'm sure you two will have a *lot* to talk about!"), a series of essays that are less a hermeneutics or an erotics of art than an aesthetic manifesto of really daunting irrelevance.

California, January 1983

The Bob McFadden Experience

The Beat Generation: fragile souls and desolation angels, sainted junkies and Madonna-like pansexuals—well, not right now. After four or five decades *The Beat Generation* is three CDs in a box. Produced with great affection and no respect by James Austin with Stephen Ronan and Gordon Skene, this aural documentary ranges all over the place, Jack Kerouac voicing his word jazz, William Burroughs running his cracker-barrel-philosopher-with-a-big-.38 shtick on *Naked Lunch,* John Drew Barrymore declaiming "Christopher Columbus Digs the Jive," Edd "Kookie" Byrnes (private eye's carhop sidekick in fifties TV series *77 Sunset Strip,* never mind) saying cool stuff, Howard K. Smith of CBS radio news digging into the zeitgeist, and on, and on—everything is smeared together until the smart make the stupid seem worth a second listen and the dumb cast even the geniuses into doubt. Kerouac never sounded so much the smug, flip phony as he does here, or Howard K. Smith so much the good-hearted liberal trying not to miss the point—and not missing it, either. As reconceived, ripped up, and reassembled by Austin's production team, *The Beat Generation* uncovers the strange tale of a subculture as it was received by mass culture, and then as it turned into mass culture. It's a ludicrous, horribly embarrassing, sometimes thrilling story.

This is not the way the history of the beats is usually told. The conventional account follows the brave adventures of a small band of brothers struggling to find a way out of the prison of the Cold War and in the process setting free a whole generation of young men and a few women who *did not even know they were in jail.* The names of the pure are harked: Jack, Allen, Bill, Neal, and whoever else can jump on for the ride at any given moment. Writing in Venice, California, Lawrence Lipton got in on the ground floor in 1959 with *The Holy Barbarians,* and that's pretty much been the line ever since. At the head of a vast crew, Ann Charters may have made the best career out of incense-burning hagiography (soundtrack, ever since Neal Cassady died in 1968 at forty-one and Kerouac the next year at forty-seven: hush of elegiac whispers, then hearty laughter—*they would have wanted it that way*). She published the premature *Kerouac: A Biography* in 1973 and followed with the two-volume encyclopedia *The Beats: Literary Bohemians in Postwar America,* her own photo collection (*Beats & Company;* presumably you're supposed to call up Shakespeare & Co., Sylvia Beach's bookstore in the golden age of expatriate literary bohemians in post[first]war Paris—*solid*), and the 645-page *Portable Beat Reader.* You'd never know from her books—and the spinning discs of *The Beat Generation* don't let you forget—that from the beginning Kerouac & Co. were about mystification, myth-making, and making it. These were—as they often tried to find ways to say without exactly letting the secret out—good American boys. They wanted to be larger than life. They wanted success. They wanted fame. They wanted everyone to be like them—which is not the same as wanting to change the world.

Now, it is said (by John Arthur Maynard, in his obsessive 1991 study of the artistic and moral desert of *Venice West: The Beat*

Generation in Southern California) that from "1948 through at least 1962, Henry Luce"—founder and editor-in-chief of *Time,* and in the 1950s the absolute embodiment of anticommunism, Americanism, and white-Anglo-Saxon, heterosexual, Protestant rectitude—"was in the habit of receiving a fortnightly briefing paper on the activities of the avant-garde throughout America, prepared for him and his senior editors by a shrewd and very canny researcher named Rosalind Constable." I don't actually believe this; it's just too good to be true. The *Beat Generation* set makes it credible, though—if you assume its programming is the result of shuffling a bunch of Constable's old memos. That's what it sounds like: a great leveling. The point, Maynard reports, quoting a summary attributed to Constable herself (no source given, in an otherwise carefully documented university press publication), "was to 'draw attention to the more off-beat events, sometimes the very ones that are causing such consternation among the critics. . . . And the weirder the better, if there is reason to believe that the author knows what he is doing. It is just possible (as history has sometimes proved) that he is inventing a new language which takes most people, including most critics, time to learn.'" That's a decent critical theory, and Austin & Co. take it to its limit. In their hands, comic Ken Nordine sounds as significant as harrumphing literary colossus Kenneth Rexroth—and after you've been through the jive talk of Babs Gonzales, a riff from Lenny Bruce, Dizzy Gillespie's "Oop-Pa-a-Da" and Nelson Riddle's "Route 66 Theme," "But I Was Cool" from Oscar Brown, Jr., and Lord Buckley's "The Hip Gan" (Gandhi laying down his world-historical revolutionary rap), the Lambert, Hendricks & Ross psychoanalysis-on-its-own-couch "Twisted" (none of these people appear in *The Portable Beat Reader*), radio and TV features from WNYC and NBC (audio only, of course), plus a lot more from Kerouac, Charles Kuralt's 1959 investigation of "The Greenwich Village Poets," and so on into the night, Nordine's nervous, alone-in-the-dark monologues make Malcolm Cowley's voice-of-my-generation routine sound like the fraud it's always been. A few words from Carl Sandburg (Newsman: "Mr. Sandburg, as a sort of elder statesman of American literature, what do you think of this beatnik movement?" "Well, there ought to be a beatnik movement at all times. I was part of a beatnik movement—1915 to 1924. I point to some of my pieces as a challenge to the modern beatniks") carry more weight—the dignity and peacefulness in Sandburg's voice (that is, the cool) is bottomless—than the cranked rants of Venice poet-scenester Stuart Z. Perkoff about the dank side of the American dream (he's one step away from telling you the CIA is trying to send him messages through his fillings). Greenwich Village poets crowd the open mikes of network interviewers, but tourists and passers-by seem to have more to say—or anyway a more believable tone of voice.

When I think of the beats, one image inevitably crowds out all the rest. It's from an old *Saturday Night Live* skit, set in a perfectly clichéd beatnik nightclub: there's a bit of bad jazz, Laraine Newman vamping in black tights and long ponytail, and then the poet comes on. It's Steve Martin, all shades and sly strut, ready to suck up the emptiness in the lives of the people in the audience and throw it all back in their faces. He only needs a few lines and he's rolling. "MR. COMMUTER!" he bellows. "*Not for me* your life of . . ."

That's the beat critique in one. On *The Beat Generation*, Kerouac (backed by Steve Allen on piano) seems to be imitating Martin when he lets go with the 1959 "October in the Railroad Earth," dripping contempt for the "neck-tied" commuters catching the 5:48 down to Millbrae and San Carlos from San Francisco while he, son of the big sky and the open road, gazes fondly at freight trains and talks to "Negroes" (the very word, as he pronounces it, going gooey with sex and freedom). It's unbearable—

but by this time, all through the fifties, really, Kerouac was already imitating himself as surely as Steve Martin would one day imitate his imitators. So stale, so fast—while, as Carolyn Cassady, Neal's wife, would later report, Kerouac enjoyed the comforts of her nice, neat, respectable, perfectly bourgeois home down the same damned Bayshore freeway that carried the gray-flannel devils back to their martinis and picture windows.

Against this, the very second track on *The Beat Generation* sings with an odd kind of life. This is, appropriately enough, the infamous "The Beat Generation," a 1959 Brunswick single by "Bob McFadden"—otherwise known as Rod McKuen. McKuen had an interesting career. Born in Oakland in 1933, he claimed to have worked on psychological warfare during the Korean War, and soon after popped up snapping his fingers in various early teen-exploitation flicks, most notably the 1956 Sal Mineo vehicle *Rock, Pretty Baby*, which also featured Fay Wray of *King Kong* fame. In the 1960s he moved to San Francisco and became a sort of proto–Michael Bolton, cultivating a beard, long hair, sad face, and an infinite wallowing in sensitivity. He recorded a slew of albums of his own poetry (*Stanyan Street and Other Sorrows*, *Listen to the Warm*, etc.), and made a fortune repackaging the stuff into gift books and greeting cards.

For "The Beat Generation," though, he's very gruff. "I belong to the *beat* generation," he snaps—and the leap ahead almost twenty years to Richard Hell and the Voidoids' 1977 "Blank Generation"–rewrite is almost implicit in the performance. McKuen's voice has the force of a squirrel's, but the patent fakery of the performance runs up against the backing comments of one "Dor"—while McKuen rejects middle-class life, steady work, Mr. Commuter! Dor is there mouthing "make the scene," "yeah man," "so out it's in!" "weirdsville," as if he'd actually like to, you know, check it all out. McKuen is aiming at a good ripoff, but he can't keep his sarcasm from showing; Dor makes the thing seductive in spite of itself. He sounds like every high school kid who got the idea there might be something more interesting out there—"reefer," "chicks," "on the road." The great gift of *The Beat Generation* set is that as it makes subculture indistinguishable from mass culture, it allows the likes of Rod McKuen to reveal the mere showmanship of Jack Kerouac and Kerouac to reveal the spark of blocked desire in the likes of Dor.

There is another story—one the set only hints at. In 1960, CBS radio ran a series called *The Hidden Revolution,* anchored by Howard K. Smith; the segment on the beats was called "The Cool Rebellion." The idea was that, since the end of the Second World War, the world had been put through profound upheavals, which were paradoxically so quiet and, in a way, secret—with atomizing cities replacing smaller communities, increased hierarchy in everyday affairs, growing distance of business and government from ordinary people, the removal of centers of information and power from democratic control or indeed any sort of public accountability—that these drastic changes were felt rather than understood. This was "The Hidden Revolution," which produced "The Cool Rebellion"—a withdrawal, a refusal, a small, then growing band of exiles in their own country.

The documentary made to illustrate these premises is serious, considered, giving people a lot of time to speak; it's so serious, in fact, that when Smith wraps up with "There is, perhaps, a grain of truth in the overall protest," you're surprised, because he's convinced you there's a lot more than a grain of truth. The struggle, he's made clear, is about materialism and soullessness, empty abundance and the need to create, the monolith and the self: "the battle for survival," he says finally, "of the individual personality in a tragic century."

This is true and eloquent—more eloquent, unfortunately, than the dispensations Kerouac and so many of his epigones so easily granted themselves. It defines what's missing from most of their work, and almost everything else on *The Beat Generation,* cool or square: that sense of tragedy, a fate too big and awful to escape, a fate that is shared, not simply passed on to the commuters while the beats dance on down the road and their women keep the soup on the stove. But tragedy isn't altogether missing on these discs. It's there—along with modesty, humor, and courage—on the last track of the set: Allen Ginsberg's "America."

Written in Berkeley in 1956 and recorded in 1959 for Berkeley's Fantasy label, "America" is a slowly building cry in which the queer Jewish commie anarchist dope fiend refuses the internal exile his country has offered him and demands instead full citizenship. At the same time, this poet redefines citizenship. "America" can be read alongside the Declaration of Independence because that is what it is: a declaration that each American must in one way or another declare independence of and from America, without having to surrender the slightest connection to it, before he or she can fully and freely join it. On and on Ginsberg goes, making odd incidents from his childhood yours, bringing you into his tale. He's not cool. His rage becomes your rage, he takes you off your feet and away from anything like home, makes home unrecognizable, unwanted, and then leads you back.

He burns with resentment, yet he speaks easily, smoothly, leavening his hatred with affection, his fire with wit, his rabbi's tones now a good salesman's come-on. As Ginsberg begins to tower over the blasted bad faith of his country, its landscapes of pettiness and fear, you realize that America will have no choice but to accept Ginsberg, and that he has no choice but to accept his country. On *his* terms: in a great common effort, string section up, one fine closing John Ford shot. In the famous last line of the poem: "America I'm putting my queer shoulder to the wheel."

Thus does *The Beat Generation* roll to its end—with a number that rolls right off the beat the rest of the scene so carefully cultivated. Yet if the beats did nothing more than make the setting where this work could appear, almost any dumb tribute to these self-celebrating soul rebels would be justified. And they did do that. Without the camaraderie Ginsberg found and made with Kerouac, Burroughs, Cassady, and so many more, without the loving acceptance they gave him, without the openness of spirit with which they prized his special gifts, his voice could have been stilled from the first. The history told on *The Beat Generation* is a grand retrieval of a practical joke certain people once played on themselves—a shaggy dog story, you can begin to think somewhere between Perry Como's "Like Young" and Don Morrow's "Kerouazy"—a great escape that followed the route of a closing circle.

Puncture, Spring 1993

The Expanding Vacant Spot

I n 1936, with the Depression still the biggest story in town, *Fortune* magazine assigned staff writer James Agee, who co-opted government photographer Walker Evans, to produce a series of articles on white Southern tenant farmers. Fifty years later, *Sacramento Bee* reporter Dale Maharidge and *Bee* photographer Michael Williamson set out to discover what had become of the people Agee and Evans found, and what happened to their descendants: to re-create their history from 1936 into the present.

Agee and Evans found three neighbor tenant families who grew cotton in Alabama. Most of their crop went to landowners; the families lived on loans, furnish (advances of equipment, seed, fertilizer, food), and, when they were lucky, a few dollars a year. In some ways they lived like peasants on latifundios in El Salvador today; in almost every way they did not live in the United States as, even during the Depression, it was commonly understood. Living at the very margins of the economy, they were all but outside of history.

The story Agee came up with was rejected by *Fortune*. The book he then made out of the story was finally published in 1941, under both his name and Evans's, as *Let Us Now Praise Famous Men,* sold something over five hundred copies, and was mostly forgotten; by then the Depression was yesterday's news. Reissued in 1960, five years after Agee's death at the age of forty-five, it became a classic—but such an obvious phrase is no good for a book that is anything but obvious. *Let Us Now Praise Famous Men* is a romance and a horror story, and a reminder that the romance and the horror story—think of *Wuthering Heights,* or *Frankenstein*—were never so far apart. In its combination of poetic meditation and plain reportage on everyday life, of weather and landscape and eruptions of love and bitterness—and I'm speaking more of Agee's 428 pages of text than of the 61 pages of Evans's photographs that open the book cold, without captions or notation of any kind, the pictures you see before you see the title page—the book is a landlocked *Moby Dick.* The whale, Leviathan, is the cotton economy; the tenant system; capitalism; the American republic; the American dream. Agee is at once Ahab and Ishmael. The three families, to whom Agee gave the pseudonyms "Gudger," "Woods," and "Ricketts," are the crew still manning the *Pequod,* now a beached wreck that will never move. "And I only am escaped to tell thee," Agee almost says.

What Agee saw in Alabama was a peonage at the base of the American market. Save for Maggie Louise Gudger, a bright, sunny ten-year-old Agee thought might become what she wanted to become, a teacher or a nurse, Agee saw no future for the twenty-two members of the three families. They were ciphers in the market, tools to be discarded or replaced according to the needs of the market, and so Agee drew them as contingent individuals a reader quickly came to know, to like or dislike, to respect and, ultimately, to more or less forget: people who, as the lines from the Bible from which Agee took his title run, "perished, as though they had never been; and are become as though they had never been born; and their children after them."

Maharidge and Williamson's *And Their Children after Them*

opens with the irony of Maggie Louise Gudger's suicide in 1971: at the age of forty-five she took rat poison. Maharidge sums up a life shaped by cotton tenancy, early childbearing, the early death of a beloved husband, city labor for bare wages: "Each passing year mocked the dreams she had dreamed with Agee, reducing her a little each year, so that at the end of each year the vacant spot inside her took more and more of the space that defined her to herself. Maggie Louise finally discovered she could no longer aspire to anything, because the part of her that used to aspire was no longer there."

Maharidge also notes the irony that of the many individuals presented in *Let Us Now Praise Famous Men,* some of whom Agee predicted would die young, it was Agee—like Gudger an alcoholic—who was the first to go. As with the Maggie Louise opening, it's a cheap irony, and altogether representative of the lack of imagination, empathy, terror, and style—the essential glibness—that defines *And Their Children after Them.* Despite the image of the expanding vacant spot, Maggie Louise's story is soon reduced to sociology, to "the cultlike brainwashing of the cotton system." By the book's end Maggie Louise no longer exists as an individual—worse, you get the feeling that her death was tragic, that it made an irresistibly ironic opening, because, once (when Evans made her picture in 1936, the sixth photograph in the original editions of *Let Us Now Praise Famous Men*), she was so pretty. And there is an undercurrent of glee supporting the irony of Agee's short life. Never directly, always sideways, Maharidge works to reduce him, too. A serious accident suffered by Claire Bell Ricketts (a small child, pictured on the cover of the 1966 paperback edition of *Let Us Now Praise Famous Men,* whose eyes probably influenced Walter Keane) that Agee, or Evans, "might have caused" in the course of a game becomes "an accident caused by Agee." Agee is introduced as a "cult figure," and *Let Us Now Praise Famous Men* as his "best-read work, at least among the most dedicated of the cultists"—as if the book were on a par with *The Teachings of Don Juan* or *Dianetics,* and not exactly worth the effort it demands.

Maharidge's book alternates the eloquent journal entries of Emma Woods, seventy in 1986, and remarkable tales about the utopian social vision of the men who invented the cotton-picking machine, with titillating accounts of degradation and hopelessly potted histories. He presents as accepted fact the twisted notion that the civil rights movement of the 1950s and 1960s was primarily a political reflection of or compensation for the collapse of the tenant system. The family members are often treated as poorly, and not only in Maharidge's use of the long-discredited eugenicist theory of bad genes. Margaret Ricketts, also seventy in 1986, had two children by her father, Fred Garvin Ricketts; she and her surviving son, Garvin, forty, speak at length to Maharidge, who speaks in turn of "reeling from horrors" and describes the squalor of Margaret and Garvin's house with shock and disgust.

But Maharidge never asks why the two are comfortable urinating into pots by their beds and defecating in weed patches, as Margaret was raised to do, or why Margaret seems at peace, and happy—"I'm rich-poor," she says—with the fact that her son is her brother. If the people here are sociological tools, such questions don't have to be asked; Margaret Ricketts too can be subsumed into the "brainwashing of the cotton system." But if she is a contingent individual, capable of making choices no matter how circumscribed or oppressive her environment, such questions have to be asked.

Agee was an employee dispatched to produce an objective report on a social problem. From his first pages you can sense his struggle to smash the distance inherent in the assignment. Almost as quickly, you can feel that the distance has been smashed. *Let Us Now Praise Famous Men* is full of violence rising out of ordinary descriptive passages, and what results is anything but an objective report or, from Evans's side, documentary photographs. Maharidge works under cover of objectivity (cameraman Williamson is just along for the ride); he is determinedly, almost hysterically self-enclosed, an anthropologist among savages, as appalled by an Alabama sheriff's cigarettes as by Margaret Ricketts's ease with incest. A fatal sense of difference—precisely what Agee fought against by making himself a character in the tenant families' story—is in *And Their Children after Them* not only not escaped, it is embraced.

Though Maharidge goes out of his way to explicitly deny it, he turns his subjects into adversaries, and Agee into an enemy. He tries to slip the charge, noting that his project was "marked by difficulties" (unlike other books, presumably), that it is unlikely to make much money, that any profits will go to an educational trust for "the children of the descendants of the tenant families," and that he and Williamson may be "criticized by some for following two legends of journalism." "This book is in no way intended to imitate, parody, or otherwise denigrate the work of Agee and Evans," Maharidge says, as if setting forth a legal disclaimer; "in keeping with the form and spirit of our predecessors," he writes in typically muddled syntax, Williamson's photographs, which appear in *And Their Children after Them* in the same manner as do Evans's in *Let Us Now Praise Famous Men,* "are meant as a separate but equal statement to the text." This does in fact mean to follow Agee, though it doesn't. Evans's photographs, Agee wrote, "are not illustrative. They, and the text, are coequal, mutually independent, and fully collaborative. By their fewness, and by the impotence of the reader's eye, this will be misunderstood by most of that minority which does not wholly ignore it." Still, it's a remarkable slip, that "separate but equal."

It sounds fair; it sounded fair in 1896, in Plessy v. Ferguson, the Supreme Court decision that validated racial segregation. It sounded fair to most even in 1954, when in Brown v. Board of Education the court said unanimously that it wasn't fair, that the idea was a contradiction in terms, and so consigned the phrase to the oblivion of cheap irony. Of course we are talking about a book, and for a book "separate but equal" sounds harmless enough, but it isn't.

In *Let Us Now Praise Famous Men,* from a literary perspective, there is no way 61 pages of pictures can equal 428 pages of text. Yet in terms of the way the book has actually become part of American history and American life, there is no way in which the text equals the pictures. Evans's photos are far better known, and far easier to seem to understand—"better read"—than anything in Agee's narrative. If there is any real equality between the two parts of the book, it's in the way each side unbalances the other. Though the pictures are not printed alongside the text, the pictures and the text are not separate; each constitutes a magnetic field on the other. As you read Agee you constantly turn back to the Evans portfolio, not just to match an unnamed but perhaps identifiable face to a description, but to see if Agee is truly translating Evans, or vice versa—to see if they are speaking the same language.

They aren't. It's an argument, a violent argument. Evans, his pictures so flat, so seemingly artless, so documental; Agee, his prose so excessive, fabulist, literary—the authors are fighting, because they've sensed that the story they've found, the people who make up that story, contain the whole of life, and as contingent individuals Agee and Evans do not see life in the same way.

The whole of life—the American republic as a ship, the *Pequod,* or as a monster, Moby Dick—that sort of pretentiousness, those kinds of stakes, are at the heart of *Let Us Now Praise Famous Men,* and justify both the fury of Agee's writing and the coolness of Evans's photographs. It's this that secures the distance Evans purposefully insists on as Agee breaks that distance down, the immediacy that Agee creates for the reader, the removal Evans dumps on the viewer like a bucket of ice water freezing Agee's writing as romantic conceit; then you turn back to Agee, turn back again to Evans, and the conceit, an aesthete's conceit, is his. In 1936 he was far closer to Edward Hopper than any Depression documentarian. Evans shoots, crops, and prints like a coroner; Agee writes like a faith healer, as if he thinks he can bring the dead back to life. Thus almost half a century later, the book itself remains alive, and most of all unstable—as unstable as a country where, as Rep. Thomas Downey of New York recently reported for the House Subcommittee on Human Resources, "the mean family income of the poorest 20 percent of the population declined by 6.1 percent from 1979 to 1987, and the [20 percent] highest-paid Americans saw family income rise by 11.1 percent." "You're not going to have enough locks on the doors or police in the street to protect you from a generation of people who are not part of the mainstream of American life," Downey said.

Maharidge notes this great shift—as something that, he says, happened on the "watch" of the administration in power for most of those years, as if it were a natural development, a change in the weather, not a social project meant to turn contingent individuals into tools to be discarded or replaced. And so the Depression, too, recedes into mystery, and Maharidge can write as if Evans didn't notice the fear in the faces of the children he photographed—as if the discovery is Maharidge's own. You can look at Evans's picture of a Ricketts daughter in a necklace and a hat (the thirty-fifth picture in *Let Us Now Praise Famous Men*), and imagine it was only the fear Evans meant to shoot, as if it belonged to him, as an artist, as if not even the families' expressions belonged to them.

California, June 1989

■ In 1990 *And Their Children after Them* was awarded the Pulitzer Prize for general nonfiction.

Jan and Dean as Purloined Letter

George Lucas's teen-dream epic, *American Graffiti,* opened the door for *Dead Man's Curve: The Story of Jan and Dean*— a made-for-TV movie that ran on CBS—and that may be the best thing to be said for it. Lucas's movie left me feeling depressed, cheated, and unsettlingly distanced from my own past. Set in northern California in 1962, *American Graffiti* jammed a whole summer into the night before two of the characters, Ron Howard (class president) and Richard Dreyfuss (sensitive intellectual, but no square), were to leave for college. I'd gone to a high school much like theirs at the same time; I'd cruised many of the same roads in the same spirit, and took heart from the teenage urban legends Lucas's kids actually got to act out—in real life, the kid who chained the rear axle of the cop car always left school the year before you got there. But I didn't recognize much of what Lucas put on the screen. As he created them, the boys and girls of *American Graffiti* were kept so busy turning themselves into pop myths, or just keeping up with the pop myths Lucas bought into long ago, that they never had time to feel out their roles, play with their faces, or bounce self-pity off narcissism—that last being my idea of what High School U.S.A. was all about. Even Chuck Berry would accept that role playing was much closer to what teenagers of Lucas's time were faced with than the mythicizing of the self, let alone the era, and in those days eras didn't come prepackaged with names. It was only some years later that people began to think about what kind of history they might be making before they embarked on a political act, or bought an album. *American Graffiti* was depressing because it made every received, even culturally determined gesture you might remember as a spontaneous response seem like a self-conscious calculation.

Dead Man's Curve made history real by evading what passes for it. What was so liberating about this little movie was that it took for its subject the career of two of the myth-makers themselves—Los Angeles surf and hot-rod music princes Jan Berry and Dean Torrence—and let the story tell itself as if it were itself real: that is, as if it had a claim on the public's attention regardless of whether or not the adventures of two middle-class white youths from southern California provided a clue to the legacy of the sixties, generational identity, the sexual revolution, or anything else bigger than themselves.

Jan and Dean were high school seniors when they made their first record—a national hit—in 1958. It was a garage production, utterly tuneless, energetic, and forgettable, Jan and Dean's version of doo-wop. On through college, they cut records and toured for eight more years, but it was only during 1963 and 1964 that they made a difference in anyone's life. Suddenly, their career and their music took shape, humor ran wild, and their sound exploded off the radio. With "Surf City," "Drag City" (the seemingly necessary follow-up, "Fuck City," never appeared; today, thanks to punk, it would—or, for all I know, has), and "Dead Man's Curve," Jan and Dean made surf, cars, and simply being between the ages of thirteen and eighteen seem like a mid-sixties version of God's grace. There might be more to life than this, one felt, but it could wait.

Jan had always been the creative agent and the driving force of the team. In 1966 his medical school deferment lapsed, and after an angry confrontation with his draft board, he tore down the highway, hit a truck, and ended his career. He lived, barely; part of his brain was gone. Paralyzed, a permanent victim of aphasia, he spent the next years trying to relearn how to walk, talk, and think. He made two 45s in the 1970s, and to him they must have seemed like the first steps of a great comeback. To those who worked with him, or the few who heard the records, they could hardly have seemed like more than therapy.

Based on a superb *Rolling Stone* story by Paul Morantz, *Dead Man's Curve* followed this basic outline. Screenwriter Dalene Young and director Richard Compton must have assumed there was an audience that knew about Jan and Dean and would be interested in what happened to them—must have assumed the story didn't need to be justified on any other terms. The result was a pop culture movie that, because it was about character, dissolved the myths that have become so encrusted around the pop artifacts of the last twenty-five years: myths of freedom, folly, excess, and weird clothes. What you could feel with *Dead Man's Curve* was the naturalness of pop culture: not its Significance, or its appeal as a Version of the American Dream, or its Basic Shallowness, but pop culture as a good context in which to live your life—obvious, energizing, and limited.

As defined by the filmmakers, Jan Berry's personality was allowed to evade the teenage myths that provided the commercial basis for the production. He was shown as representing no one but himself: as irresponsible, disloyal, maniacally egotistical, obsessive, and not a little crazy. That his cold perfectionism on the night he and Dean made their first record was not justified by the quality of the music that resulted was not commented on. One was left to draw one's own conclusions, or to follow the scene where it led: as a first sign of Jan's growing contempt for other people's rules, other people's ideas, and just other people. As Jan,

Richard Hatch made his eyes show cruelty when he taunted Dean about his casual commitment to their career; there was an even crueler set-piece halfway through the film, when Dean hooks a skateboard to Jan's Corvette, water-skiing style, and Jan, speeding up to sixty, nearly kills him. We see Jan cutting Dean out of their partnership, cheating on his girlfriend, treating life as a joke he plays on the world. He's no monster, merely someone you'd go out of your way to avoid—if you could resist the pull of his personality, which Dean (played by Bruce Davison as honest, loyal, and fundamentally bewildered) cannot. Never is there a suggestion that it is pop music, or the myths of pop culture, that have made Jan the way he is. That is something new, because in pop movies, personality is always explained in terms of myth, which is to say personality is always snuffed out by it.

Halfway through, *Dead Man's Curve* shifted into a medical drama; here Jan, terrified, makes as bad a patient as he did a friend, refusing all help, relying solely on his ego to reconnect his nerves. He can't or won't accept reality: music becomes his life, as it never really was when he was able to make it his career. He can hardly speak two words in sequence, but in a recording studio he sings; the result is flat, straining, you can hear every missing brain cell, but it is not pathetic.

The basic TV conceit may be that every bastard gets his, but if Jan's accident is comeuppance, he doesn't see it that way, and in *Dead Man's Curve* what happens to Jan isn't set forth as punishment. To the degree that he's physically capable, he continues to do what he's always done. After months in a coma and years in a hospital, he moves back into his own house; hippies invade it, take it over. Dean comes over one day, bringing a new "Jan and Dean" album he has recorded entirely by himself, singing all the vocal parts. There are strangers all over the place and he can't find Jan. He asks a stoned trio where his friend is. "You mean that freak who lives here?" comes the answer—and it's as chilling a moment as I've seen on television in a long while. Finally, Dean finds Jan and puts on the new record for him; Jan listens for a second, then scratches the needle straight across the surface. You can rehabilitate my body, he's saying; not me.

Dead Man's Curve covers more than fifteen years. The cultural shifts that take place from the late fifties to the seventies, while shown, are never brought to the forefront. People grow older, their hair is longer—they grow up or they don't. The presence of dope-smoking hippies in Jan's house is jarring, creepy—it's the displacement of the late sixties invading a place still frozen in the early sixties—but we aren't told, "The world had changed, and Jan couldn't keep up with it." It's assumed we know changes took place, that anyone interested in watching this story took part in those changes, deflected them, or were sucked in by them. The history of the Jan and Dean generation, for the first time, is presented not as anomaly, not as delayed adolescence, but plainly as history. Here we think no more of its surface changes than we'd think of styles of dress changing in a film biography of Howard Hughes. This may seem trivial; it isn't, because pop culture—all culture that takes pop music as its focus—is never handled this way. From *Rock around the Clock* to *Saturday Night Fever* it's been set forth as less than real—as a delusion to be thrown off or outgrown. Until now, nothing about pop culture has been treated casually, which means nothing has been allowed to reach its true level of significance or triviality. People didn't wear clothes in pop movies; clothes wore people.

I wonder, given the many pop-history movies set for release— *The Buddy Holly Story* and *American Hot Wax,* based on the life of disc jockey Alan Freed, are only the most notable—if *Dead Man's Curve* will prove to be any more than an oddity. It never pandered to nostalgia; the likes of *American Graffiti*'s slogan, "Where were you in '62?" would have been irrelevant, because all that slogan says is, "Weren't we weird then? Didn't we look funny? Can you *believe* we really acted like that?" Meaning, we really didn't, it didn't quite happen; meaning, the past can't be integrated into one's life; meaning, there is no real history in the things we've done. Pop movies offer a version of our history in which we, fans and stars, didn't exist; only the symbols to which we attached ourselves existed, and we were merely functions of those symbols.

It didn't seem that way in *Dead Man's Curve,* and for one reason aside from those I've mentioned: the film used Jan and Dean's music, rather than rerecording the songs for the actors to pantomime. The music sounded good, and Hatch and Davison's performance of it looked good. You felt the producer's respect not only for Jan and Dean's story, but for their audience. But oddly, the most affecting moment of the show came when the old records weren't used. Probably as fully recovered as he will ever be, Jan tells Dean he wants to perform one more time. He can barely get the words out, but not because of his disability; he can't humble himself to ask for a favor. He attacks Dean, insults him. Finally, the woman who takes care of Jan forces him to ask; Dean agrees. "I can't sing," Jan says. "We'll have to . . ." He can't think of the word. "Lip-synch," Dean says.

So they take the stage, ready to fake it in front of a tape of "Surf City"—which, at a concert in 1973, Jan and Dean actually did. In the middle of the song the tape breaks and they're stranded; the audience erupts in boos and jeers. (It's one of the few false moments in the show; no crowd would have been fooled by a tape, as the crowd Jan and Dean in fact played to was not.) Shamed, Jan explains what's happened to him; he decides he'll try to sing the song for real. So he does—the words don't cohere, the melody isn't there, but he gets through the opening lines. I sat watching, stunned at the way an old surf ditty could turn into the most heartbreaking soul music, finally understanding what the Rolling Stones meant when they said it was the singer, not the song.

Then, of course, the camera pulled back, and Jan and Dean finished the song in triumph, singing perfectly, the crowd on its feet, cheering. In 1973, it didn't end that way, but I didn't care.

Politicks, 28 March 1978

Dead Man's Curve

It's difficult to make a movie about the pop past that's more than a cheap joke or a sentimental fraud, because pop culture pretends to exist without reference to time. If you're working from the inside of a pop sensibility, the past appears hokey by definition. The temptation to condescend to the past through nostalgia, or to pump up fragile details of clothes or slang with a significance they can't support, is almost irresistible. But because details are easy to catch, they're used as a sort of bogus cinematic reality principle: they make what one sees on the screen seem real enough to connect to. Filmmakers focus on surface pop detail, evading the feeling that was invested in styles and trends—the feeling that made them seem special, even revelatory.

At the same time, the movie version of the pop past shows only isolation. No future, not even change, is ever implicit in a story— except, as in *The Lords of Flatbush,* being forced into marriage and breaking-up-that-old-gang-of-mine. The very immediacy of pop, its crazy intensity—and it's this that distinguishes pop, which is altogether postwar, from simple popular culture—makes any sense of the future nearly impossible. In 1959, when Danny and the Juniors sang "Rock 'n' roll is here to stay," they weren't promising their listeners they'd grow up with their new music, they were promising perpetual adolescence.

It's ironic—also wonderful—that it was the first promise, not the second, that pop fulfilled, but pop itself (as idea, culture, way of life) has still failed to come up with the conceptual framework to make such a fact real. That people are beginning to wonder about this problem is indicated by statements rock stars such as Bob Dylan and Bob Seger have been making lately: they figure they'll just keep on keepin' on til they drop, just like the great blues and country singers. Which is fine, but begs the question: it turns pop into folk music. What's lost is the pop burden of novelty, which demands a constant attempt to reach new audiences as well as the attempt to continually absorb change and turn it into novel music.

Given all this, it's no surprise that when the movies chart pop history—or when we put all the movies from *Jailhouse Rock* to *Privilege* together—we find not continuity, not an unfolding generational epic, but a series of utterly discrete moments. What would it mean for a filmmaker to take up the sadomasochistic vision of *Performance* and apply it backward to tell the story of Frankie Lymon, the black teenager who became a huge rock 'n' roll star in 1956 and died in 1968 of a heroin overdose? The pop fifties provided no concepts that could make sense of such an event; the pop sixties did. Why not link them? But eras and concepts are never linked in pop movies; you can take your whole self into the theater, and the film will take it away from you.

Pop life comes to seem like a joke the postwar generations have played on themselves—certainly that's how it was with *All You Need Is Cash*, a hilarious mock documentary about mock Beatles, "the Rutles," which aired on NBC not long ago. The Rutles dropped themselves into every memorable incident in Beatle history, which meant that ten years of pop history were covered on the premise that the real thing had been such a cosmic sham that one's memory would be easily subverted by inspired parody, and, correct or not, the premise worked. Seeing the Rutles during their "early days in Hamburg," or during their addled "spiritual phase," I got nervous. My God, I thought, had I—and virtually everyone I knew—put so much of myself into so little? In the movies, even straight pop history is usually parody in spite of itself, and you instinctively distance yourself from what you're seeing. With *All You Need Is Cash* I was ready to leave town.

In the middle of the show, a commercial for a local radio station's "All-Beatle Weekend" appeared, complete with Beatle film clips. For a second, the Beatles looked like they were imitating the Rutles; every clip showed a moment in Beatle history the Rutles had just trashed.

Nothing like this went on in *American Hot Wax,* a movie centered on the life of Alan Freed, the rhythm-and-blues-loving disc jockey who came out of Cleveland in 1954 to lead the early rock 'n' roll years in New York City. Directed by Floyd Mutrux and written by John Kaye, *American Hot Wax,* despite countless historical smudges and cheats—you get the impression rock 'n' roll was born and nearly killed off in a week-long period in the fall of 1959—peddles neither mythic icons nor cheesy stereotypes. Instead, it relates the thrill of pop culture to characters recognizable as people, and vice versa. The movie has been written off as a fairy tale pandering to pop narcissism, or as a slick gloss on some very tricky issues, and while this isn't exactly untrue—Freed was a martyr, but he was no Jesus; if rock 'n' roll scrambled racial categories, it didn't liberate its artists, fans, or entrepreneurs from racism—I don't think it's of much importance. Questions of time and pop culture are questions of reality, and they present themselves in the form of distance between film and viewer; in the best of *American Hot Wax* I found no distance at all. Details of who did what, when, and how aside, it's the most emotionally accurate movie about pop culture ever made.

Broken by indictments for payola and tax evasion, out of work and an alcoholic, Freed died in 1965 at the age of forty-three. The movie catches him at the height of his fame and power—as DJ, concert promoter, record producer, and all-around music industry middle man and proselytizer. Yet Freed is about to fall and he knows it, and Tim McIntire's performance is pitched on this high wire: his Freed is smart, open to strangers, yet insulated even from friends. He's like a man who's been diagnosed with terminal cancer but gets too much out of life to slow down for the sake of a few more weeks.

What plot the movie has centers on the last of the big rock revues Freed staged at the Brooklyn Paramount. The district attorney, with an octopus of an intelligence apparatus at his command, thinks Freed is mongrelizing the races and corrupting the youth with smut. He's out to stop the show and break Freed in the bargain. We see Chuck Berry and Jerry Lee Lewis in the big on-stage finale (Lewis lights his piano on fire, cops burst into the hall and cause a riot), plus performances by artists whose records Freed is supervising, including the Chesterfields, a fictional black vocal group he's picked up off the street. Complete with the cop who ends up thinking, "Hey, this music's not so bad after all," this is a post-Watergate update of *Don't Knock the Rock,* in which the real Alan Freed, playing himself, starred in 1956 (today cynicism about authority is not only palatable, it's soothing).

Clichés in order, the film proceeds to transcend them. The spirit of the music—its place in life—is right from the start. In the pre-credit sequence, we see a stocky man walking down a dark, wet street. Save that the movie is in color, the setting is pure film noir, and there's nothing remotely glamorous about the man: he seems fed up, wasted. It's all in the way he walks; a lot is being communicated here, but it's disorienting. We've paid our money to see a movie about rock 'n' roll, and straight off it looks like we're being set up to watch a mugging.

The man steps into an office building, walks through deserted corridors to a small studio, looks at a pile of singles marked "DON'T PLAY," picks the top one, cues it up, and points his round, bitter face at a microphone. "I'm Alan Freed," he says, "and this is rock 'n' roll." And it is, with a dramatic lift never before seen on a screen. The record is Little Richard's still-astonishing "Tutti Frutti"; it's ridiculous that a "DON'T PLAY" list would be accompanied by a stack of records not to play, but the first notes of the music swallow the absurdity, and the movie cracks wide open.

The tension generated by McIntire's tight, nervous presence is blown away. Suddenly we see other faces reflected in the glass partitions of the studio, and a nasty, satisfied smile from Freed. With three quick cuts into Freed's radio audience—a white teen-age girl stuffing her bra with Kleenex, a white twelve-year-old boy smoking and dancing in his room, three of the Chesterfields bopping out of the fourth's apartment—the whole world seems to be moving to Freed's beat. In something under two minutes, the film dramatizes the sense of isolation that draws people into pop culture and the sense of community that ties them to it. It seems like a miracle that the disparate people we've been introduced to could be sharing something as intensely as they share the record Freed is playing, but they did. And now we do.

It's a moment of true magic, and again and again the picture matches it. Such moments, in fact, are what *American Hot Wax* is all about. The usual components of history are scrambled by the immediacy of the film's epiphanies. Here the real events of Freed's career, such as his troubles with the law, don't seem quite real, because they were pop-movie clichés even before they happened. Long since absorbed by pop myth, the true events are inaccessible except as ready-mades. They seem quaint, like set-ups, and we draw away so as not to be fooled. But coming off the same screen, the music, and the depth of response people bring to it, seem anything but quaint.

In one amazing scene, Freed, with about two dozen people in tow, arrives at a recording studio. The Planotones, a fictional white doo-wop group, are trying to cut "Come Go with Me" (actually a 1957 hit for the Del-Vikings, a black and white doo-wop group), but they're sluggish, and arrogant about their sluggishness. Their producer, played by Richard Perry, gives the Planotones a hook: "Four 'doms,' then a 'dom-de dooby wah,' OK?" Perry sounds like an idiot speaking rock 'n' roll nonsense syllables with the earnestness of a priest, but the group picks up the phrase and locks into the song. The place erupts with joy: you can see Freed's eyes bugging with excitement, and the grin that splits Perry's face when one of the Planotones hits his high note is worth all the records Perry, who makes his off-screen living producing pop-rock in Hollywood, has ever made.

Even stronger is a scene with the Chesterfields. After Freed has taken them under his wing and then apparently dropped them, they gather under a roadway to spend the night throwing songs at each other. It's all a cappella, of course; they've never sung with accompaniment. But what begins as a laugh, a way to pass the time, quickly grows into something much deeper—or perhaps it's the very idea of passing the time that grows deeper. As the Chesterfields move from one rhythm and blues standard to another, the feeling of warmth that comes off the screen is so strong it makes present-day pop music seem like an obscenity of contrivance. William Fraker's camera moves effortlessly with the loose, snapping beat, catching a singer in close-up, then framing all four, never burdening a singer with more time than he can visually or vocally carry. The emotion is so direct, so purposeless, so utterly validated by itself, that when the plot returns—in the person of Freed, who's checking out the group again for a last-minute spot in his show—it's an intrusion. We don't care any more whether the Chesterfields get their chance at the big time. We just want to hear them sing, to go further into the image of harmony they're making—an image that implies the community of strangers pop has always promised.

McIntire's characterization of Freed is the perfect counter-rhythm to such an easy moment of freedom. His Freed knows he's going to pay for moments like this one; he knows, and makes us understand, what they're worth. The fact that in the person of McIntire Freed looks to be in his mid-forties (Freed was thirty-seven in the fall of 1959) drives this home—and if we're in our thirties or older now, McIntire's performance might have a special pathos. His Freed is as profoundly in touch with rock 'n' roll as any teenager has ever been, and this makes him more than a promoter, or even a fan. It makes him a harbinger of the audience that, in the years to follow, would grow up and keep listening.

With his world falling apart around him, he holds on to the music as if it's the last thing he can be sure won't trip him up. This is a constant of McIntire's performance, rendered best when we see Freed getting ready for his Brooklyn Paramount show, sitting in his dressing room and swigging Scotch out of the bottle. He has the radio on; the song is Maurice Williams and the Zodiacs' "Stay." As he buttons his shirt, smooths his hair, he idly keeps time; then he presses the rhythm with greater insistence; and finally, as one of the Zodiacs begins his climb toward the insane high note that tops the music, McIntire, watching himself in the dressing room mirror, silently and lovingly twists his face around the note and swallows it.

It's a scene of absolute empathy. The forced distance between the audience and what's on the screen that's always been inherent in pop-history movies—the distance that makes the community and the continuity of pop seem like delusions without ever letting a viewer understand why people have been able to take such sustenance from that community and that continuity—is bridged. What we've watched is the dissolution of distance between a culture and one who's part of it, and that's what we've felt.

"In the worst of times music is a promise that times are meant to be better," Robert Christgau has written. The premise of *American Hot Wax*—the premise you draw from its texture, not its plot—is that pop culture is about shared access to feeling in a world that keeps people separate and feeling at a distance; that pop culture is about the unpredictable interplay between three-minute utopias of sound and ordinary life. Never has the utopian-ism of pop been presented on the screen in so undeniable a fashion—and that means that when you leave the theater and return to ordinary life, it no longer seems quite ordinary. It seems like a gift.

Politicks, 9 May 1978

When You Walk in the Room

On the Social History of Art" is the first chapter in T. J. Clark's *Image of the People: Gustave Courbet and the 1848 Revolution.* Writing over the winter of 1969–70, Clark was looking for the ways in which the social dimension of life—the political and economic facts of life, certainly, but also, in a great formulation, the always spectral body of the public as a kind of analogue to an individual's unconscious—finds its way into works of art, and how in such works the presence or the shape of social history can be discerned. Clark was asking how there could be, in a thing made by an individual, a kind of social doppelgänger.

Clark insists on how hard it is to see the "transactions" in which the private and the individual keep company with the social and the public, and vice versa; how looking for the "process of conversion and relation" is like looking for a subatomic particle that is at once proved and yet invisible and unfound. But a good deal is at issue: the question of how, in certain times, in certain hands, images of possibility or negation that can speak beyond their time are left behind. It's patent in *Image of the People* that the future depends on, among other things, a few images from Courbet. After the defeat of the 1848 revolution, Courbet made his greatest paintings, Clark argues; with one notion of life defeated, another rose, in another form, presaging yet another formation— the continuation of a story that, as told by other voices, was already over. "Still!" Clark ends *Image of the People*, quoting Baudelaire. "In spite of everything!"

So the stakes are high. As Clark wrote twenty years later, looking over "On the Social History of Art," he wanted not "a recipe for reading 'social content' out of art works," but "a framework within which it might be possible to rethink, histori- cally, the very process by which a particular work produced its meanings and lost them."

Sometimes, though, the question needs to be twisted. Clark's question makes sense for high or fine art—for art self-consciously made and received within a tradition that has, for works that pass certain tests, so to speak preapproved their illumination. For low art—or vernacular art, or everyday art—one always has to begin with an argument that a work produced in, or dropped by, this sort of tradition, has any meaning at all beyond ego, commerce, or sociology. The notion of works that in some way or another contest their time is basic to the criticism of fine art; no critic approaching vernacular art has ever really beaten back the premise that work in popular culture is made by its time. Clark rightly dismisses the idea of a work of art reflecting its era, or some facet of it, but such a dead and deadening notion rules in the criticism and the history of popular art—and when you work within the terms of cultural reflection, you always find exactly what you're looking for.

For popular art—art made within a tradition the operating premise of which is to replicate a work and sell as many copies as possible as fast as possible—the question is not that of letting the social into the art. It's a question of freeing the art from the social—and here too the stakes may be high. It may be that unless certain works of art can be loosened from the social circumstances that seemingly produced them, there can be no history, social or otherwise—no history we have to answer to, a history that is more than the sum total of, to quote Clark again, "the topical needs of the moment." Everyone knows Walter Benjamin's dictum that history is a matter of seizing "hold of a memory as it flashes up at a moment of danger." As the critic Howard Hampton puts it, though, history does not simply flash up, and flash out. As history flashes up, it "demands that the present account for itself." To refuse to account for ourselves—or to be unable to, to be unable to see history as the product of certain choices made at certain crossroads, a commingling of private motives brought to bear on public works—is to leave nothing to writing history but burying the dead.

As Marx loved to say, let the dead bury the dead. Some artists are dead to the degree that they are subsumed by the social, and alive to the degree that the social can be distanced from their work; as with any attempts to bring the dead back to life, it's easier said than done.

More than half a century ago, in late November 1936, a twenty-five-year-old blues singer from Mississippi made his first records in San Antonio, Texas—among them "Terraplane Blues," "Come on in My Kitchen," "Walking Blues," "If I Had Possession Over Judgment Day." In January 1970, a month after Altamont, the all-day Rolling Stones rock festival where I'd witnessed the worst violence I'd ever seen in the flesh, I walked into a record store, not looking for anything in particular; I just wanted to buy a record. I flipped through the blues rack and saw the name Robert Johnson. It didn't mean much to me; I'd noticed it as a song-writing credit on Cream albums, for tunes called "Crossroads" and "Four Until Late." The previous fall, I'd watched the Rolling Stones play a pristine version of "Love in Vain," a track on their soon to be released *Let It Bleed,* but I didn't know it was Johnson's; they had credited the song to someone called Woody Payne.

I was just starting out as a rock critic, though after Altamont I felt a hundred years old. I thought I ought to know where Cream songs came from, so I bought the Robert Johnson album, *King of the Delta Blues Singers,* included as part of the bizarrely named series Thesaurus of Classic Jazz. It was one of those moments when you get your life changed—like picking a college course that leads you to think for the first time, or walking thoughtlessly into a room and falling in love. I took the record home and put it on: I knew nothing about country blues. I knew almost nothing about the Deep South in the 1930s—I'd never even read Faulkner. All I had were memories of *Life* magazine photos of lynchings, Richard Wright's autobiography, and the autobiography of one of the Scottsboro Boys (both mediated through the ever-changing Communist Party line on the race question). All I had, really, was a liberal upbringing and a lot of socialist realism. I brought virtually no context to the record. I simply took it home, put it on, and had my life changed.

I heard a sound I'd never heard before, but which, for some reason, I connected to. It was what Herman Melville called the shock of recognition—and for me the shock has always been the realization that you have recognized something nothing could have led you to expect to recognize. The question turns out to be not what-makes-the-music-great, but why you recognized its greatness when, all things considered, you shouldn't have understood it at all, or even stumbled upon it in the first place. I've been married for more than twenty years; sometimes, like anyone married that long, I wonder what my life would have been like if, on a certain meaningless day, I hadn't walked into a certain meaningless room. Sometimes I think my life would be more or less the same; sometimes I think I wouldn't have a life at all. I feel the same way about Robert Johnson.

Predictably, playing the Robert Johnson album, I didn't like his 1936 version of "Cross Road Blues" as much as Cream's 1968 version. Cream's performance, a live recording, was a firestorm; this was too quiet. As the album played, I read the liner notes. This is how they began: "Robert Johnson is little, very little more than a name on aging index cards and a few dusty master records in the files of a phonograph company that no longer exists."

Those lines were poetry to me. I still think the cadence of the prose is poetry—the movement from "little, very little" to the hard stop of "no longer exists." I turned the record over and found myself frozen by "Stones in My Passway"; my nice living room was suddenly invaded. To get away from what was happening, I read on: "Robert Johnson appeared and disappeared, in much the same fashion as a sheet of newspaper twisting and twirling down a dark and windy midnight street." This wasn't poetry—it was corny—but it reminded me of the cover on my copy of Camus's *The Rebel,* a picture that has stayed with me with far greater force than almost anything in the book itself. The cover showed a sheet of newspaper, with headlines in a smear of different languages and alphabets, all carrying reports of revolution and upheaval, blowing down the street to nowhere. The likes of the Paris Commune in 1871, the Berlin rising of 1918, Barcelona in 1936—all such events expelled from history by those with the power to get history written, published, censored, and taught, the incidents appearing, when they appeared in the record at all, like a list of perversions in a sex manual on healthy married life. I experienced those words on the Robert Johnson album, and Robert Johnson's music, as an invasion of a world I had taken for granted—an invasion of an urban, modern, white, middle-class, educated reality I had taken as complete and finished, as a natural fact.

Robert Johnson's music was a rent in that reality, a violent rip, a negation, a no. I suddenly realized I was sick of rock 'n' roll; sick, after Altamont, of what it could do and what it had already produced. Altamont showed me blood and death. I'd seen people beaten to the ground with lead-weighted sticks, seen naked people with their teeth knocked out, and I'd left the place only to hear on the radio that, as I'd stood behind the stage on top of a van to hear the Rolling Stones, a young black man had been knifed, kicked, and bludgeoned to death. There was death in Robert Johnson's songs—but it always stopped short, stopped short at the point of choice. As I listened, full of ugly memories, Robert Johnson's music talked to me as the voice of a new world, where everything was at stake, and nothing was resolved. Every choice was open, made real—what happened was up to me.

This wasn't socialist realism, or even liberal realism, which says that all people are products of great historical forces in a world they never made: that all people are sociology. Robert Johnson's music wasn't merely a rent in the bourgeois life I'd lived; it was a rent in the theories of the leftists who'd fought against that life as natural fact, who reached their high point in the thirties, at the very moment Johnson was singing. The bourgeois view of the world said people like Robert Johnson didn't count; the socialist realist view of the world said he'd been made not to count, and that if by some miracle he'd made his voice heard, it was as the voice of the irrepressible will of the people—in other words, as sociology. As an individual he didn't exist. But this wasn't what I heard. I heard a particular person, someone no sociological construct could have predicted, or even allowed for. Years later I would read Albert Murray's comments on Bessie Smith: he noted that many writers had tried to tie the expressive power of Smith's music to the pain and suffering of black people in America, and then he wondered why four hundred years of slavery and oppression had produced only one Bessie Smith. Albert Murray, a black American critic, was trying to rescue Bessie Smith from socialist realism; he was trying to give her back the subjectivity, the autonomy, that is automatically granted any urban white artist. She was, Murray was saying, a genius.

With Robert Johnson, in 1970, I wasn't ready to think on this level, only to respond. Instead of trying to understand the voice I tried to understand the form—the genre, the sociology. I became obsessed with Mississippi country blues—primitive blues, it was called in the notes to the Robert Johnson album. I learned a lot about it. I bought everything I could find. I learned about the first country blues performers to record, men much older than Robert Johnson: Charlie Patton, Son House, Willie Brown, Skip James, Garfield Akers. I heard a music that was rich, fierce, funny, and bitter. But I kept listening to Robert Johnson, and what I learned still didn't touch what he was doing.

I learned that blues had come into being—was invented, was discovered, I don't know the right word—around 1900, probably in the Mississippi Delta; wherever it came from, the sound was soon heard across the South. Everyone, black and white, who heard this sound—all those with enough education to write down their thoughts on what they heard—said the same thing. It didn't matter if it was some benevolent rich white woman or W. C. Handy of Memphis, who later named himself "Father of the Blues." They all had the same reaction, used the same words: "Weird." "Strange." "Eerie." "Unearthly." "Devilish." "Terrifying." "Not of this world."

The blues was something new. Just as Robert Johnson's music made a breach in my white, middle-class, modern world, around 1900 blues made a breach in the known world of Southern blacks. It wasn't like the old field hollers, work songs, animal fables, ring shouts, spirituals, though musicologists have traced the lines back so that you'd think a breach had never been made. A leads to B and B leads to C, and who can deny it? But the testimony of those who were there counts—and what those who were there said was that they'd never heard anything like this before, and they weren't sure they ever wanted to hear anything like it again. A white woman heard her black teenage maid moaning to herself as she folded laundry—whatever the song was about, the white woman testified, if it was a song, if it was about anything, it wasn't laundry. W. C. Handy was waiting for a train late one night; two men with guitars sat down beside him and began to play; later he wondered if it hadn't been a dream.

What was this? Robert Johnson attracted international attention in his lifetime; *Melody Maker*, the British music weekly, ran an item bemoaning the fact that Johnson's record company wasn't known for encouraging protest songs. Obviously, blues was full of pain and suffering; therefore at its heart it had to be a protest against white oppression. On the page, that wasn't hard to understand—why was the sound so hard to understand?

It was hard to understand because blues was music born not of oppression, but of freedom. It was not a protest against racism, sharecropping, even lynching—it was, like *The Sound and the Fury*, a protest against life.

Blues was invented by one of the first generations of black Americans not to be born slaves—to be born with the freedom of movement that from the time of Daniel Boone was enshrined as the first principle of American life. They were among the first African Americans to escape of their own free will the ties of hometown, home plantation, family, church—and, most important, work. The black church as well as white sheriffs pushed the singers back—and they pushed back against the church no less than against the sheriffs. No, they said, I do what I like.

A whole new, common language grew up around that negation, that affirmation: "No, I do what I like." It was a shared language of guitar riffs and lyric phrases ("My black mama's face shines like the sun," "The sun gonna shine in my back door someday," "Minutes seem like hours, hours seem just like days"), a set of fragments reaching for some all-encompassing blues parable that every blues singer presented in pieces. You could say, as blues chronicler Peter Guralnick has, that the tradition itself, not the individual artist, was the poet—and that the tradition came about as a poetic opposition to playing by the rules. In that sense, of course, blues was a protest, but blues singers—me, not you, him, not them—didn't see it that way. They considered themselves free men, as good as anybody and better than most—if not better than most, more free. Their music was made out of a conviction that, like all Americans, they were masters of their own lives, or should be. When they ran into the limits of their mastery—the inability to hold a woman, to keep a dollar in hand, to live without fear—they found themselves face to face not only with the particular racial, economic, or social conditions of the Deep South in the twenties and thirties, but also face to face with the facts of life. Those facts could be summed up very easily: men and women were not at home in this world. It was the same fact Melville had discovered in *Moby Dick*, that Faulkner was raging against in *The Sound and the Fury*, that the writers of Greek tragedies had chewed over more than two thousand years before that. That was why, to those who heard the blues around the year 1900, the sound was strange, scary, confusing: the new blues singers were singing about things people had *never* wanted to talk about. For the first time, these folk were taking alienation as a first principle. These modern individuals were acting like free people, running into the wall that separates desire from its realization, and makes that separation into consciousness.

It took me a long time to glimpse this—or to believe it. For a long time, what I heard in Mississippi country blues, and always most intensely in Robert Johnson, was a contradiction. The music reached me directly, went straight to the heart, seemed to call forth answers from the blood; at the same time the music was impossibly distant, odd, and old. For black people in the twenties and thirties, the Mississippi Delta was full of horses and wagons; it was ruled through peonage. There weren't any telephones and there weren't any toilets. No black people were allowed to vote. Most couldn't dream of learning to read and write. The first contact most would have with a world outside the one into which they were born was when their sons were drafted to fight in World War II—and many of their sons were given farm deferments, arranged by white landowners to ensure that their workers would never see a world outside the one into which they'd been born.

But I've fallen back into sociology—what's at issue is a different sort of distance, a different sort of oldness, a different sort of oddness. I grew up on *The Twilight Zone;* Mississippi blues was twilight zone stuff. The singers, recorded in their twenties and thirties, seemed in their voices to have been old before they were born. Robert Johnson was a ghost—out of a past I'd never expected to confront, he was years ahead of me every time I listened to him, waiting for me to catch up.

I am writing about Robert Johnson because if any of the things I have been saying are true, they are titanically more true of him and his music than they are of any other singer of his place and time. Once one has been through the tradition, many of the great singers and most of the minor ones—and scores of black men made records in the South in the twenties and thirties—recede into that tradition; the tradition speaks for them; finally, they become sociology. Their music makes sense sociologically—and after that it may not make any other kind of sense, or make non-sense out of whatever preconceptions a listener might bring to it. Charlie Patton, considered the founder of Mississippi Delta blues, sounds like a founder. Son House sounds like an exponent. Skip James and Tommy Johnson, both of them with highly de- veloped individual styles, sound like eccentrics, isolates within a tradition that is itself isolated from the America, be it political or artistic, where history was supposedly being made. In 1936, with the New Deal coalition utterly dependent on what was, at times, called White Democracy, FDR had no trouble mapping the black world within the Mississippi Delta as another country.

Compared with Skip James or Tommy Johnson, Robert

Johnson does not sound particularly individualistic. He sounds very traditional—and also as if the tradition, this particular racial/economic/social/religious happenstance, is meaningless, as if it had never existed. In his music you seem to hear what everyone else was reaching for, what everyone else was trying to say, what no one else could touch, what no one else could put into words, into the twist of a vocal, the curl of a guitar line—or for that matter into a passage of prose, the scene of a play, the detail of a painting. Robert Johnson takes the tradition as a given, in the same way that we take it as a given that the people we meet will speak, eat, and sleep; he then goes beyond the tradition to such an extent that concepts of speaking, eating, and sleeping lose their meanings, or acquire entirely new ones.

Robert Johnson, his music says, worked and lived with a deeper autonomy than other blues singers, most of whom came forth to affirm autonomy. He made his music against the limits of that autonomy, limits he discovered and made real, and he did so with more ferocity, and more tenderness, than other blues singers, all of whom encountered similar limits. The difference is this: other blues artists dealt with that problem within the bounds of the tradition, within the bounds of the form of Mississippi Delta blues, speaking that common language. If the tradition allowed them to refuse the limits on their lives, they accepted the limited power of the tradition to affect those limits, to make sense of them.

Robert Johnson did not do this. As an individual, sparked by the blues tradition to want more out of life than he might have otherwise demanded, he refused to accept the limits of the blues tradition itself—a tradition that, as an aesthetic form, at once inspired and limited his ability to make demands on life, to protest against it. Just as around 1900 blues made a rent in black American life, in 1936 Robert Johnson made a rent in the blues.

Blues was his language, his only means of making a mark on

the world, of leaving it even slightly different than he found it. He mastered the tradition—he formally extended the vocabulary of blues guitar, formally raised the level of song composition, deepened its formal possibilities for vocal strength and delicacy. Yet he also found the tradition inadequate—and you can hear this in his greatest songs, in "Stones in My Passway," "Hellhound on My Trail," "Come on in My Kitchen," "Traveling Riverside Blues." The tension of wanting to say more than the tradition can say explodes the tradition. "Stones in My Passway" and "Hellhound on My Trail" neither sound nor feel like other blues. It doesn't matter how well any musicologist can track their melodies or their lyrics back to any other performers. You run into a wall of emotional, aesthetic fact: sociology can explain Mississippi Delta blues, but it cannot explain Robert Johnson any more than four hundred years of pain and suffering can produce two Bessie Smiths.

Most traditions of any sort decay, fall into ruin, wear out. It's rare to see, to hear, any tradition actually be blown up—to be taken to a critical mass of possibility and desire and then destroyed. That's what happens in Robert Johnson's last recordings, made in 1937, the year before he died. It seems impossible that there could be any Mississippi blues after those last recordings—and in a way there weren't. Nothing new; just refinements, revivals, footnotes. Many of Johnson's more conventional compositions—"Sweet Home Chicago," "Dust My Broom," "Cross Road Blues"—became blues and then rock 'n' roll standards in the years and decades after his death; it's interesting that almost no one has even tried to make a new version of "Stones in My Passway" or "Hellhound on My Trail."

Once it's truly heard, Robert Johnson's music takes shape as a mystery—and confronted with a mystery, the human impulse is to try and solve it. Robert Johnson is no longer a name on a forgotten index card; since *King of the Delta Blues Singers* was released in 1961, almost every fact one might care to know about him has been discovered. There are enough facts for a full biography; not long ago there was mostly legend, tall tales, superstition. And yet Robert Johnson's music has not been reduced, has not been contained, has not been made sense of. You hear a man going further than he could ever have been expected to go—even if you know nothing of the particular limits of Mississippi blues, you can hear those limits being smashed, or hear the artist fall back violently before them. What you hear is a struggle more extreme, and more fully shaped, than you can accept. So you begin to ask: What would it mean to want that much? What would it mean to lose that much?

Carlos Fuentes once spoke about the difference between literature that can be contained within the bounds of sociology and ethnography and literature that cannot. "Perhaps *Babbitt* and *Main Street* could only have been written by a perfectly determined North American writer born in Sauk Center, Minnesota, in the year of grace 1885," Fuentes said of Sinclair Lewis. "But *Absalom, Absalom! Light in August* or *The Sound and the Fury* could, in their mythic essence, have been told by a wise savage in central Africa, an ancient guardian of memory in the Himalayas, an amnesiac demon, or a remorseful god." Sam Charters, one of the first to write in detail about Mississippi blues, once said that only a black man, living in the Mississippi Delta in the first third of the century, could possibly understand what Son House meant when he sang "My black mama's face shines like the sun." Maybe that is true, in the same way that what Fuentes says about Sinclair Lewis may be true. But nothing similar is true about Robert Johnson, any more than one has to be anything like Faulkner to understand what he wrote.

For all this, Robert Johnson remains a figure in a story that, as it is usually told, is already completed: that is, he is a sociological exemplar of an ethnographic cultural incident that makes complete sense within the bounds of American sociocultural ethnography. No one talks about Melville, Hawthorne, Dickinson—or even D. W. Griffith, John Ford, and Orson Welles—this way. They are discussed as people who took on the world and, for whatever reasons, made something of it; what they made of it is what gets discussed, and discussed in the most wide-ranging way, connecting to and informing anything that might connect to or inform it. Such talk makes their work richer, and the world richer, more interesting. But there are few American black artists discussed in these terms, and no blues singers. Formal objections are easy—how can you compare a handful of two-and-a-half-minute songs to Melville's books, or just *Moby Dick?* Can you really say there is a labyrinth as deep and twisting in "Stones in My Passway" as in *The Sound and the Fury?* Well, put it this way: could you tell Johnson or Melville or Faulkner there isn't?

Village Voice, 9 December 1986; revised for *Texte zur Kunst,* Spring 1991

Cretins, Fools, Morons, and Lunatics

ome time in the 1980s, at a Milan vanity press specializing in the occult, the three middle-aged editors who suffer the plot of Umberto Eco's *Foucault's Pendulum* chafe under countless stupid manuscripts on the Holy Grail, gnosticism, Stonehenge, the Rosicrucians—most of the thick, smeared piles of paper insisting on a single plan beyond the ken of science, a plan to rule the world. Like smart people with a good crossword puzzle, in their idle moments the editors are also intrigued, and most of all by the mysteries surrounding the Knights Templar: the pious Christian order of crusader-monks, founded in the early twelfth century, which gained unprecedented autonomy and wealth in Europe in the thirteenth century, and was destroyed by the king of France in the early fourteenth century as a cult of devil-worshippers. Who were they, really? Did they possess the Grail? Did they have their hands on the Plan? Who cares? Who doesn't?

"There are four kinds of people in this world," says one of the editors in a drunken reverie: "cretins, fools, morons, and lunatics." He defines the types:

Cretins are of no interest to us. They never come to publishers' offices. . . . Fools don't interest us, either. They're never creative, their talent is all second-hand, so they don't submit manuscripts to publishers. [Unlike cretins, fools] don't claim that cats bark, but they talk about cats when everyone else is talking about dogs. . . . [Morons] get their reasoning wrong. Like the fellow who says all dogs are pets and all dogs bark, and cats are pets, too, and therefore cats bark. . . . A lunatic is easily recognized. He is a moron who doesn't know the ropes. The moron proves his thesis; he has a logic, however twisted it may be. The lunatic, on the other hand, doesn't concern himself at all with logic; he works by short circuits. For him, everything proves everything else. The lunatic is all idée fixe, and whatever he comes across confirms his lunacy. You can tell him by the liberties he takes with common sense, by his flashes of inspiration, and by the fact that sooner or later he brings up the Templars.

For fun, the editors dive into "the blueprint": the Templar MacGuffin, the "self-generating," unread directives behind all the unholy texts that, from pre-Christian esoterica to *The Protocols of the Elders of Zion,* "migrated from one conspiracy to another," throughout history, before history, as a prophecy of the end of history. Armed with a computer, the editors brainstorm their way across thousands of facts, pseudo-facts, and anti-facts to invent their own Plan of the Templars, the perfect reflection in the Hall of Mirrors of the Temple of What Cannot Be Known. Bits and pieces leak out of their offices, enough to alert the credulous army of epistemological monsters whose manuscripts the editors exploit for a living; the editors find themselves under siege, their lives in danger, trapped in their own device. Like the Templars, they are forced to give up their secret—which, like the Templars, whom Philip the Fair exterminated solely for political reasons, they don't have.

The Templars were tortured, some burned over slow fires until the flesh and sinew vaporized (one survivor collected the bones of his feet, and exhibited them in a plea for alms); the editors succumb in turn. The first to go merely perishes from cancer, but it is the most significant death. He dies from an AIDS-like wasting, a semio-flesh disorder, his body a metaphor for the occultist's destruction of knowledge and language. Dying by inches, he is proof that language, like the phony Plan, is an invention, an arbitrary assemblage, a mirror that can produce only a horrible reflection of the God who gave Adam the power of perfect naming, the absolute language in which each sound actually was what it signified.

"I'm dying because I convinced myself that there was no order, that you could do whatever you liked with any text," the editor says to his comrades. "I am experiencing in my body everything we did, as a joke, in the Plan. . . . Have you ever reflected that the linguistic term 'metathesis' is similar to the oncological term 'metastasis'?" "Don't talk nonsense," says a second editor. "It's a matter of cells."

And what are cells? For months, like devout rabbis, we uttered different combinations of the letters of the Book. GCC, CGC, GCG, CGG. What our lips said, our cells learned. What did my cells do? They invented a different Plan, and now they are proceeding on their own, creating a history, a unique, private history. My cells have learned that you can blaspheme by anagrammatizing the Book, and all the books of the world. And they have learned to do this now with my body. They invert, transpose, alternate, transform themselves into cells unheard of, new cells without meaning, or with meaning contrary to the right meaning. There must be a right meaning and a wrong meaning; otherwise you die.

"Superstition brings bad luck," runs one of the epigraphs to Umberto Eco's 641-page entertainment. Fifty-seven-year-old academic semiotician (*The Role of the Reader, The Aesthetics of Thomas Aquinas,* etc.) and best-selling novelist (*The Name of the Rose),* Eco could have used a line from Stevie Wonder: "When you believe in things that you don't understand / Then you suffer."

This is the gist of *Foucault's Pendulum*. Like any other big novel on the occult, it's both good airplane literature and hard to follow. There comes a point—there come a lot of points— where you don't have any idea what's going on but you press ahead just to see what happens or, as with all such books, what doesn't. Eco has written a trendily pre-millennial book, and he's here to tell us that despite AIDS or the greenhouse effect or whatever portent of doom you might name, the millennium will not be the Millennium: the year 2000 (or, to be strict, 2001) will be just another year.

The subtext of *Foucault's Pendulum* is more properly histori- cal—the 1980s of the novel measured against the events of a premature Millennium, the year 1968—but at the same time that subtext is in its way as evanescent as the king's charges that putatively devout Templars were initiated by carrying out the commandment to kiss the anus of a black cat. Nineteen sixty- eight was the year of incipient revolution in the modern world—a casting back, Eco seems to be saying, to an archaic belief in an apocalyptic transformation of all things under the sun, an instant of absolute upheaval. The editor Casaubon, Eco's narrator, re- members it; he can't forget it. The memory of what didn't happen in 1968 is what drives him toward the Plan.

Behind the endless arithmetic of occult reconstructions of What Never Was, Eco's book is about a moment when the world suggested it was about to change. Casaubon recalls the near overthrow of the French state, or its near dissolution: thousands of students rioting in Paris in May 1968, then workers across the country refusing to work but occupying their workplaces to argue over the shape of the future, the whole event somehow spoken for in a single punning gnostic slogan: I TAKE MY DESIRES FOR REALITY BECAUSE I BELIEVE IN THE REALITY OF MY DESIRES.

Casaubon recalls as well the worker-student revolt against the Italian state, a revolt that ultimately revealed the state as a mere postfascist construct, itself intertwined with bizarre conspiracies and secret societies, the plaything of the Q2 Masonic lodge and the Vatican Bank, an invention no less arbitrary than the Plan.

In 1968, authority was suddenly a hall of mirrors that produced no reflection whatsoever. People tried to destroy the mirrors, and the notion of reflection itself. Some demanded that in politics as in art representation yield to the presence of the pure self; others turned to murder. "It was extraordinary," Elsa Gili says in Ronald Fraser's *1968: A Student Generation in Revolt.* "We felt that we belonged to a powerful movement that was changing the relations of power, changing history." "I found myself killing people, yes," testifies Silveria Russo of what, in Italy in the years after 1968, changing history came to mean. "I'm one of the two who fired at policeman Lo Russo. I killed him, I remember it as though it were now. . . . He was a prison policeman, known as a torturer. For me it was like a work routine. For us, there were friends on one side and on the other enemies—and our enemies are a category, symbols, not human beings—so that our relationship to them was an absolutely abstract one." Between 1969 and 1980, 322 people died from terrorism in Italy, from the bombs of the right and the guns of the left.

"For some, the next thing was God," says one of Eco's mouthpieces of the '68ers, "for some, the working class; and for many, both"—in any case, "a fixed point." "The other day I went personally into that bookshop," the head of the Milan press says to his editors, "you know, that place where six or seven years ago they sold anarchist books, books about revolutionaries, Tupamaros, terrorists—no, more, Marxists. . . . Well, the place has been recycled." Now the store sells books about the Templars. Defeated, revolution turns to magic. Two decades after May '68, as Casaubon arrives in Paris to solve the mystery of the Plan he and his fellows have created, students are again rioting—about what it is not said. "In the Latin Quarter groups of people were shouting and waving flags. On the Ile de la Cité I saw a police barricade. Shots could be heard in the distance. This is how it must have been in '68." For Casaubon, convulsed against his will by specters of a hollow earth and final truths, this is as close to heaven or hell as he wants to get.

There is the suggestion that this unexplained 1980s Paris event represents the rising of occult forces, of an esoteric, hermetic claim on the absolute—on the unknown secret, the unspeakable power. There is the suggestion that what happened in Paris in May '68 was nothing less and nothing more. It's as if the casual, trivial crossword puzzle of the hapless editors sparked this present-day refusal, and all the lived history behind it, all the murderous history that followed.

As a good piece of airplane literature, Eco's book reads as a pox on any embrace of the absolute, left or right, seemingly real ("Workers of the world unite . . .") or unreal (the secret of the Templars is the secret of the . . .). Still, as the editors pursue their fairy tale, the book can be read as a lament for a time when the prospect of the transformation of the world, as promised in a certain year, by real people of all sorts, seemed more real than anything else. There is a secret, Eco almost doesn't want to say, but does—as a semiotician, as a best-selling novelist, as whoever he is, he is telling his secret under his breath, between the lines of the kitsch noise of his tale—and the secret is that though the world seems to be only as it is, the world is not what it seems.

As a lark, *Foucault's Pendulum* may finally hold a certain danger, and not simply because of the price Eco's editors pay for fooling with history and time. To fool with history and time can be a crossword puzzle, it can mean corpses stacked for no reason and no future, but how else, Eco may be asking, is history made? Eco's entertainment is a considered rejection of all things traveling under the numerals 68; it is as well a shamed call for them. Like a dream it is desperate, unclean, meaningless, and terrified, full of the energy of wishing.

NEWS ITEM—Berkeley, the *Express*, 1 December 1989: Late in the evening of September 29, heavily armed officers of the Berkeley Police Department staged raids at Merkabah House and Thelema Lodge, two temples of the pantheistic Ordo Templi Orientis (Order of the Templars of the East), the first located on 8th Street in Berkeley, the second on 63rd in Oakland. The warrants show that the object of the raids was drugs; nevertheless, residents of both houses report that the raiding officers took an extreme interest in religious articles as well, desecrating their altars and seizing items of purely religious interest. . . . The group is among many claiming descent from the 11th century Knights Templar. . . . Michael Sanborn, [one] of those arrested, stated that, "In jail, it became apparent that those of us imprisoned on this arrest had been labeled as 'devil worshippers.' One policeman came down the hall asking us in our separate cells, 'Who here's into Satan?' As no one was, no one stood forth."

California, February 1990

Old-Time Religion

I n 313 A.D., Constantine the Great officially opened the Roman Empire to Christianity. He sent Zeus and Jupiter, Aphrodite and Venus, Athena, Minerva, and all the rest into oblivion— but, Camille Paglia declares at the start of *Sexual Personae: Art and Decadence from Nefertiti to Emily Dickinson,* her 718-page first book, "Judeo-Christianity never did defeat paganism." She is saying that the gravity of the absolute authority of a single, omniscient, omnipotent God, an absolute creator-judge, the source of all values, has never matched the pull on the Western imagination of the panoply of warring, jealous, spiteful, all-too-human pagan gods.

Paglia is also arguing that this isn't ancient history. "A critical point has been reached": today, she says, paganism may be on the verge of a final triumph, in which the ethical absolutes of Western monotheism, the very notion of distinguishing good from evil, may be dissolved. Her position on this claim is unclear. When she writes that "with the rebirth of the gods in the massive idolatries of popular culture, with the eruption of sex and violence into every corner of the ubiquitous mass media, Judeo-Christianity is facing its most serious challenge since Europe's confrontation with Islam in the Middle Ages," she can sound as if she's cranking out scare letters for Pat Robertson—who considers Halloween a pagan festival and wants it banned. But well before this forty-three-year-old professor of humanities at the University of the Arts in Philadelphia is done with her book, you may get the feeling that she, like the gods whose story she tells, has been biding her time for nearly two thousand years, waiting for the right moment to reclaim the earth. That is because the sexual personae of her title, icons she believes have always determined the forms and subjects of Western culture, *are* pagan gods: Apollo in the shape of Michelangelo, Madonna no less than Medusa, Prince no less than Perseus.

Paglia marshals a vast array of canonical cultural materials with a radically subjective voice derived, she says, from "sixties acid-rock lead guitar." As a scholar, she's old-fashioned enough to say, "But art is what transcends and survives. Of all truths it is the finest," and sure enough of herself to refer to the Beach Boys' "immortal 'California Girls.'" "My method is a form of sensationalism," she says, and she's not kidding. "Enough of brains, on to lungs," she writes of Emily Dickinson. She's talking about Dickinson's lust for mutilation and dismemberment: brains and lungs, on Dickinson's pages, ripped out of the body, along with hearts served up on plates. By this point, Paglia has traced paganism from its beginnings to the nineteenth century, orchestrated it as an imaginative mode of being in which sexuality renders the body unstable, *unfixed* in the most extreme sense of the term, moving from Athena's birth out of Zeus's head to the baroque atrocities in de Sade (of which, Paglia says charmingly, "even I cannot stand many passages, despite . . . a summer as ward secretary of a downtown hospital emergency room").

Approaching the end of the book, the reader is prepared to feel Dickinson's kind of lust as an inevitable undertow in the Western tradition—a tradition in which, as Paglia defines it, destruction always catches up with creation, and supersedes it. "Enough of brains, on to lungs"—Paglia's words soften you up, destroying whatever image of Dickinson as genteel neurasthenic nature lover you might harbor. Paglia gets the reader to take lines she has excavated from Dickinson as if they mean exactly what they say— a triumph for any critic—to accept their gruesome blasphemies. "The auctioneer of Parting / His 'Going, going, gone' / Shouts even from the Crucifix / And brings his Hammer down," Dickinson wrote, and Paglia finishes up: "Christ turned money-changer is conducting a slave auction from the cross." This is sensationalism, but also close to poetry, and it's typical of the writing in *Sexual Personae*. As a set-up, it allows the Massachusetts virgin (in Paglia's words, "Amherst's Madame de Sade") to locate the paganism of culture in a Christian world, where the gods, now ghosts, drive out God: "Nature is a Haunted House—but Art—a House that tries to be haunted."

The Western artistic tradition, as Paglia reconstructs it out of sculpture, painting, and literature, is white, Eurocentric, and mostly male. Antedating her subtitle, she begins with a Paleolithic female figurine, the 30,000-year-old Venus of Willendorf from Austria, jumps to Egypt, crosses to Greece, leaps into the Italian Renaissance, then moves on through Spenser, Shakespeare, Rousseau and de Sade, Blake, Wordsworth, Coleridge, Byron, Shelley, Keats, Balzac, and Baudelaire, burning her way out of her book with the Pre-Raphaelite Brotherhood, Emily Brontë, Poe, Hawthorne, Melville, Oscar Wilde, and Our Lady of Brains and Lungs. It's a broken but finally unbreakable line, followed according to Paglia's sense of protean events in pagan culture— when it ruled and, more vitally, when, enveloped by Christianity, it again and again erupted out of its catacombs beneath the church—the pagan, Olympian tradition of heroism, excess, folly, and sexual confusion, over which, in this story, the certainties of Christianity are merely a veneer, a lie the West has told itself.

"I try to flesh out intellect with emotion and to induce a wide range of emotion from the reader," Paglia says, and she succeeds on the level of Norman O. Brown, or for that matter Stephen King. When I finished her chapter on *Wuthering Heights* I was shaking with fear, and not because of her analysis of Emily Brontë's attack on all pieties, as in "Sometimes the cruelty is quite subtle. When Catherine falls ill with fever, Mrs. Linton visits Wuthering Heights to nurse her, then insists on taking her to Thrushcross Grange to convalesce. Nelly recalls: 'But the poor dame had reason to repent of her kindness; she, and her husband, both took the fever, and died within a few days of each other.' The sudden exit of the elder Lintons," Paglia as M. or Mme. de Sade writes, "always inspires me with admiring laughter. They die so fast we nearly hear their bodies hitting the floor."

This is pagan revelry, but not what Paglia uses to make *Wuthering Heights* so fearsome. To do that, she homes in on "Lockwood's terrible dream of Catherine's ghost"—that hideously uncanny passage, coming early in *Wuthering Heights,* in which the old man hears the dead Catherine, as a child, rapping at his window. He breaks through the glass and grabs Catherine's arm. Lockwood remembers what happened next: "finding it useless to attempt shaking the creature off, I pulled its wrist on to the broken pane, and rubbed it to and fro till the blood ran down and soaked the bedclothes."

Paglia slows the passage down. Through her cool, careful questioning of what manner of forgotten gods Brontë, Catherine, and Heathcliff, now burrowing up out of the Western unconscious to bestow identity or seize it, might be, Paglia somehow makes the reader go through the bad dream over and over, until the passage seems to contain the whole of her book. Creating such an effect is what it means to reconstruct a cultural tradition: not only to seek out sources and stack them up, but to be ready to imagine that all along some goal was coded in each artifact. It's as if Brontë's ancestors, as Paglia identifies them across the centuries, have worked their way out from under the strictures of Christianity just so a dream like Lockwood's could finally be said out loud.

Paglia roots her book in the tension between the pagan gods Apollo and Dionysus. In her hands this is no high school formula (the classics equivalent of that biology-class standby, "When in doubt, say 'osmosis'"). It's an intellectual torture rack, the thing she uses to get her subjects to talk. Her Apollo is no Pericles, her Dionysus no god of wine and happy orgies. The Apollonian for her is selfish, severe, discriminating, narcissistic, making a mind that quickens not to wholeness but to separation—and, first, the separation of humanity from nature. Paglia is not unsympathetic. It is culture, self-consciousness made into representations, that distinguishes humanity from the rest of the world, she says; thus "everything good in western culture has come from its battle against nature." The extensions of this statement have no limits: that is why, with the unstable, unfixed pagan body, the ultimate body is hermaphroditic, or parthenogenetic, overwhelming biology. When Paglia says of Rousseau's elevation of nature over the artificiality of social life that "we cannot escape our life in these fascist bodies," in which male is male and female is female, it is hard to imagine a more Apollonian protest, and then easy to imagine that sex-change operations, following the transformations of the Olympian gods, are less modern science than pagan reversals.

If the Apollonian is against nature, the Dionysian, Paglia writes, "is no picnic." Because so many see the Dionysian as literally that, a bucolic romp, Paglia uses a less familiar word: "chthonian." It means, she says, "'of the earth'—but the earth's bowels, not its surface. . . . It is the chthonian realities which Apollo evades, the blind grinding subterranean force, the long slow suck, the murk and ooze." This is consciousness in hiding from Freudian insight, the body in which chromosomes resist hormonal therapy and sex-change surgery: the irreducible, the font of sex and violence that, today, Paglia sees invading our structured, Apollonian world, a world that is the product of a war with nature, against a wilderness where incest is inevitable and bodies exist only to merge into others. Forget Christianity (in this book, it barely exists); the Apollonian is civilization, but the chthonian is the barbarism that can never be fully expunged ("The rapist is created not by bad social influences but by a failure of social conditioning"). The chtonian, with us always, is Darwinian, blind, indiscriminate, devouring, the instinct for self-preservation driven not by the Apollonian ego but by Dionysian genes.

Within such a framework, the whole of culture, of history, takes on a perverse, destructive, seductive aura. "The continuum of empathy and emotion leads to sex," Paglia writes. "Failure to realize that was the Christian error. The continuum of sex leads to sado-masochism. Failure to realize that was the error of the Dionysian Sixties. Dionysus"—nature in human form—"expands identity but crushes individuals . . . the god gives latitude but no civil rights. In nature we are convicted without appeal."

Throughout her rewriting of Western culture, Paglia's language is always capable of its own chthonian violence, breaking down preconceptions with shock technique ("The excretory voiding of one person into the mouth of another is a Dionysian monologue, a pagan oratory"), a good joke ("Supreme western works of art . . . are morally ungraspable. Even the *Venus de Milo* gained everything by losing her arms"), or plain speech: "this bloody pagan spectacle," she says of *Wuthering Heights*. After what she's found in *Wuthering Heights*, after what she's made you feel, after she's made you flinch, you can perhaps identify the emotions behind her phrase—disgust, exhilaration, displacement, homecoming—but you can't separate them. Such a smear is anti-Judeo-Christian; it is pagan, an epistemological charnel house.

Paglia makes no apologies: it is paganism, she says, that "has produced the modern aggressive woman"—the woman who can, on pagan terms, change her sex, "who can think like a man and write obnoxious books." She has written to change the way we see the world, to banish God and strand us in uncertainty. This, to her, is history, ancient and modern. This is where we are, whether we know it or not. The gods don't care.

California, July 1990

A Change in the Weather

And thy desire shall be to thy husband, and he shall rule over thee.
—Genesis 3:16, King James Version

To your man's body your belly will rise, for he will be eager above you.
—*The Book of J*, 8

T wo different worlds are contained in, are implied by, the differences between those passages on God's curse on Adam and Eve and their expulsion from the Garden of Eden. The first is overwhelmingly, almost fascistically, familiar. The second is off our map, and both new and ancient. *The Book of J* is about those different worlds, and a version of a lost world.

The Book of J is an attempt to extricate a first, original strand of biblical narrative from the Old Testament—the story from the Creation to the death of Moses. As translated from the Hebrew by David Rosenberg, and accompanied by a long interpretation by Harold Bloom, the result is a great change, in the way one sees the human condition, one's own ancestry, one's own inheritance: an explosion.

"In Jerusalem, nearly three thousand years ago," Bloom writes, "an unknown author composed a work that has formed the spiritual consciousness of much of the world ever since." An unsteady consensus amidst a school of biblical scholarship long ago identified a single, first voice embedded within the Five Books of Moses, or the Pentateuch (specifically, in Genesis, Exodus, and Numbers), even though, as Bloom says, there is "no agreement upon the dating of what I am calling the Book of J, or upon its surviving dimensions, or even upon whether it ever had an independent existence at all." ("J stands for the author, the Yahwist, named for Yahweh [Jahweh, in the German spelling; Jehovah, in a misspelling]"; thus "J"). Relying on earlier textual detective work, and on their own sense of J's self-distinguishing ironies, wordplay, and tone of voice, Rosenberg and Bloom offer a microcosmic Bible, only about 25,000 words, that is so at odds with any one has read or heard or absorbed it carries the uncanny recognitions and absolute uncertainties of a dream.

Before a plant of the field was in earth, before a grain of the field sprouted—Yahweh had not spilled rain on the earth, nor was there man to work the land—yet from the day Yahweh made earth and sky, a mist from within would rise to moisten the surface. Yahweh shaped an earthling from clay of this earth, blew into its nostrils the wind of life. Now look: man becomes a creature of flesh.

The differences between this passage, the first in *The Book of J,* and the corresponding lines in the King James Bible, Genesis 2:5–7, are many and profound, from the absence of the entire first chapter of Genesis to the replacement of "man became a living soul" with "man becomes a creature of flesh"—without the distinction between soul and flesh, Christianity, or what some call "Christianism," dissolves. But perhaps the greatest upheaval is in that simple "Now look." Again and again in *The Book of J,* "Now look," "Now listen," "Watch," and their like go off like little bombs. Speaking directly, writing less as a storyteller than as a witness, J makes the reader into a witness as well. The immediacy, the sense of contingency and happenstance, is undeniable, and it carries the thrill of vertigo. Every shape is recognizable, but shaded away from what it seemed to be. You see handholds everywhere; they disappear as soon as they're touched.

Whether or not Rosenberg and Bloom believe they are rescuing a possibly mythical J or making a true J up out of supposition and wish, they are playing for high stakes. In fact Bloom's introductory line about the unknown author shaping the spiritual consciousness of the world is just a tease, a hook; his real argument is that *The Book of J* is not meaningfully spiritual, or even ethical, at all. "We, whoever we are," he says a few pages on, "have been formed in part by strong misreadings of J." And this itself is merely an opening hedge, or a wedge in the wall of Mosaic wisdom and righteousness Bloom knows his readers will bring to whatever he, or Rosenberg, or J, has to say.

Bloom insists that the three thousand years or so since J wrote have been based on a reduction and suppression of a work that today can be perceived only imperfectly, perhaps only by half: the narratives produced by the various later writers of the Pentateuch, or by the editor or editors who in about 400 B.C. wove the several versions into the beginning of the Bible as we know it, are "all revisions or censorings of J." Politically and socially, in the here and now, as a familiar of the lives we lead, this means that the fragmentary, broken, smoothed-out voice of J is that of "an author not so much lost as barricaded from us by normative moralists and theologians, who had and have designs upon us that are altogether incompatible with J's vision." Leaving aside for the moment what the content of that vision might be, Bloom is saying that the millennia that separate us from J have been rooted in a seizure and a distortion of a single view of the meaning of life—that our world is a vast edifice of misconstruction built less to incorporate than to conceal and deform what we might have received from the unknown author. In other words, the argument is that within Jewish, Christian, and Islamic civilization, certainly within Western civilization, at its heart—or at its foundation—is a ruin.

Now listen: all the earth uses one tongue, one and the same words. Watch: they journey from the east, arrive at a valley in Sumer, settle there.

"We can bring ourselves together," they said, "like stone on stone, use brick for stone: bake it until hard." For mortar they heated bitumen.

"If we bring ourselves together," they said, "we can build a city and tower, its top touching the sky—to arrive at fame. Without a name we're unbound, scattered over the face of the earth."

Yahweh came down to watch the city and tower the sons of man were bound to build. "They are one people, with the same tongue," said Yahweh. "They conceive this between them, and it leads up until no boundary exists to what they will touch. Between us, let's descend, baffle their tongue until each is scatterbrain to his friend."

From there Yahweh scattered them over the whole face of earth; the city there came unbound.

That is why they named the place Bavel: their tongues were baffled there by Yahweh. Scattered by Yahweh from there, they arrived at the ends of the earth.

It's hard to decide which does greater violence to what we think we know: the reconstruction of the ruin of *The Book of J* as a convincingly whole, unitary work one can read in a sitting, or the argument that surrounds the work—and the argument is violent in ways that go beyond, or through, its formal theses, or even anyone's interpretations of what J's original vision might have been.

The notion that our world is based in the refusal of the vision of a single, ordinary individual is not just biblical but epistemological, historiographical heresy; Bloom's particular argument, within these parameters, is very nearly bizarre in its specificity. "I will put all my cards on the reader's desk here, face up," he says. Trying to imagine the author, working with no conventional facts, Bloom argues for J as a woman, descended from King David, part of the court of King Solomon and then of his son Rehoboam, king of Judah after Solomon's empire broke up upon his death in 922 B.C.—a woman who, writing in a time of strife, pettiness, jealousy, and decadence, looking back as if from a prison of nostalgia, crafted her tale with murderous, laughing irony, to recover and re-create a sense of vitality, possibility, loss, and grandeur.

Though Bloom's argument about J's motives ultimately does the most to undo our sense of how our history was made, at first his sublime certainty that J was a woman is more displacing. Formally, he makes his case mostly by focusing on the difference between male and female characters in *The Book of J*, and the argument is a good one. Throughout, from Abram (Abraham) to Moses, the men are confused, small-minded, short-sighted, fundamentally unreliable; the women, from Sarai (Sarah) to Rachel to Tamar, are inventive, funny, opportunistic, smart, fundamentally willful. For me, though, the real proof was in the act of reading. The old controversy over whether the author of the sadomasochistic classic *Story of O* was a man or a woman derives from the fact that as one reads no author's gender holds; reading *The Book of J*, I found it impossible to think of the author as anything but female. Once the suggestion was made, it seemed obvious.

Part of this obviousness—and it's a liberating obviousness—is hinted at in Bloom's pronouncement that *The Book of J* is the most blasphemous book ever written. What he means is that there really are no lessons, rules, or morals in *J*—no basis for social control. (Not only do the Ten Commandments go unmentioned, the endless prohibitions and statutes of Leviticus—the fine print of the Commandments, so to speak—are nonexistent.) Life is a struggle and an adventure played out on a field planted by

Yahweh, but Yahweh is not only the Farmer. Yahweh is like the weather personified.

He is arbitrary, capricious, enraged, peaceful, all meaninglessly. Yahweh is less unpredictable—though he is almost always that—than unreadable. As the giver of life, he means to govern it, but he has no idea what he wants to do with it, what he wants it to be, save that, having created life to stave off his own boredom, for his own amusement and fulfillment, he means to keep his hands on the prize: to remain more alive than anyone else. The only crime in *The Book of J*—there are, in its ethical desert, no sins—is to seek to match Yahweh's vitality, his power, or his "fame" (thus J's version, or Rosenberg's version of J's version, of the Tower of Babel, with all of its puns and wordplay, "bound" to "boundary" to "unbound," "scatter" to—a translator's triumph—"scatterbrain"). Here as throughout *The Book of J* and ever since, it's men who seek to play god by constructing architectural wonders and ethical systems to match, and supersede, the natural order; it's women who, keeping their own company, pursue the living of life on terms of temporal victory and defeat. Or at least this is the story told in *The Book of J*. It's not God, or Yahweh, that is brought down to earth, but humanity.

All that said and put aside, one dramatic cultural, historical disordering is brought forth by Rosenberg and Bloom's book: one great shift. Never before has it been possible to read the Bible as, in a line of unknown provenance Louise Brooks once quoted, "a subjective epic composition in which the author begs leave to treat the world according to his point of view"; now it is possible. As one reads, one imagines the author smiling to herself, then pressing down on her scroll in a moment of anger. This changes everything. It weds the subjectivity of Bloom's interpretation, and Rosenberg's translation, to the veiled, suppressed, always shamed subjectivity of the reader, and frees it.

California, November 1990

Lost and Found

U sing mostly reproductions rather than original artifacts—casts of sculptures, photographs and photomurals of cave paintings, graphic reconstructions of engravings—*Ice Age Art* is less a presentation than a dramatization of prehistory: the world-vision of peoples who lived from more than 30,000 to 10,000 years ago, from France to Siberia. The show insists on a complex cultural experience rather than a staged confrontation with official masterpieces or a desultory contemplation of the leavings of primitive tribes. In a society that measures its history in centuries and takes history itself to be a straight, ascending line from intellectual poverty to mastery, the exhibit is revelatory, and it is also unsettling. Again and again, the categories of cultural time

---

In 1979, in San Francisco, the California Academy of Arts and Sciences in Golden Gate Park opened *Ice Age Art*, an exhibition prepared by the American Museum of Natural History in New York City, and curated by Alexander Marshack, an archaeologist associated with the Peabody Museum at Harvard University. It was the first exhibition of its kind ever mounted in the United States—and, as a depiction of fragments of lost rituals, it was a kind of ritual itself, an exhibition of an origin myth, with anyone who wandered through perhaps pulled in close to any of its unmarked gathering spots, to circle around tale-tellers' fires last lit no one knows when.

one brings to the exhibit dissolve. You see cave art; portraits of people who lived 13,000 years before Christ, engraved by their contemporaries; animal figures beautifully made as personal ornaments or as part of involved seasonal compositions; tools; notations, probably of lunar cycles, marked on bone; tiny sculptures of mammoth, horse, woolly rhinoceros, lion, and the female figurines known as Venuses—some rendered so crudely as to enforce an impossible sense of distance, some created with such grace as to smash distance altogether, and with it the idea of progress. You look at the hugely enlarged photo of a tiny sculpture of a horse, 32,000 years old, from Vogelherd, Germany. The aesthetic finality—the completion of vision—engages you so fully that the image comes to represent not only a horse but human sensibility as such. It is a struggle to go back to the very beginnings of Egypt and Sumer, and then back again, and again, and again, and again—back four times more to reach the time when this horse was made.

The exhibition reaches a sort of climax when one comes to Jean Vertut's overwhelming photomural of a famous scene from the Paleolithic sanctuary of Lascaux, dating to about 17,000 years ago. Distance and recognition somehow come together. In orchestrated movement—too much movement to take in all at once, so much movement it seems to produce noise—more than a dozen animals flash across a cave wall, heading toward each other; then they meet. Two huge bulls (in the cave of Lascaux, they are more than life size), the one on the left preceded and followed by black and red horses almost as big, face each other; between them are little stags. Along the bottom on the left is a series of smaller horses. At the far left—waiting, not running, as are the others—is a pregnant, cowlike animal, its humped back marked with red ovals, and protruding from its head not the horns of its apparent species, but two long straight lines, the horns of no animal that ever lived.

Though the images on this wall were made at different times, the tableau carries an inescapable sense of composition, of totality: of definitive, coherent, perhaps cumulative vision. The scene is not realistic. The animals shown did not run together, let alone under the gaze of the oddly silent, neutral figure of the imaginary animal. And yet every moment of the composition is supported by realistic detail—including, by means of blanks at the tops of the animals' back legs, perspective. The great bull on the right, pulling up short, apprehending the massed procession heading toward it, is so forceful and kinetic an image, so direct and unencumbered, that it seems less to have been painted on the wall than to have appeared there. Its realism animates the far more stylized horses it faces, just as the symbolic abstractions of the horses intensify the symbolic qualities of the realistic bull.

What are we to make of all this?

The people who are the subject of this exhibition lived thousands of years before the invention of writing. That they possessed language, ritual, and even music (photos of a four-stop flute and an ensemble of bone percussion instruments, from Siberia, are part of the exhibit) can be established; the purposes and content—the motive and meaning—of such cultural systems are unknown. Archaeologists and paleoanthropologists are beginning to show that art-making Paleolithic Europeans—generally known as Cro-Magnons, and barely distinguishable physically from contemporary men and women of European descent—were hardly the rootless nomads they were once thought to be, but questions about how they evolved anatomically, where they came from, their gender roles, and their social organization remain unanswered. The record, pieced together since the first Neandertal discovery in Germany in 1856–57, is full of contradictions and lacunae; almost all theories are more easily disproved than proved. This lack of certainty—a wealth of artifacts, few social facts—has led to a shrinking of questions, and to a shrinking of our sense of who and what the Cro-Magnons were. It has led to a reduction of prehistory to subsistence and superstition. *Ice Age Art* moves in the opposite direction.

The exhibition is based in the theories and discoveries of Alexander Marshack, and the whole thrust of his work in Paleolithic culture has been against simplistic assumptions about the nature of behavior, consciousness, and motive in the distant past. In 1963, an almost chance insight, sparked by a *Scientific American* article on the excavation of the 20,000–25,000-year-old site of Ishango, in Zaire, led Marshack—then a popular-science journalist—to guess that marks on Paleolithic bones, previously thought to be random scratches, hunting tallies, or doodles, were really lunar records and calculations about the future: protean calendars. The pursuit of that insight, and its nearly endless implications about the cognitive abilities and practices of the Cro-Magnons, led to a re-envisioning of the cultures of Ice Age peoples, and became Marshack's life's work. It was a classic example of the thesis that scientific revolutions are made by outsiders, the thesis being that of Thomas Kuhn, in *The Structure of Scientific Revolutions:* "Almost always the men who achieve these fundamental inventions of a new paradigm have been either very young or very new to the field whose paradigm they change."

Using microscopic and infrared photography to reveal previously unknown detail in artifacts excavated over the last century, Marshack and others have begun to rescue the productions of Cro-Magnon culture from characterization as childlike cause-and-effect magic, meaningless decoration, automatic realism, or plain indecipherability. Marshack has been able to show that engravings, paintings, and notations were "time-factored," or "storied," and that they were made and passed down, sometimes across hundreds of generations, within an intellectual matrix of complexity and depth. The microscope has revealed that notations were made with different points over long periods, thus establishing an awareness of time. There were also compositions linking animal and plant images, telling stories of seasonal change with precise naturalism. Animal images were "renewed," and their meanings perpetuated or changed.

Originally, Marshack argues, the various symbol systems—glyphs, notational sequences, representations of animals and humans—were kept separate from each other. The cognitive, associative leaps between them had not been made. The combining of these systems—as on the 15,000-year-old antler from La Marche, France, which includes a probable lunar notation marked down over seven and a half months and two renewed, reengraved horses—"represents," he has written, "one of the great intellectual achievements of man." It represents the association not merely of two techniques but of two versions of reality.

The most confusing part of the exhibition is the section on people. Here one finds the very early statuettes of women—mostly pregnant, faceless, with exaggerated breasts, hips, and buttocks—that began to be made across Europe 30,000 years ago. There are examples from France, Austria, Siberia, Italy, and one from the extensively excavated site of Dolni Vestonice, in Czechoslovakia. They move beyond the narrow context of fertility magic, to which they used to be consigned: again, cause and effect. They suggest instead an attempt to connect to the mystery of procreation—there is no evidence that Paleolithic peoples understood biological conception—which itself suggests the mystery of human beginnings: the dim shape of a creation myth, a concept that is a prerequisite to the idea of a soul. In a way that the exquisite Vogelherd horse may not, the Venuses represent a fundamental act of self-recognition—"Who are we?"—the basis of the long process that led human beings to stand outside themselves, to think, to move backward and forward while standing still.

To take the words of Mircea Eliade in *The Myth of the Eternal*

Return, the question the female figures raise is "how and why for the man of the premodern societies certain things become real." As one looks at the radically abstracted or stylized Venuses, it's easy to imagine that the culture in which they were produced was one in which reality was purely symbolic—where reality had no prosaic dimension. Three extremely schematized statuettes (two from Dolni Vestonice, a woman reduced to breasts in one and vulva in the other; a pendant of female buttocks from a much later Czech site) deepen the impression. But a few feet away in the exhibit are two tiny bone faces of women, from France and Dolni Vestonice, that are as early as the Venuses, well over 20,000 years old. With their well-defined faces and intricate hairdos, they seem to be images of actual people, of individuals, as the Venuses do not—and the exhibit does not mention that in the case of the face from Dolni Vestonice, there is a mature female skeleton from the same site with a skull deformity, a paralysis of the left side of the face, that matches that of the sculpted head.

Still, these faces cannot be simple portraits. Only one individual from Dolni Vestonice was singled out. The deformed woman was elevated, or memorialized, perhaps as a symbolic ancestor, perhaps as a living link to a specific body of mystery. No matter how specific or generic, once both possibilities are present, the little heads signify—among other, unknown things—a movement from the iconic to the actual and back to the iconic.

The ability to move back and forth along that line may be the essence of consciousness, and on the wall above the tiny Venus heads it is orchestrated by hand-drawn copies of 15,000-year-old engraved stones, again from La Marche in France. The stones come from an extensive cache discovered in the late 1930s. There are many multiple images, and most are covered with hundreds of intentional marks and lines, made by hundreds of people, or by one. The stones were not definitively rendered and published until 1976, when Léon Pales completed the work and his two-volume *Les gravures de La Marche* appeared in France; the images from that work have never been exhibited before.

Here, rather than a community subsumed into an icon, is the community itself. There are men, women, adolescents, infants and elders, naked and dressed, smiling, frowning, in postures we see as prayerful, dancing, showing fear and delight. Some seem storied, engaged in ritual; some as if they simply meant to have their portraits made. There's a great shock of recognition when one views these images. You've seen these faces before, and here they are so animated you begin to see them on the street as soon as you leave the exhibition.

Contrasted with the abstract or schematic Venuses, these pictures embody a strikingly casual realism. But while an immediate, prosaic aspect is surely present, implying that in the minds of Ice Age peoples the prosaic was now real, that aspect can be deceptive. The smiling, seemingly praying woman, perhaps pregnant, perhaps not, reaches us as an actual person. But she is also clearly a continuation of the tradition of the faceless Venuses, and possibly a transformation of it. The apparently male ghost figure, shown opposite the woman in the exhibit's graphics, is on the original stone intermingled with her, indeed seems to be diving into her. This would make the story that begins with the Venuses a new story, linking male and female for perhaps the first time. But even if this is a misreading, which it probably is, it is inescapable that this representation of a female is at the very least doubled. This is a monumentally potent, fundamental mythic symbol, already rooted 15,000 years in the past—not our past, but the past of the people of La Marche; part of the "single religious system," as André Leroi-Gourhan writes in *Treasures of Prehistoric Art,* that "seems to underlie the works of art from Russia and the Ukraine to Spain"—and also the image of an ordinary woman. The elements of individuality, an empathetic warmth an icon cannot convey, remain, coexisting and combining with the symbolic aspects of the image. And this suggests that those engravings from La Marche shown in the exhibit that seem free of symbolism—a laughing youth, an old man—may not be.

What these drawings appear to say is that by 15,000 years ago, the purposeful movement from the actual to the iconic, from the iconic to the actual, and the recognition of places in between, was not simply a possibility of culture, but an ordering principle. The existence of an individual could be expressed, as could symbols independent of individuals, the individual or the collectivity absorbed into the symbol, or the unity—the relationship—of individual, collectivity, and symbol. This is not a reality we have progressed beyond. If anything, it is a reality we inherited, have broken into parts, and can no longer put back together.

Of all that you can take away from this exhibition, most disturbing might be the sense that you cannot understand what you've seen as the work of a primitive people. The idea of the primitive has no real meaning save as a description of people who live almost solely within limits: within imaginative and technological restrictions that do not simply define the perimeters of life but are its essence. Primitive people are culturally stagnant, immobile, often regressed from a more active state—and a definite artistic and probably technological regression took place across Europe about 12,000 years ago, when the last Ice Age ended and Cro-Magnon cultures began to break up. The Cro-Magnons' technology—their tools included knives, needles, spear-throwers, paints, oil lamps, grinding stones, firing kilns, rope, and the like—could perhaps be called primitive, even though Marshack's analysis of notations (the idea that Paleolithic peoples practiced notation was heresy only fifteen years ago) has convinced him they solved problems as we do. But the cultural dynamic of the Cro-Magnons was not essentially technological. It was ontological and artistic, less a matter of shaping a tool than of recognizing and shaping the world.

Technology can function very well within the limits of necessary utility, but there are no limits on the mind's demand for meaning once the perception and representation of meaning have become the basis of life. What we see in the Cro-Magnons' close observation and visual representation of animal anatomy and behavior, in their intensification of symbolism, in their expansion of technique in order to render an increasingly complex vision, is an enormous reach beyond limits—a reach that opens imaginative and intellectual possibilities rather than, as in a primitive milieu, closes them off. The art of the Cro-Magnons does not look primitive to us because it is not, and it is not because it was motivated by demands on the world that were not primitive.

Ice Age Art allows us to enter the cosmology—not the cult, not the magic—that gave meaning to life 15,000, 20,000, and 30,000 years ago: the symbolic and iconographic construction of the world. The cosmology of the Cro-Magnons must have been to them the apprehension of reality, and an attempt to pierce and enter its mysteries; to us that cosmology can represent the invention of reality, its founding. Even though it is out of reach as one looks and thinks, the feeling that some unifying myth lies behind each artifact, each image, is present; so, as one looks again at the Lascaux photomural, is the feeling that, as William Irwin Thompson writes in *At the Edge of History,* "myth is not an early level of human development, but an imaginative description of reality in which the known is related to the unknown through a system of correspondences in which mind and matter, self, society, and cosmos are integrally expressed in an esoteric language of poetry and number which is itself a performance of the reality it seeks to describe."

Within a cosmology, all things are related in special, storied, intentional ways. A complexity of motive, perception, action, and belief builds on itself, deepens. A sense of time emerges and becomes inseparable from the creation of an image and the way in which that must be seen and used. Nothing is random. There can be no such thing as a doodle, and no such thing as a meaningless mark on a bone. There can be no such thing as a single, contained meaning for a painting, or an engraved face, or a carving, or an act.

In the cave of Pech Merle, in France, there is a painting of two large horses—one of the most stunning tableaux in prehistoric art, and fully reproduced in the exhibit. The composition is completed with red and black dots, hand prints, a circle, and a fish. Marshack has been able to show that the outlines of the horses were made first, then filled in with dots, and that more dots, and the hand prints, came last.

Hand prints, here and elsewhere, are a fundamental motif of preliterate art, whether in 20,000-year-old cave paintings in Europe or Australia or in the painting of present-day children anywhere. Those at Pech Merle have been much interpreted: as signifying human control over the horses (ensuring that they could be killed), or as a Kilroy-like I-was-here. Both ways of seeing are quaintly modern, stressing aggression and ego as motives; both say more about the mind of the present than that of the past. One can see something richer: the act of people joining themselves to the composition, not so much as its masters or creators but as members of the cosmology it speaks for. It is a connecting of the individual, the group, or the human species as such to the whole, and as dramatic a statement of the shape of our culture as there is.

The shape of its first fully realized form is reappearing now in outline; it remains to be filled in. One can deduce the presence of legends and symbol systems without knowing their content. The Cro-Magnons surely had an explanation of their own origins, a myth perhaps shared all across Europe for tens of thousands of years; for the moment, *Ice Age Art* can be understood as a version of the myth of our own origins.

New West, 26 March 1979

Escape from New York

Everybody knows *Guernica*. In 1965, in *The Success and Failure of Picasso*, John Berger called it "the most famous painting of the twentieth century," and surely it is. Most people know what it's about: the 26 April 1937 terror bombing of the pro-republic, anti-Franco Basque town of Guernica by the Nazi Condor Legion, Franco's helpmates in the Spanish Civil War. An experiment in modern warfare, as historians summarized the event, a fascist tune-up for World War II. Faced with an atrocity, Picasso offered a protest, now conventionally seen and understood as a cry of anguish at the horrors of war—any war.

But the atrocity was specific, as was its context, as was Picasso's reply. The re-creation of that specificity, its return to the everybody that knows *Guernica,* is the first step of Herschel B. Chipp's *Picasso's "Guernica": History, Transformations, Meanings*. With art, politics, art-politics, and political art all seamlessly combined, Chipp quickly takes a reader back five decades. The details are not new, merely forgotten—part of *Guernica*'s canon, so to speak, but long since stripped away by the universalist ideology that has smothered the picture for half a century.

Chipp tells a story: in January 1937 an emissary of the embattled Spanish Republic speaks in Paris with Picasso, and asks him, as a son of Spain, to contribute a work to the Spanish pavilion meant to be part of the great Paris Exposition of that year, due to open in May. Notoriously apolitical, Picasso is noncommittal. He does not work to order, and clearly any work he might produce, no matter what its theme, will because of his name be propaganda, not a painting of whatever it might be a painting of but a poster affirming the health and determination of the republic. Picasso might paint an artist and his model in a studio, which is what, on 18 April, he began with; the context in which the work would be shown, in which it would be used, would make everybody see the picture as news before it could be seen as art.

With a brief but intense account of Picasso's January 1937 prose poem and etching series, "Dream and Lie of Franco," Chipp demolishes the notion that Picasso was untouched by the events that were tearing his homeland to pieces. The question, Chipp makes plain, was "less one of Picasso's politics than of his way of expressing himself." The "Dream and Lie" etchings leave no doubt. They are repulsed and repulsive, studded with purely Spanish-Catholic references, corrosive and rotting with specters of church and army as creatures from some awful swamp: all in all a little horror movie, a hideous comic strip, a few feet of the Bayeux Tapestry now driven by blasphemy and rage. Still, Picasso could not bring himself back to the civil war until Guernica was hit; five days later, on 1 May, he made a sketch, indistinct figures overshadowed by an outstretched arm, and twenty-five days after that his mural was finished. Every stage of the work was documented in drawings and photos; in Chipp's book the piecing together of the painting, the May-first gestalt and the choices that followed, are set forth like a detective novel in which both the character of the investigator and the name of the killer are clear from the start. You know what happened, who did it. The how and the why provide all the suspense you could ask for.

Chipp goes on to follow the painting through time, its tours in Europe and the United States after the fall of the republic, its reception and then apparently permanent installation at the Museum of Modern Art in New York in 1939, then its return to the Prado in Madrid in 1981, eight years after Picasso's death, and six years after Franco's. Of course it was no return, the painting had never been in Spain before—in 1966 even a letter from Czechoslovakia franked with a stamp bearing the image of the painting was considered illegal and returned to its sender—but the arrival of the work was felt as a return, a homecoming, and symbolically it was. The symbology said that after so many years, after all the killings of the war and the deaths of so many who had committed them, Franco most of all, official Spain was ready to accept its own history; from the time Franco took power in 1938, it was official Spanish history that Guernica was not bombed by fascist airplanes but torched by retreating republican troops. Paris papers Picasso could have read in 1937 bought the line straight off, just as the *San Francisco Chronicle* and the *Los Angeles Times* dutifully reported Ronald Reagan's claims that the mutilated health workers and murdered babies of Nicaraguan cooperatives were victims not of Reagan's contras but of disinformation: of Sandinista troops dressed up in contra uniforms.

Chipp tells a rich tale, but the tale begs the question of the painting itself. "Picasso's greatest work," Chipp says—that is not so clear as his story. If *Guernica* is the most famous painting of the century, it can also seem like the most obvious: a comic strip of suffering, a simple transposition of post-cubist tricks into headlines, or vice versa. Picasso's 1907 *Demoiselles d'Avignon* still has mystery, so does his 1917 *Portrait of Olga Koklova*—is there really any mystery in *Guernica* today? Was there ever?

In 1965, when I moved into my first college apartment, one
of my roommates tacked a poster of *Guernica* up in our kitchen.
It was an odd thing to eat under, people said, all those mute
screams and twisted shapes; we'd turned a cliché, the requisite
famous art in a student apartment, into a conversation piece, but
we got used to it, and soon the carnage was just decoration. When
I went to see *Guernica* in New York that summer it communicated even less than our poster. Huge, dramatized by its place-
ment at the end of its own gallery, it was so important it was hard
to see. As a protest it has been successful, if not ensuring the
survival of the republic at least sealing a memory of fascist crime,
but in 1965 the painting superseded the event—by then the event
was memorable not because it was a terrible and specific crime,
but because it had served as the occasion for a sanctified work of
art, just as Lincoln's speech at Gettysburg ("The world will little
note, nor long remember what we say here") has superseded the
battle ("but it can never forget what they did here"). *Guernica*
had made history, but it was a history that transcended its victims.
After nearly thirty years, what the picture protested it also erased.

A year after my roommate put up the poster, I went to hear a
lecture by Herschel Chipp, since 1953 professor of art history at
the University of California at Berkeley; a friend taking his class
said he was good. Chipp's theme that day was the paired motif
of the horse and bull in Picasso's work, from boyhood bullfight
sketches through sexual allegories to *Guernica*. Of all the lectures
I heard in nine years at Berkeley, this one, from a class I wasn't
taking, by a man I'd never heard of and have not heard lecture
since, is the one I remember most vividly.

The central chapter in *Picasso's "Guernica,"* "Transformation
of Themes and Characters," is that lecture played out and
finished: a distillation and an expansion of Chipp's life's work. As
in the chapters on Picasso's politics, the civil war, the Guernica
bombing, its press coverage, the reception of the painting in

1937, and its odyssey thereafter, the lecture made indelible connections. Chipp brought obviously linked and seemingly disparate drawings and paintings into the world of common
knowledge and public events; he took art works away from that
world and made them talk to one another in their own salon, at
once insisting on their private language and translating it. Before
a roomful of undergraduates he did it all with such quiet delight
and evident love it was possible to leave the room and never again
engage a painting one had reason to care about (or a novel, a
poem, a piece of music) without beginning to imagine it as part
of a story—and, yes, a mystery. There was, Chipp demonstrated
with his slides and arguments, a matrix of happenstance and
possibility, inheritance and creation, error and serendipity, desire
and realization, surrounding any work of art worth talking about.
To construct that matrix, as Chipp did in his lecture and as he
does in his book, is to make the work talk, to make the world
talk—to let them talk. You can, within such a matrix, play with
the work, with its details. For one: Chipp recounts how, in 1939,
with the republic a memory, *Guernica* toured the United States
to raise funds for refugees. John Berger writes that by the 1960s
Picasso was so famous he was King Midas: "Just after the Second
World War Picasso bought a house in the south of France and
paid for it with one still life. . . . Whatever he wishes to own, he
can acquire by drawing it." You can fantasize that were *Guernica*
to be auctioned today, it would likely bring more than $100
million, no doubt more than the market value of all the real estate
in present-day Guernica. By having drawn Guernica, Picasso—or
his heirs—could now own it. But Chipp goes on to note that on
the 1939 tour, two New York symposia devoted to the painting
brought in precisely $41 for the support of Spanish republicans
in exile. The detail is tiny; it brings the painting down to earth.

Chipp's guided tour through the permutations of the
horse/bull symbology in Picasso's work is intricate and daring—

gender signs are unstable, the symbology itself is generative, alive on its own terms—but he does not exhaust the symbolism. For Picasso, the bull mostly symbolized notions of maleness, the horse those of femaleness, but the tortured horse and terrorized bull in *Guernica* cannot be enclosed by any arguments about sex or bullfights, and the reason may be out of reach. As symbols, the horse and bull go back to the Paleolithic, and on Picasso's own ground: to painted caves in France and Spain more than 15,000 years old. While such scholars as André Leroi-Gourhan and Annette Laming-Emperaire believe each animal represented one or the other sex, they disagree over which animal represented which—and that, one might think after reading Chipp, is why the symbolic pull of the two animals in *Guernica* is so great. Here these archaic symbols embody no specific meaning, not maleness or femaleness or (as pedants Chipp quotes have it) Franco or the republic, but symbolism as such: the possibility that certain images, placed in certain contexts, can generate endless meaning.

There is one modest documentary illustration in *Picasso's "Guernica"* that, today, after Guernica's passage from protest to masterpiece, ideology to cliché, may be worth more than any color plate of the painting—but it is only the matrix Chipp builds, all of his plates of Picasso's preliminary sketches and drawings, archival photos and dozens of relevant reproductions, that allows this illustration to say anything at all. It's a black and white reproduction of *La visita*, a 1969 painting by Manuel Valdés and Rafael Solbes, two Valencia artists then working under the name Equipo Crónica: a painting that shows *Guernica* in a museum gallery. The great work covers a wall; a few tiny people stand in a doorway, as if unsure about entering the room. But they are only functionaries here, at best witnesses, for in this imaginary room *Guernica* has begun to return to its event, to the history it made and the history it failed.

A woman, and the head and arm of a man, have left Picasso's

painting; they remain exactly as Picasso made them, but now they are on the floor. They leave blank spots in *Guernica;* with all the desperation in the painting, powered by all the years that desperation has been enclosed by roofs and walls, they are trying to crawl out of the room and into the streets.

California, March 1989

A Dream of the Cold War

In *The Manchurian Candidate,* a Hollywood movie released in 1962, it's about 1954. Major Ben Marco, played by Frank Sinatra, is lying on his bed, fully clothed in his uniform, dreaming the same dream he dreams every night. He's sweating; as his lips twitch, the camera moves in and we enter his dream.

We're in an old hotel in Spring Lake, New Jersey: a meeting of the Ladies Garden Club is in progress. On the platform, one Mrs. Henry Whittaker is speaking; seated on either side of her are all the members of the patrol that Major Marco, then Captain Marco, led in Korea in 1952. The soldiers look bored out of their minds. The talk they're listening to, that we're listening to, is beyond boring: "Our Friend the Hydrangea," more or less. The scene is striking: the ghastliness of Mrs. Whittaker's floral print dress is topped only by her hat.

The camera begins a circular pan around the room: an audience of women dressed just like Mrs. Whittaker, most of them over fifty, a few of them young, listening attentively, taking notes, whispering discreetly to each other. It's a long, slow pan; when the camera returns to Mrs. Whittaker's lectern, the scene is completely different. Yen Lo, a fat, entertaining Chinese Communist scientist played by Khigh Dhiegh, is now speaking; the soldiers are seated at his sides, as in the New Jersey hotel room. They're in a small, steep, modern auditorium; the seats are filled with Soviet and Chinese Communist cadres. Behind Yen Lo are huge photos of Mao, Stalin, workers, peasants—an ultra-modern, post-dada montage of great style and elegance.

Yen Lo explains that the soldiers—betrayed by their interpreter, Chunjin, played by Henry Silva—were set up for an ambush while on maneuvers in Korea, then flown by helicopter to a hospital in Manchuria for what Yen Lo calls "conditioning"—"Brainwashing," he says, laughing, "which I understand is the new American term." The soldiers have been made to believe they are waiting out a storm in a New Jersey hotel. Whatever Yen Lo says, all they hear is flower talk.

Mrs. Whittaker now reappears—speaking Yen Lo's words in her own voice, though speaking a bit harshly now, with an edge of contempt. Behind her are Stalin and Mao. Yen Lo appears as himself in the auditorium. He speaks as himself, in the New Jersey hotel. From his point of view, we see the audience, the Ladies Garden Club. Mrs. Whittaker speaks Yen Lo's words in the auditorium. In the hotel, Yen Lo speaks as Yen Lo, with Communist cadres filling the garden club seats.

In the audience, a cadaverous Chinese demands an end to Yen Lo's pedantic explanations of the wonders of mental conditioning—Yen Lo, or Mrs. Whittaker, has lost himself, or herself, in footnotes and bibliographies. The question, the man in the audience says, is Lieutenant Raymond Shaw, an upper-class prig played by Laurence Harvey—who, in the opening minutes of *The Manchurian Candidate*, we've seen returning to the United States from Korea to be awarded the Congressional Medal of Honor, for leading his supposedly lost patrol back to safety. The question is, says the Chinese in the audience, "Has he ever killed anyone?"

Mrs. Whittaker replies in Yen Lo's words, and then addresses Raymond Shaw. Yen Lo continues speaking as himself, in the garden club. A member of the club is cradling a bayonet like a kitten, smiling. Mrs. Whittaker is about to take it when a Soviet officer, in the auditorium, objects: "Not with the knife, with the hands." The officer turns into a member of the garden club, gaily waving a handkerchief.

Yen Lo is present in the auditorium as himself: to prove the efficacy of the experiments he has performed on Shaw and the others, Raymond, who (Yen Lo has explained) has been programmed as an assassin who will have no memory of his deeds, will now have to kill the member of the patrol he most likes. "Captain Marco," Shaw says. "No," says Mrs. Whittaker, with Stalin and Mao at her back, "we need him to get you your medal." So Shaw chooses the soldier he likes next best, and begins to strangle him with a towel. The soldier protests—"No, no, Ed," says Yen Lo in a friendly voice. The soldier is polite—he relaxes—it's just one more moment in "Our Friend the Hydrangea." Throughout the sequence, the soldiers have acted naturally, not at all brainwashed, just bored. So now this soldier is, again, bored. Raymond Shaw kills him, and the dead man topples off his chair. No one reacts. It is 1952; back in 1954, Major Marco wakes up screaming.

The sequence is structured around the same principles of New Sobriety graphic design that shape the photomontage backdrop Yen Lo and Mrs. Whittaker speak against. It's visually irresistible, lucid, as anything beautiful is lucid, and at the same time it's unacceptable—confusing, at first, then an impossibility, then again perfectly possible. The sequence is set up as a dream, but it doesn't come off the screen as a dream, doesn't communicate as a blur, with soft edges, dissolves, milky tones—it's severe, mathematical, a fact, true. It's real. You realize that this actually happened.

It's here, in this moment, that *The Manchurian Candidate*, a movie based on a best-selling 1959 trash novel by Richard Condon, takes off. It's here that you realize something is happening on the screen that you haven't seen before, that you're not ready for. Even if you've read the book, you aren't ready. All Condon made up was the setting—the soldiers in the hotel—a setting which in the book lies flat, like Condon's dialogue, so much of it used in the film, alive and frightening on the screen, dead in print. Condon imagined none of the cinematic shifts that nail the details of the event, that make those details almost impossible to keep straight—I took notes, and I'm sure I haven't gotten it all just right. You sense, suddenly, that this movie you're watching, a movie that promised no more than an evening's good time, can go anywhere, in any direction—that there's no way you're going to be able to predict what's going to happen next, how it's going to happen, why it's going to happen.

The Manchurian Candidate may be the most exciting and disturbing American movie from *Citizen Kane* to the *Godfather* pictures because this scene is not a set-piece: it is a promise the movie pays in full. To see Raymond Shaw strangle the soldier—and, later, in another patrol member's matching dream, to see Shaw shoot another, teenage soldier through the head, to see a wash of blood and brain matter splatter Stalin's face—is to be shocked, and not to be prepared for the atrocities that follow, much quieter, almost silent atrocities, and all the worse for that. And yet there is no message here, no point being made, not even any felt implication that Communists are bad and Americans are good, nothing like that whatsoever—this is all, somehow, taking place in an atmosphere of moral neutrality, of aesthetic suspension. All we're seeing is people. We're seeing the director, John Frankenheimer; the screenwriter, George Axelrod; plus Frank Sinatra, Laurence Harvey, Henry Silva, Khigh Dhiegh, Angela Lansbury (Raymond Shaw's demonic mother), and more—all of them working over their heads, diving into material they've chosen, or been given, in every case outstripping the material and themselves.

Before and after *The Manchurian Candidate,* John Frankenheimer was a crude director without an interesting idea in his head. Frank Sinatra was a good actor, sometimes much better than good, instinctive and wary, but he never came close to the weight, or the warmth, of his performance here. You could say the same for almost anyone involved in the project. Something— something in the story, something in the times, in the interplay of various people caught up consciously in the story, and consciously, unconsciously, or half-consciously in the times—came together. Something in the story, or in the times, that had to have been sensed, felt, but never thought out, never shaped into a theory or a belief or even a notion, propelled these people out of themselves, past their limits as technicians or actors or whatever they were, and made them propel their material, Richard Condon's cheap paranoid fantasy, past its limits.

There's a special thrill that comes when you recognize an author working over his head, over her head—and in *The Manchurian Candidate* everyone, from Frankenheimer to Sinatra to the unnamed actor who flies across the stage in the midst of the carnage at the end of the film, seems like an author. Bob Dylan was not working over his head when he made "Like a Rolling Stone"—he was realizing a talent, and a vision, that was implicit in his previous work. The same was true with Aretha Franklin, when after years of suppressed, supper club standards she stunned the world with "I Never Loved a Man (The Way I Love You)." But reading *Uncle Tom's Cabin,* even if you've never read the novels Harriet Beecher Stowe wrote before or after, you can sense an author driving her story and being driven by it—being driven by her times, by the smallest, most subtle details inherent in every character or setting she's invented, or borrowed, or stolen: the provenance becomes irrelevant. Here clichés turn into horrors. The ordinary becomes marvelous. Anything can happen. Even with a screenplay, where the director and the actors are playing out a script, where every moment may be storyboarded, defined, fixed in advance—even here, nothing is fixed in advance. There's no storyboard, no script, no director's intention, no actor's intention, that can call up, that can demand, that can account for the complexity of Major Marco's smile when he finally proves that his dream was not a dream, but a memory—when he begins, finally, to break the case, when he knows that what he dreamed was real. His smile is warm; it is sadistic. It's happy; it's determined, against all odds. A whole life is in that smile—and a promise of a happy ending, a happy ending the movie won't provide, the ending that the smile, so all-consuming and complete as it appears on the screen, won't get.

The plot of *The Manchurian Candidate* is simple nonsense, an exploitation of terrors floating in the air in 1959: the terror of McCarthyism, of Communist brainwashing, good hooks from the news of the day. The Soviets and the Chinese have made a zombie assassin out of an American soldier and contrived to have him awarded the Medal of Honor, to place him above suspicion, beyond reproach. Their comrade in the United States is Raymond Shaw's mother, the wife of Senator John Iselin, Raymond's step-father (played by John Gregory), a stand-in for Senator Joe McCarthy. Posing as rabid anti-Communists, Senator and Mrs. Iselin are Communist agents. Ultimately, Senator Iselin will win the vice-presidential nomination of his party, Raymond Shaw is to assassinate the presidential nominee as the nominee delivers his acceptance speech, and then Senator Iselin will take his place with a great patriotic address—"defending America even if it means his own death," Raymond's mother explains as she gives Raymond his assignment. And then Senator Iselin, or rather Raymond's mother, will be swept into power, which she will exercise as pure sadism, for its own sake, betraying her one-time comrades, destroying them and, the implication is, everything else. The United States. The republic. Herself. All for the pure pleasure of the act—for the pleasure of its violence.

There is no point in pausing over this plot as a clue to anything, save for the plot as the clue to a certain state of mind. The plot, in this movie, is an excuse—an excuse for the pleasure of the movie's violence. That is, you're going to get to see everything you ever believed was fixed and given suspended in the air and then dashed to the ground. That's a thrill. You're going to believe the notion that a single person could, by means of a single bullet, change history, transform it utterly. Nonsense—even if it happened, in the years after *The Manchurian Candidate* was made, again and again. Historians tell us that it didn't happen; that solitary individuals, even solitary individuals acting out great, historic conspiracies, don't make history. History is made by invisible hands.

As it plays, *The Manchurian Candidate* raises none of these questions. It revels in absurdity, works off of it, takes absurdity as a power principle: the power of entertainment. The movie—and I can't think of another movie that in its smallest details is so naturalistic and in its overarching tone is so crazy—is first of all fun. It's slapstick, as Pauline Kael said, who loved the film; "pure jazz," said Manny Farber, who didn't love it, but who had to be talking about bebop—this movie is not Duke Ellington. You can see this spirit, this heedlessness, this narrative irresponsibility, in a scene that didn't have to be anything more than a transitional device, a counter in the plot.

Major Marco's schizophrenic dreams have led him to a near breakdown; the army has relieved him of his duties and reassigned him as a public relations assistant to the secretary of defense. The secretary is holding a press conference, with Marco by his side.

"Mr. Secretary," says a reporter, "can you explain the cut in budget?" The secretary, bulbous and impatient, with a hint of Lyndon Johnson in his vehemence but with none of Johnson's savvy, explodes. "Since you've asked a simple-minded question," he roars, "I'll give you an equally simple-minded answer." The secretary goes on to explain, in words so straightforward you can't imagine them being spoken today (and with a logic so straightforward you can't imagine it ever applying to a bureaucracy), that because no naval power threatens the United States Navy, there is no need to build more ships; thus the cut in budget. We see a room filled up with reporters, cameras, TV monitors— like Major Marco's dream the scene is at once whole and all cut up. Now we see the secretary directly, then on a TV monitor, then again directly, then from the crowd, then the room from his point of view, everything moving fast.

The secretary is responding rudely, with great humor. You're caught by a violation—the violation of plain speech, of all the rules of bureaucratic propriety. Who is this man? How did he get appointed? This is more lively, more real, than government is supposed to be, but it's just a warm-up. As Major Marco tries to end the press conference, Senator Iselin stands up in the back of the room. Mrs. Iselin, sitting off to his side, is silently mouthing the words Senator Iselin is going to speak, words she's written: the accusation that there are two-hundred-and-some card-carrying Communists in the Defense Department.

In utter chaos, the camera moves from the secretary to Iselin to a TV monitor fixed on the secretary, the monitor then panning—blurring, sliding, ripping—to pick up Iselin. He speaks both from the monitor and in the room—it's a kind of epistemological violence, a set of media contradictions fed into an actual

event, or vice versa. But the event is dissolving; even as it pro-
ceeds, all that's left is its representations. The secretary is beside
himself. He doesn't answer Iselin's absurd charge; he says,
"Throw that lunatic out of here! You claim to be a senator?
Senator of what, I want to know! If this man is ever here again
I want him thrown out, *bodily*. Never, do you understand me!
Not EVER!"

You lose any real sense of the development of the plot; you're
captured by the weird spectacle of a high government official
saying exactly what he means. You forget that, of course, the
secretary of defense would know who Senator Iselin is. You revel
in the secretary's disbelief and refusal. "Not EVER!" Wouldn't it
be wonderful, you think, if our government actually talked like
that? That's the pleasure; that's what stays in your mind. You
don't care about Senator Iselin, about the strange and hideous
conspiracy that's unfolding. You want to see the secretary of
defense keep talking, you want to see him take over the story.
And he does, in a way. Even though we never see him again, his
spirit—breaking all the boundaries of what you've come to expect—is what the movie is about: what it's for.

When you look at this 1962 black-and-white Hollywood movie
made up out of bits and pieces of Hitchcock and Orson Welles,
out of *Psycho* and *Citizen Kane,* out of a lot of clean steals,
workmanlike thievery, a second-class director using whatever he
can get his hands on, what's so overwhelming is a sense of what
the movie does that movies can no longer do. The momentum
of the film is so strong you may not catch this dislocation until
the second time you see the picture, the third time, the tenth
time—but that sense, that itch, may keep calling you back.

I remember first seeing it, alone, when it came out in the fall
of 1962, at the Varsity Theatre in Palo Alto, an old-fashioned

Moorish wonderland of a movie palace. The first thing I did when it was over was call my best friend and tell him he had to see it, too. We went the next night; as we left the theater, I asked him what he thought. "Greatest movie I ever saw," he said flatly, as if he didn't want to talk about it, and he didn't. He said what he said stunned, with bitterness, as if he shouldn't have had to see this thing, as if what it told him was both true and false in a manner he would never be able to untangle, as if it was both incomprehensible and all too clear, as if the whole experience had been, somehow, a gift, the gift of art, and also *unfair;* and that was how I felt, too.

We saw—as anyone can see today—too many rules broken. It's one thing to have Raymond Shaw, the nice, boring prig, made into an assassin; the zombie state he's put into when he has to kill is not, really, so far from his everyday life. When his controllers make him kill his boss—in 1954, two years after his conditioning in Manchuria, to see if the mechanisms are still functioning properly—Shaw doesn't do the killing all that differently from the way he speaks or gestures to the people he works with. But it's something else to see him enter the house of Senator Iselin's nemesis—the liberal senator who is also, for one day, Raymond Shaw's father-in-law. On orders from his mother, his "American operator," Raymond shoots the liberal senator. It's not horrible—until, after shooting the senator through the heart, from a distance, Raymond approaches the body, bends over it, and puts the necessary, professional second shot into the dead man's brain. As Raymond does so, his wife, the senator's daughter, comes running down the stairs, into the frame—and then Raymond, who has been programmed not only to kill his target but to kill any witnesses to any killing, coolly, casually, without the slightest human response (though he still, somehow, seems to be himself, a real person), turns and shoots his wife through the forehead.

At the end of the movie, at the party convention, as Raymond perches high in Madison Square Garden, hidden in a spotlight booth, positioned to assassinate the presidential nominee—at the end, when Raymond instead shoots his stepfather, Senator Iselin, there is an instant cut to Raymond's mother, seated next to the senator, as she realizes what's coming. A second bullet goes through her forehead, and her hands jerk to her head, just as President Kennedy's hands would go to his neck. But by this time we have come to see Raymond Shaw not only as a prig, but as an individual, a man who for all his demons might possibly have a life to live, who deserves that chance. When he commits the final, necessary, fated, heroic crime, when he kills his mother, in that instant, the movie stops, and you stop, and you realize what's happened: the horror of every death is doubled. His father-in-law, his wife, his stepfather, his mother, then himself—he has to kill them all. It's right—but you can't cheer, not even inwardly, when Raymond Shaw shoots his mother, the villain. You think: My God, he's killed his mother. What can he do next? He has to kill himself—but that's not the ending you want. And you can't accept it.

This kind of violation, this kind of extremism—presented, for all of its impossibility and absurdism, in a mode of naturalism—is not all there is in *The Manchurian Candidate* that is not in movies today. There is that sense of people working over their heads, which is really a sense of playfulness: What can we get away with? That's what's happening with the casting of Joe Adams, a black actor, to play an army psychiatrist—one of the few truly sympathetic characters in the film, along with Sinatra's Major Marco and Khigh Dhiegh's Yen Lo—Yen Lo, always a joker, a regular guy, someone you'd love to spend an evening with. Here we are, in 1962, and a black man is playing a professional, a thinker, and it's not commented on, it's not an issue, but still it's a shock. The man is just doing his job, and no one pays it any mind. How many other American movies use a black actor to play what audiences expect to be a white character without even bothering to point it out, to clap themselves on the back, to congratulate themselves? In a way the black psychiatrist is as displacing as Raymond Shaw's murder of his mother. And that's people working over their heads: Let's do it! Let's mix it up! Who cares!

Finally, though, there is another dimension to *The Manchurian Candidate* that is part of this displacement—not, one might think, part of the glee with which those who made the movie made it; not part of the glee with which they let it happen, played it out, but a dimension that confronts us now, almost three decades later. That is, we are watching a movie made in another world.

There are obvious moments that take us out of our own time, as we watch the movie today, moments that seal the movie as a curiosity, as a relic, that take place around the edges of the action. There's the glimpse we get of the elevator operator in Raymond Shaw's apartment building, who smokes in the elevator. Far more than the sight of late-fifties, early-sixties cars on the screen, or the use of the Korean War as a social fact it's assumed everyone understands, or Joe McCarthy as a monster or a hero everyone only recently reviled or applauded, this is odd: we know elevator operators can't do that any more, that even if we get another Korean War, another Joe McCarthy, we won't get any more elevator operators smoking in elevators. Such tiny details, as we see them today, make the movie safe, today—protect us from it. Maybe, subliminally, as the movie plays itself out, we try to hold on to such details, because the rest of the movie is too familiar.

The Manchurian Candidate, plunging toward the assassination of a would-be president, climaxing with the assassination of the man who's going to take his place, was taken out of circulation not long after it was released. Not that quickly, not right after the assassination of President Kennedy; even after that, the film ran on television. Then it was withdrawn—because it was, in some manner, not right. It wasn't that the movie in any way predicted the events that followed it, the ultimately incomprehensible assassinations that filled the 1960s and the years after that, all the assassinations and near assassinations: Medgar Evers, John F. Kennedy, Malcolm X, Martin Luther King, Jr., Robert F. Kennedy, Andy Warhol, George Wallace, Gerald Ford, George Moscone, Harvey Milk, John Lennon, Ronald Reagan. On the part of those who controlled the film, there must have been a feeling—an unexplainable feeling—that the film might be part of these incomprehensible events, of this unexplainably but definitely whole, complete, singular event, of this current in our public life: a transformation of what was taken as open, public life into private crime or hidden conspiracy. There must have been a feeling, as the film was withdrawn, as year after year it, too, stayed hidden, that our real history, our history as we live it out every day, the fundamental premises of all our work and leisure, love and death, might be a kind of awful secret we will never understand.

It's not that *The Manchurian Candidate* ever prefigured, let alone prophesied, the events that followed it. It didn't. It is a fantasy in which Joe McCarthy, as Raymond Shaw's liberal father-in-law says, "could not do more to harm this country if he were a paid Soviet agent"—a cheap irony. What *The Manchurian Candidate* did prefigure—what it acted out, what it played out, in advance—was the state of mind that would accompany the assassinations that followed it, those violations of our public life: it prefigured the sense that the events that shape our lives take place in a world we cannot see, to which we have no access, that we will never be able to explain. I think we will find out someday, Gore Vidal once wrote of Who-Killed-Kennedy; I don't believe we ever will, not to the satisfaction of any of us. And that disgusting acceptance is, today, part of what *The Manchurian Candidate* is about.

As the movie ends, in its final scene, Marco, Frank Sinatra, understands the whole story—why it happened, how it happened—and he can't accept it. "Hell," he curses. "Hell." That's the end of the film: misery, regret, fury, the secret he has to hold inside himself. It can't be told, that the Soviet Union and the People's Republic of China conspired with apparent American fascists, who linked themselves with fascist tendencies in American life, in order to destroy the American republic: the repercussions would be too great. Marco will have to take the secret to his grave. The truth of the life and near death of the republic cannot be told to the people who make up the republic. It will be buried, for our own good.

So you look at the movie, lost in its visual delights, cringing at its violence, wondering what it says, if it says anything—wondering what happens. A lot of what happens is unburdened by any moral weight at all, such as the great karate fight between Sinatra, Major Marco, and Henry Silva, Chunjin—in 1954 sent to New York by his masters to watch over Raymond Shaw, and thus working as his houseboy. Sinatra rings the doorbell to Raymond Shaw's apartment, Silva opens it, Sinatra sees Silva, the whole betrayal in Korea comes back to him, as a fact, undeniable, and he slams Silva in the face. After the fight has gone on and on, not a second too long, there is a moment when Sinatra has Silva down on the floor, is kicking him in the ribs, again and again, each movement as precise as it is fierce, Sinatra asking Silva what happened in Korea, what *really* happened—and then the cops arrive and Sinatra, not thinking, acting in the real world, responds to a grab around his shoulders by elbowing the policeman in the stomach, and the cop falls away, and the scene is cut. It's a purely instinctive act—and it sums up so much of what's alive about this movie.

But that's not all. After so many years, or after you see the movie now, more than once, another element enters. You see that, here, everyone acts politically: the villains, the heroes, the characters that barely register, that simply come and go. Everyone acts as a citizen of the republic, or as an anticitizen. What's at stake is a commonwealth. As the movie closes, in that final scene, Sinatra rewrites the dead Raymond Shaw's Medal of Honor citation. "Made," he says with a long pause, "to commit acts—too unspeakable to be cited here. He freed himself, and in the end, heroically and unhesitatingly, gave his life to save his country."

The words carry enormous weight—the weight of the idea of one's country, one's community, one's social identity. Of course this is no less an absurdity, no less a fantasy, than anything else in the movie: the idea that a single person could ruin the commonwealth, or save it. But *The Manchurian Candidate* has, perhaps without intention, played against this idea of the single, all-powerful hero, or all-powerful villain, throughout its length. In this film, everyone, hero and villain, minor character and star, has appeared not as a function of the plot, but as someone who acts as if the life of the republic depended on his or her actions, on his or her convictions, beliefs, his or her will, motive, desire.

This is, today, an odd idea—as odd as the casting of a black actor as a psychiatrist, or the characterization of Major Marco as an intellectual: "You don't want to hear about my mother," Raymond Shaw says to Marco in a drunken moment. "Sure I do," says Marco. "It's like listening to Orestes gripe about Clytemnestra." "Who?" says Raymond. "Greeks," Marco says. "Couple of Greeks in a play." The idea of everyone as a citizen is as odd, once one has been subsumed into the world of the movie, as a speech by President George Bush on education. "Bush Rallies Businesses to Invest in U.S. Education," runs the headline. "The businesses that are involved with local schools, developing the workforce at its source," Bush says, "are making fail-safe investments." An anonymous wire-service reporter finishes the story: "Bush mentioned no specific reforms or initiatives to give workers the skills and background that will be demanded by economic changes and technological advances." But this is no criticism. The reporter accepts the terms of the president's world, of the republic he speaks for: the antirepublic.

Just as, today, the paranoia of *The Manchurian Candidate* is absurd, so, within the world defined by the movie, is this little news story. Here, now, the citizen of the republic is reduced to part of "the workforce," as in the People's Republic of China, today; in the movie, all people are citizens, concerned with a commonwealth greater than themselves. They are acting, in small or great ways, purposefully or thoughtlessly, to save or ruin it. And that is the issue. The idea that any man or woman could be merely part of "the workforce," private, concerned only with his or her personal fortune or lack of it, is in *The Manchurian Candidate* as foreign and strange as the smoking elevator operator is to us today.

In the end, *The Manchurian Candidate* is about patriotism—the idea of a life where private acts have public consequences. This is no longer the world we live in. This is the shock of the movie, now. This Hollywood movie, based on a commercial novel, from long ago, or not so far away, is a dream of a life we could be living. A dream, a fantasy—not so different, in certain ways, from the last shots of a John Wayne war movie. But there are no parallels, really, to Frank Sinatra, smiling as he breaks the case, and then almost dead with sorrow and guilt as he recites Raymond Shaw's epitaph, and says "Hell . . . hell." Thunder crashes, but it's not melodramatic, just the sound he has no words for. He looks down, away from himself, as if he cannot bear to look at himself; and the movie is over.

Threepenny Review, Summer 1989

■ *The Manchurian Candidate* was rereleased theatrically and issued for the first time on video in 1988, and in 1989 offered for network television viewing. ABC, NBC, and CBS all turned it down. "They didn't feel it was appropriate for prime time," said Norman Horowitz, president of MGM–United Artists Telecommunications.

John Wayne Listening

W hen a much-loved (and secretly feared) public figure dies or falls gravely ill, the tendency is to sentimentalize his or her career, to smooth it out. John Wayne is getting the treatment now, but in fact it has been underway for some time. In the last decade, John Wayne became so venerated as an American symbol, became so obvious and banal an icon, that he is now safe. Even liberals, some contriving elaborate rationalizations for his mythic stature, have forgiven him his politics. Ultimate professional ("I got paid for it," Wayne told film critic Jay Cocks, when asked if he wasn't disappointed so few people saw *The Searchers* at the time of its 1956 release), professional American, he wears the mantle of Manifest Destiny easily, happy to represent America to the world, to itself, and to himself. And yet what Wayne represents is not, after all this time, very interesting. Today, forty years of memorable and forgettable films blur into a single, indelible, seemingly inevitable image: a big man, in the big country, in cowboy gear, aging but indomitable, shilling for Great Western Savings on TV.

It's an absurdly incomplete image, but we are vulnerable to it—for it's that image, not Great Western, that Wayne is really selling. He seems to have taken one last opportunity to connect himself and us to a heroically decent America we can neither rationally credit nor emotionally surrender. As we listen to what is by now a kitsch-mythic voice, whatever Wayne might have shown us about the country and ourselves stiffens, as if, as a legend—the man who, on screen or off, stands tall, certain in the knowledge that he is always right, waiting quietly to make his move—he were already the freeze-frame we will get at the close of the tributes that will appear on each network the day after he dies.

Because Wayne's legend has become encrusted with the myths he has acted out (or maybe vice versa), it's no longer satisfying to ask what, as a kind of statue-in-waiting, John Wayne means. We can do better looking for the psychological and historical territory he has explored and others have avoided. This is wild, unsettled, unsettleable territory: almost a blank spot on the map of Wayne's career as the media floats it before our eyes, but also the site of his greatest and most frightening triumphs—triumphs so frightening, in fact, it's as if Wayne's legend has taken shape and been accepted precisely to exclude those moments, to render them invisible.

The Wayne we know best is the Wayne of Howard Hawks's *Rio Bravo* (1959), a perfectly focused version of a persona that consistently develops from *Stagecoach* (1939, directed by John Ford) to *Dark Command* (1940, Raoul Walsh) to *Back to Bataan* (1945, Edward Dmytryk) to *Fort Apache* (1948, Ford) to *The Quiet Man* (1952, Ford) to *The Man Who Shot Liberty Valance* (1961, Ford). This Wayne is not remotely a cartoon. In *Rio Bravo*, as John Chance, a sheriff holding a prisoner against great odds and slowly coming to accept the help he needs, Wayne acts out a toughness that is inseparable from his restraint. When he's arrogant, or even wrong, you're utterly convinced he's earned the right to be so. This is a man who has truly *learned*, and is still learning. He—the sheriff, but also Wayne the actor, Wayne the representative man—has invented and discovered himself out of necessity and out of curiosity about life. His natural superiority, and his unmistakable menace—his readiness to kill his enemies, his honest belief that some people don't deserve to live—is redeemed from cynicism by open humor, which keeps the character alive. This John Wayne is flawed just sufficiently to be wholly admirable, and he leaves behind an overwhelming, almost fated sense of moral symmetry: nothing so hard as justice, more like fairness.

What makes the John Wayne of *Rio Bravo* so convincing is that he does not take his role for granted. Underneath the assurance and experience he must communicate, he is feeling out the role moment to moment—constantly judging himself and others, weighing choices, posing moral alternatives and, once he has acted, sanctifying his actions by agreeing with them.

I don't mean simply that as a mature actor Wayne betrays no distance between himself and his character, or that he loses himself in his role. He doesn't. Rather, the distance between Wayne as an individual and the role he is playing is always present, and, over and over again, you can see him close it.

This is an extraordinarily intense style of performance—and within the basically smooth good guys vs. bad guys matrix of most good John Wayne movies, that intensity is not as threatening as it probably ought to be. The moral uncertainties that push to the surface as Wayne the man sanctions what his character must do are easy to miss, or forget. If Wayne's films dramatize a heroically decent America, then their essence is the story of how the hero achieves decency and passes it on to others, and the ultimate outcome is not in doubt. It's when the same style of performance is brought to bear in much rougher territory that the heroically decent America comes unglued, and Wayne emerges as an actor less easy to track.

If in other movies Sheriff Wayne is, to take a figure from *Moby Dick,* Starbuck armed—the god-fearing man acting forcefully within limits—then in Howard Hawks's *Red River* (1948) and John Ford's *The Searchers* Wayne is plainly Ahab. He is the good American hero driving himself past all known limits and into madness, his commitment to honor and decency burned down to a core of vengeance. This Wayne is better than other men not in a social sense—because someone must do society's dirty work; because he has a stronger idea of right and wrong—but for his own dark reasons. The sin of pride is all mixed up with a bitter, murderous defiance, and before our eyes Wayne changes from a man with whom we are comfortable into a walking Judgment Day, ready to destroy the world to save it from itself.

In both *Red River* and *The Searchers,* the main action gets underway in Texas after the Civil War. In *The Searchers,* Wayne plays Ethan Edwards; still wearing the pants from his Confederate uniform, he returns to his Texas relatives under a cloud so heavy thunder seems to be breaking over his head as he enters their house. The family is soon wiped out by Comanches—except for Edwards's young niece, who is abducted. Edwards sets out with his adopted nephew to find her; five years later, after searching from Canada to Mexico, he does. But by then she is a woman, no longer innocent, defiled by the Comanche chief under whose hand she has lived, and we realize that what Edwards has gained from his long search is the knowledge that he will have to kill her, and the will to do it.

In *Red River,* Wayne plays Tom Dunson, cattleman. His adopted son returns from the war to find the Dunson ranch on the verge of bankruptcy; Dunson decides to risk everything and take his ten thousand head of cattle to the new markets in Missouri. No one has ever made this drive before. The trek begins with exhilaration, but it's not long before Dunson is pushing his men too hard. Discipline begins to crack; Dunson bears down harder. He refuses advice from men he's trusted most of his life, takes to the bottle, sleeps with a gun, and, in a truly staggering coincidence, if that is what it is, slowly and surely begins to look like another Texan—the embattled Lyndon Johnson, fighting off quitters and cowards as he struggled to hold on to his war and his sanity.*

The whole camp twitches with fear; finally, after a ruinous stampede, some men desert. Dunson has them brought back. They are prepared to be shot for stealing provisions, but in a horrifyingly determined moment Dunson announces he will hang them instead. Violating the code everyone understands, he will replace justice with sadism.

With this act, Dunson crosses over into territory where none will follow. Faced with rebellion, he goes for his gun, and it's shot out of his hand; his son takes over the drive. Wounded, leaning against his horse like some forsaken god, Dunson is left behind, but not before swearing to chase down his son and kill him.

The grandeur of the settings of these movies—the Red River as the huge herd enters it so gracefully, Monument Valley in *The Searchers*—ennobles their characters even as it dwarfs them. But as Edwards or Dunson, Wayne refuses to be either ennobled or dwarfed. He has other business. As the conflict his characters insist on deepens, as they greet madness as a spell they have cast on themselves, their resistance seems to encompass not only the actions of others, but the natural scale of things. If Ethan Edwards gazed too long on the wonders of the country through which he pursues his niece, he might realize that his quest was,

---

*As Lawrence Wright wrote in 1988 in *In the New World,* after being driven from office by antiwar protesters and the North Vietnamese army Johnson "came home to Texas and let his hair grow down to his shoulders." The symbolism of that line is bottomless. Was Johnson's long hair the hair of the people who shouted him down? The men who died at the Alamo? George Custer? Regardless of whose it was, it was also that of Wayne's Dunson; once he begins to crack his gray hair seems to lengthen by the day.

in some essential way, beside the point. And so, like Ahab, who is softened when he contemplates the beauty and the vastness of the sea, and thus turns away from it, Edwards accepts no messages from god.

We are a long way from the prosaic troubles of *Rio Bravo*. We are in a country where final, elemental murders can take place, and Edwards and Dunson have vowed that they will. That Edwards does not kill his niece or Dunson his son takes little if any of the edge off: Wayne's performances are terrifying because he has, as an individual, accepted the choices of his characters.

Shot by shot in *The Searchers* and *Red River,* you understand that Wayne is judging the motives and actions of his characters and finding them correct, necessary—satisfying. With a thousand details of expression, inflection, carriage—the tiredness of Dunson leaning on his horse, Edwards's revulsion when he sees how years of Indian captivity have turned two white women into gibbering lunatics—Wayne conveys to his audience the hard reality that were he thrown into the situations his characters face, he would act as they do, or hope for the strength to do so. That these situations are horrible—not heroic but a perversion of heroic possibility—lets us see the oddity of Wayne's way of acting them out. Very few actors enter such desperate, psychologically catastrophic crises, and when they do they protect themselves. They overact, distancing themselves and their audience from the action, or they underact and convey reservation. Or, like Robert De Niro in *Taxi Driver* or Al Pacino in the *Godfather* movies, they lose themselves in their roles and thus as individuals really do get lost—they can't be seen. In the imagination of the audience, they aren't culpable for what their characters do.

Wayne watches the action unfold even as he carries it forward; you can feel him thinking as he moves. He doesn't throw himself into his role, he edges into it, step by step, until he comes out the other side.

In *Short Letter, Long Farewell*, Peter Handke describes a scene from John Ford's *Young Mr. Lincoln*. Lincoln, played by Henry Fonda, has agreed to defend two brothers accused of murder; a drunken mob arrives at the jail to lynch them, and Lincoln faces it down. He talks; he captures the drunks "by softly reminding them of themselves, of what they were, what they could be, and what they had forgotten. This scene—Lincoln on the wooden steps of the jailhouse, with his hand on the mob's battering ram—embodied every possibility of human behavior. In the end, not only the drunks, but also the actors playing the drunks, were listening intently to Lincoln." The scene is a cinematic miracle, but it is not complete: Henry Fonda does not listen to Lincoln. He simply plays him, and there is the difference. When Ethan Edwards speaks in *The Searchers*, or Tom Dunson in *Red River*—when their vows are made, and then they are taken back—John Wayne is listening to what they say.

Los Angeles Times, 11 February 1979

■ John Wayne died of cancer on 11 June 1979. When he became too ill to appear before the cameras, various of his colleagues, among them Dennis Weaver, volunteered to fulfill the remainder of Wayne's contract with Great Western, in order to "carry on his work." Weaver remains the Great Western spokesperson to this day. In 1992 the *Los Angeles Times* noted that Great Western "has focused much of its lending efforts on Los Angeles' inner city neighborhoods," and had approval rates for loans to African American and Hispanic American applicants that were from two to more than four times higher than those of the Bank of America or Wells Fargo, Great Western's principal competitors.

Germany in a Second Language

As translated from the German by Leigh Hafrey, the just barely skewed American idioms in *The Wall Jumper* perfectly convey what Wim Wenders once called American pop culture's colonization of the subconscious of postwar West German youth. The sense of confinement that animates the best postwar Eastern European fiction merges with the naiveté of an American voice, once removed. You may come away feeling less that you've finished a novel by one Peter Schneider, forty-three, former West German left-wing activist and scenarist of Reinhard Hauff's *Knife in the Head*, than closed a bar with Schneider's unnamed narrator, a West German, a man about forty, who moved to West Berlin in 1961, just after the wall was built.

Walking away, you might feel your head spin, because so much has been said, so many good tales have spun off into world-historical arguments that devolve once more into tales when it becomes clear that nothing can be settled. Every page of the book twists with thought; if structure is subject, then the subject of this book is thinking itself; "The Berlin Wall as Will and Idea" would do for a subtitle. The man has been talking about the ability of a thing, in this case the wall, to create people, the people who live on either side of it. This is a philosophical matter, and it calls forth abstractions the mind can barely hold. The man has been talking as well about the attempts of various individuals to prove that a thing cannot create people: to prove that in the face of an object that turns people into objects of history, some will insist on being subjects of history, and will thus seek to dissolve the object in their own subjectivity. This too is a philosophical matter, and it calls forth not abstractions but stories, urban legends, perhaps, but with names, dates, jokes, accounts of heroism, tragedy, even frivolousness—for example, says the man, dropping his attempt to explain how his twenty years on the border that divides the two social systems that rule the world have forced him to become aware of how the smallest details of walk and talk are politics, are by-products of political constructions that (he is trying to make you understand, but he does not want to believe what he is trying to make you understand, so the words float away) are more profound than anyone knows (do you understand?), and will arise out of a pinball game or a love affair to subvert and destroy the most rational philosophical agreement— for example, the story of the three East Berlin boys who hopped the wall because the West offered better movies.

On their first trip they made it to the Kurfürstendamm, checked out the theaters, and chose *Once upon a Time in the West* over *The Schoolgirl Report, Part III*. The narrator is telling this tale with such respect for its wondrously blithe subjectivity that you don't catch the kick of the film title til much later, until the narrator's worry that the kids can't have crossed the wall in the manner mandated by the story reemerges from the story's wondrous frivolity, until you begin to suspect that this story has over the years been so embellished, so fully lived by each person who has told it, that it may have never been acted out at all. But it's too good to disbelieve.

The three crossed the border twelve times. Finally they were stopped by West Berlin police, who themselves couldn't believe the story: They weren't *refugees*? They didn't want to *stay*? The true irony of the wall, after all, is that the West gained at least as much from it as the East did. The East got to keep its people, and the West got to gild its symbols. As the narrator has already told you:

What on the far side meant an end to freedom of movement, on the near side came to symbolize a detested social order. The view East shrank to a view of the border complex and finally to a group-therapy absorption with the self: for Germans in the West, the Wall became a mirror that told them, day by day, who was the fairest one of all.

So much for irony, which the man dissolves by doubling: it is after all the Wicked Queen who owns the magic mirror. Irony is the currency in West Berlin—a supreme form of bullshit. ("The war was wonderful for Berlin," crowed a tour bus guide in 1967 to his all-German cohort of passengers, all German save two, who squirmed. "We got new apartments"—he pointed out the window—"new parks"—he pointed forward—"and that new stadium"—he waved back—"all thanks to the war! And all thanks to the Americans!") Irony is what the narrator finds everywhere, and tries to overcome. The currency is worthless. Cold comfort, it's always too comforting, a sort of celebratory fatalism, a way of erasing the past and submitting to the present. It's survivors' humor—which is never dangerous. The wall grins with the last laugh. The only irony is that the wall, which no one expected to endure, which was built when the reunification of Germany was the number-one issue in West German politics, has been accepted.

The narrator is trying to explain how the wall has infected the Western half of the city, or the Western half of the world, has infected its everyday life—its walk-and-talk, that realm which

normally unfolds without aggressive symbolization, without consciousness or active fantasy—with ambiguity. He is trying to
explain how the wall has infected the Eastern half of the city, its
everyday life, with certainty, which defeats consciousness. How
can this be? Who wants to live in the East? The narrator has a
story or two about people who have left the West for the East,
but they are marginal, even psychopathic; his best friend and the
woman he cannot get over, both refugees from the East, are a
thousand times more present, more real. But what they tell him
is that life in the West, while more agreeable, is not real, not real
at all, because in the West what has been constructed is assumed
to be natural, while in the East no one is fooled.

In the East, if one must live with the wall—despite ties of
family, friendship, history, language, culture, and, for many, the
maps they grew up with—then one must live with it. One must
accept its amoral command as a moral imperative, as a supersign
that allows the deciphering of every sign of everyday life. Life
itself becomes a process of deciphering, and the certainty is that
this is what it means to lead an intelligent life. Westerners, gazing
in their magic mirror, caressing their reflected features, think no
such thing. But when one shifts one's gaze from the mirror, the
wall upon which it is hung suggests that all politically ordered
societies are artificial—shows, contrivances, contraptions. Such
contraptions produce what are supposed to be their antecedents:
habits, manners, states of mind, people. Forcing this recognition,
the East leads people to read between the lines, to lead lives of
intensity and guile. Denying this recognition, the West leads
people to accept what they are told, to lead lives of passive social
narcissism. Thus when the narrator plays pinball, he reads the
instructions on the machine and follows them. His friend Robert,
late of the East, wrestles the machine, shakes it, has learned how
to take it to the very edge of tilt. The narrator never wins. As
Alexander Trocchi wrote in 1960, in his novel *Cain's Book:*

Apart from jazz . . . the pinball machine seemed to me to be America's greatest contribution to culture. . . . It symbolized the rigid structural "soul" that threatened to crystallize in history, reducing man to historicity, the great mechanic monolith imposed by mass mind; it symbolized it and reduced it to nothing. The slick electric shiftings of the pinball machine, the electronic brain, the symbolical transposition of the modern Fact into the realm of play. (The distinction between the French and the American attitude toward the "tilt" ["teelt"]; in America, and England, I have been upbraided for trying to beat the mechanism by skillful tilting; in Paris, that is the whole point.)

The certainty of the East is that societies, which are supposed to grow out of the details of walk-and-talk, are fakes, imposed from above for particular reasons and on behalf of particular interests. Consciousness is defeated because other possibilities are not in question. Talking to you—his friend Robert has left—the narrator takes up the challenge: "The advantage of this delusion is that the blame always falls on something outside of him. For good or bad, Robert is sheltered by a state"—any state—"that takes responsibility for everything; Robert himself is never to blame." Good enough—but ambiguity invades the mind of the Westerner as soon as the question of where one would rather live ceases to enclose the question of where, in fact, one does live. The narrator takes his response to his friend's delusion back upon himself:

As I consider this objection, it turns itself around. Who derives benefits from which way of thinking? Doesn't every career in Western society, whether that of an athlete, investor, artist, or rebel, depend on the assumption that every initiative is one's own, every idea original, every decision completely personal? What would happen to me if I stopped finding fault with myself, as I've been taught to do, and blamed everything on the state?

The marvel of the story of the three moviegoers—the reason, one suspects, the story has been so embellished, so treasured, so removed from any real solution to the conundrum of just how the trio crossed the border again and again—is that it escapes such questions. Shocked that the kids just wanted to catch the latest film, the cops who stopped them called a reporter; he wrote the story up. That put the East Berlin police onto the wall jumpers.

On the evening of their last excursion, the narrator tells you—as fatigue overcomes you both, and the wall, which over the years has faded from Western consciousness, becomes little more than an excuse for another Berlin architecture joke—one of the three, the boy called Lutz, had skipped back from the West to the East, to his

favorite neighborhood movie house in Prenzlauer Berg for a showing of *High Noon*. He had been standing in line a quarter of an hour when the projectionist announced that the show was canceled—the film had torn. At that moment Lutz felt that something inside him had torn too. "You run your heels off from Kurfürstendamm to Prenzlauer Berg to be on time . . . and the film is torn," he snarled at his neighbor. "That does it!"

Lutz stepped on his motorcycle's starter, raced at top speed back to the Wall, and hurried through the darkness into the West, in order at least to catch the late show of *The Big Country*.

The police arrived at his house that night; he remained in the West.

You laugh as you return home. You laugh into your mirror and the mirror laughs back. You are the fairest of them all, the mirror says. You can see *The Big Country* any time you like. The next night, you return to the bar where you have met the narrator, who has many more stories to tell: stories about the man who jumped the wall sixteen times "because it was there," about the man who happily devoted himself to destroying it, and was destroyed by it, about the man who—. But now both of you are drunk and all you know is that your presence here is an accident.

Voice Literary Supplement, March 1984

Settlements

The Deborah Chessler Story

I n an early episode of *Homicide: Life on the Street,* Barry Levinson's TV series about a team of Baltimore cops, the detective played by Ned Beatty is mooning over the coroner. Beatty's character is fat, divorced, aging: "I'm forty-eight," he says. "Approximately." He can't work up the nerve to ask the doctor for a date and he's miserable.

In the crab joint where the homicide crew hangs out, Beatty has draped himself over the jukebox, looking for tunes to quiet his soul. Very low, very distant, as if emanating from somewhere behind the soundtrack, you can just make out an ancient piece of doo-wop, young black men harmonizing on a ballad—angels of the cop's loneliness, or his lust. Along with fellow moviemaker John Waters (who once moonlighted as a bartender on *Homicide*), Barry Levinson has in recent times done the most to fix Baltimore as a real place with a real past, and he's always careful about the music he uses; in this case the singers are the Four Buddies, from Frederick Douglass High School, once the pride of Baltimore's African American community, doing their hit "I Will Wait," from 1951. It almost sounds as if the song has been waiting for this television set-up to get its due; the music feels that old, and that present.

Doo-wop was a music where the feeling put into words overwhelmed the words themselves, until the highest moments were often those when the soaring, breaking voices cut loose from words altogether. It was the first form of rock 'n' roll to take shape, to define itself as something people recognized as new, different, strange, *theirs*—the first version, as Lou Reed put it in 1989, inducting Dion into the Rock & Roll Hall of Fame, of "the sound of another life."

"The irony is," Barry Levinson says, "you can have people doing barbershop quartets—*those* are voices, right? But it's a totally different thing. With doo-wop, there's an *elusive* quality— and *that's* what gets you." It is what gets you, that drift toward nirvana in the harmonies: what you can't pin down, what floats right before your eyes, always out of reach.

Later in the *Homicide* episode, Ned Beatty has against all odds overcome his fears. Hand in hand, he and the coroner stroll along the waterfront. They pass a group of black men singing on the street, doo-wopping for change. The singers are older now, their voices rougher, but it doesn't matter; if they've lost love's wings they've found love's body. Beatty gets out a dollar, smiles at the coroner; she smiles back.

Forty-five years before, in the same city, on Pennsylvania Avenue, the main street of black Baltimore, in front of a club called the Avenue Café, a few young black men stood singing, looking for change and looking to be noticed. It was 1948; they were back from the war. They had jobs—driving a truck, waiting tables—but they had eyes for more than that.

Their leader called himself Sonny Til. Born Erlington Tilghman in 1925, he had a high tenor that seemed to have been born in the air, a delicate touch, a certain reserve. Around him were George Nelson, baritone, who sometimes took the lead from Til in the middle of a tune; Richard Williams, his place soon taken by Johnny Reed, bass; and Alexander Sharp, a bear of a man with the highest, most elusive voice of all. They were singing, perhaps, Til's favorite, "I Cover the Waterfront," or "At Night," a song written by a pal of theirs named Clifton Morris. Or they were singing copies of hits by the Ink Spots, the Mills Brothers, or the Ravens, the big black vocal groups—but singing them wrong, without polish, with too much emotion, nothing finished, nothing sealed, with the feeling the song could go anywhere at any time.

Sometimes performing inside the Avenue Café on amateur nights, with Johnny Reed playing stand-up bass and a guitarist, Tommy Gaither, sounding out the rhythm, the group had named itself the Vibranaires; before the summer of 1948 was out they would become the Orioles. Over the next months and years they would create a new music, passionate, imperfect, and open— "primitive-modernist," to borrow Jim Dickinson's phrase for Howlin' Wolf, who would come later. The Orioles would inspire singers from all over the country—the Four Buddies, Clyde McPhatter, Elvis Presley, Dion, and Lou Reed among them—to reach for something different, for something more, for another life.

When people came to write the history of pop music, they would fix on the Orioles as "the first R & B vocal group," as "the very first rock & roll band." "If their name is not a legend today," Jack Schiffman wrote in *Uptown*, a history of the Apollo Theater, "their force flows unseen through the Ray Charleses, the Aretha Franklins, the Chuck Berrys . . . through newly formed groups of hairy individuals who learned guitar the day before yesterday."

But it is not that simple. "You actually are the one that started rhythm & blues," Sonny Til said into a tape recorder in 1980,

the year before he died. "That's what really started rhythm &
blues, which led into rock 'n' roll. Your song, Deb. That was a
different type of music."

At seventy, Shirley Reingold lives with her husband, Paul Reingold, and their twenty-six-year-old daughter, Wendy, in a hand-
some, mostly Jewish high-rise condominium development near
Miami Beach, close to the edge of the ocean. Forty-five years ago,
as Deborah Chessler, a struggling Baltimore songwriter, she became the manager of the Vibranaires. As the Orioles, they sang
her songs, among them "It's Too Soon to Know," a tune so
bottomless all the music that followed can disappear into it with
no sense that anything has been lost. She guided their career
through the six years of their success. Together they made their
piece of history—a young Jewish woman and five black men in a
segregated American city, where blacks and whites did not sit
down in the same public place, not in a school and not in a
theater. Together they found the new sound.

The story is not typical of anything. "We would never have
made it if it hadn't been for you and your mother," Til said in
1980. "If we became men, in any way, you played a big part in
that. You were like our *sister* to us, and we *loved* you. And Mom
Chessler was *our mom*, too." This is not how the story goes.
Where is the bitterness? Where is the resentment of a man who
was once on top of the world and now speaks from oblivion, who
hasn't had a hit for nearly thirty years? Where did the smile come
from, and why did it last?

"We came out of nowhere," Deborah Chessler says today. She
was born Shirley; she changed her name in the 1940s when
Buddy Clark, a star singer who entered the world as Samuel

Goldberg, told her it was too Jewish by half for show business: "'Shoiley, Shoiley, Shoiley,' you'll never hear the end of it." It's a long way back, and her memory is clear and urgent. "There are times in your life when you're unhappy. Writing songs was my outlet. I loved writing songs: they came so fast, and they were through so fast. And I was always trying to make money." Her father died when she was nine, in 1932, at the trough of the Depression; Chessler and her mother were on their own, and their fear was missing the rent. "We were broke. My mother was ill a lot of the time, and money was very hard to come by." Chessler's mother sold women's clothes; so did Deborah, once she began lying about her age. At fourteen she looked eighteen, and she took advantage.

It was a time and a place, in her words, of "orderly segregation." If you played by the rules, kept your mind blank, your mouth shut, and your heart closed, there was no problem. Of course, you also had to watch your step. "I went to a swimming pool once, a public pool: you paid your way in, and I paid," Chessler says. "When I came out I needed change for the streetcar home. I went to the cashier, and that's when I saw the sign: NO JEWS ALLOWED. I was very sorry that I'd gone in—and I wanted the cashier to know. I said, 'I see your sign, NO JEWS ALLOWED—isn't that something!' She said, 'What do you mean, "Isn't that something?"' I said, '*I'm* Jewish—and I haven't ruined your pool at all.'"

It was a tiny incident. In 1938 there was a slightly bigger one. Chessler was fifteen: "I worked for a store called Hixbie's, selling ladies' wear. I'd *rush* in front to grab a customer—I was on commission! One day I recognized Ella Fitzgerald coming in the door. I ran forward. She had 'A-Tisket, A-Tasket'"—Fitzgerald's first big hit. "I grabbed hold of her, and I took her in the back, and I brought out several dresses for her to see, and she picked what she wanted, and she wanted to try them on."

This was forbidden. Black women were allowed in some Baltimore department stores and specialty shops, but even into the fifties they were not permitted to try on clothes. "I thought: 'The heck with it. Why not?'" Chessler says. "I stayed in the back and helped her try the dresses on. *She* would never remember this. There was no way for her to know what was going on.

"I sold her *five, six* dresses. She paid cash, and she left with her packages. Then my boss called me: '*What made you think* you had the *right* to take *that woman* in the back and *try on clothes* on her?' I said, '*Two* things. I *sold* them all—and I knew that this woman could buy them and would buy them if she liked them. And *you* don't even know who she *is,* do you?' I sang him 'A-Tisket, A-Tasket.' 'That's her?' 'That's her.'"

"*I* didn't have any songs then," Chessler says. "The other women in the store were against me. I was young, they were older. They were heavy, I was skinny. I could beat them to the door. It wasn't a matter of who I was selling to—the main thing was to sell, because I got a commission. Ella Fitzgerald could buy—and later on, years and years later, she recorded a song of mine." That Ella Fitzgerald would remember.

Two years later Chessler lied about her age one more time and her life blew up. In 1940, at seventeen, she ran away and got married. She was in the eleventh grade; she had to drop out of school. The marriage was an immediate disaster; her husband was a wastrel. She moved back with her mother, asked for a divorce—he refused. Soon enough, though, the war began, and there was an unexpected bonus: the draft. "The day that he was supposed to go into the service," Chessler says, "the night before, we gave him a party: *we were so happy he was going.* He went down to the Fifth Regiment Armory the next day—to *leave.* And at three or four o'clock he was home. He said: 'Well! They're not getting me!' I said, 'What do you mean?' He said [in a demented, sing-songy voice]: 'I'm a psy-co-path-ic per-son-al-i-ty! [Then threateningly] *You remember that.*'" Though she pushed him away from her life, it wasn't until the 1950s that Chessler was able to divorce him, and she had to buy him off. In 1940, divorce was a scandal; Chessler's situation was much worse. If she had looked to her future, she might have heard doors slamming all around her.

Chessler began to write. She sold her first song—"for thirty-five dollars, a lot of money"—to the organist at the Loews Century Theatre: a jingle celebrating the movie house's new air conditioning.

By the time the war ended, with Chessler in her early twenties, she was pressing harder. She sang her tunes for local disc jockeys. She couldn't read music or play piano, but she found people to write out lead sheets. Some tunes were shtick—a calypso number she got to Latin bandleader Desi Arnaz, a Yiddish-titled song the great jazz bandleader Lionel Hampton took, though neither was recorded then—and some were verging on what twenty years later would be called soul music. "I *liked* what I wrote," she says. "That gave me the strength to go after it. I'd go to the backstages, if there was someone there who recorded. I'd knock on the door, introduce myself, tell them I had a song I thought was good for them, sing it to them. I went to the Hippodrome, the Century. I went to the Royal"—the heart of black night life, Baltimore's version of the Apollo, except that in Baltimore there were no white hipsters or slummers in the audience, just a pretty white girl backstage who said she wrote songs.

Looking to get a record made, Chessler went from one person to another. A disc jockey sent her to Martha Tilton, a singer with the Benny Goodman band; she provided contacts in New York, in the Brill Building, the legendary center of the American music business—Tin Pan Alley. The result was "Tell Me So," Chessler's first recorded song, cut by Savannah Churchill, a leading black jazz singer known for her work with bandleader Benny Carter.

The treatment was sterile, and the disc didn't move. Chessler knew the song had more life in it; it was one of the first to really distill the personal disasters she was still trying to escape. She recites the opening lines today in plain speech, like an argument she means to settle: "If you don't love me, *tell me so*. Don't tell other people—*I'm* the one to know." She went backstage at the Royal and sang the song to Dinah Washington, then on the verge of the long string of hits that would make her the preeminent female R & B singer in the years before Aretha Franklin. Washington's recording was stronger, but the composition would not truly flower until the Orioles made it a Number One R & B hit in 1949. Their version was slow and aching—a tremendous emotional momentum building throughout the performance, and never let loose.

Chessler was now a small name in Baltimore: a local girl whose tune you could actually hear on the radio. One evening she was home with her mother, and the phone rang: a man named Abe Schaeffer, saying he'd heard her name on the radio, that Chessler knew his sister-in-law Thelma, that he had five guys who wanted him to manage them, he'd made demos, he didn't know what to do with them—could she help? Would she listen?

The Vibranaires sang over the telephone. "I heard Sonny Til," Chessler says with bright eyes and a warm smile. "'Two Loves Have I.' He was *so* good—and the harmony behind him. So *clear*. They already had a style. My mind was working already: no way I wasn't going to work with them."

Schaeffer and Chessler worked together briefly, but she soon outdistanced him, and both he and the group realized the show was hers to run. She found the Vibranaires work in local clubs for little money, for exposure—*off* Pennsylvania Avenue. She was aiming for the mainstream, wherever it was. She went to New York, got a line on a man who could supposedly get you on the weekly *Arthur Godfrey's Talent Scouts,* a competition show, the premier radio showcase in the U.S.A.; the connection worked. She borrowed money from her lawyer and got the group to Manhattan—where, singing a standard called "Exactly like You," they lost to the blind British pianist George Shearing and a Swedish soprano. After the Godfrey show logged five thousand calls and telegrams from all over the country—blacks and whites, young and old—protesting a travesty of musical justice, the group was called back to appear on the less prestigious daily *Chesterfield Show;* still, they went home to Baltimore penniless. "They went back to their jobs," Chessler says, "and I went back to mine." She was a saleswoman at a place called Kitty Kelly Shoes.

Traveling as always with her mother—on the Orioles' first tours, through the South and up and down the East Coast, Irene Chessler would be all but a second manager until her death, in 1950—Chessler soon headed back to New York. Working on the kind of luck you make for yourself—a luck that's equal parts nerve, will, brains, talent, charm, and bravery—the two women went for dinner at Lindy's, show business central, "sharing a sandwich, sitting there all night, just in awe of the people coming in, all names you recognized, and at the next table were two men." One was Lee Tully, a comedian; one was Sid DeMay, a record man.

Chessler left with the names of people to see at National, the Ravens' label, and Jubilee, a smaller outfit run by a man named Jerry Blaine. Because he didn't have a vocal group she went to him first, got him to listen to the Schaeffer demos. "He was a very big guy—and his eyes got all misty," Chessler says. "I was watching him." She made the deal, after talking Blaine up from zero to three cents a single for the group. Blaine renamed them the Orioles—no one had really liked the snazzy meaninglessness of Vibranaires—and contrived a new label for them, the wonderfully titled It's a Natural (though he bumped them back to Jubilee when the National label complained that "Natural" was too close to its trademark, as if you could trademark phonics). On 21 August 1948, It's a Natural released the Orioles' first record, Chessler's "It's Too Soon to Know," backed by a quickie Chessler ditty called "Barbara Lee." Willie Bryant, a black DJ who with his white partner, Ray Carroll, had the late-night shift on WHOM, broadcasting out of a storefront in Harlem, put on "It's Too Soon to Know." "The phones started ringing," Chessler says. "I don't think they ever took it off."

"It's Too Soon to Know" was like Elvis Presley's "That's All Right (Mama)," Aretha Franklin's "I Never Loved a Man (The Way I Love You)," Nirvana's "Smells like Teen Spirit"—a shock, a dead-in-your-tracks what *is* that?—a sound that was stylistically confusing and emotionally undeniable.

Jerry Leiber, who with Mike Stoller, his songwriting and producing partner, helped define rock 'n' roll in the 1950s—with the Coasters, with "Hound Dog" and "Jailhouse Rock," with the Drifters' "There Goes My Baby"—grew up in Baltimore. As a Jewish boy in the R & B world, albeit in Los Angeles and New York, filling out a role Deborah Chessler had sketched just a few years before his day came, it seemed likely he might have felt some kinship with her. I called him and asked. "Who?" he said. "The songwriter and manager of the Orioles," I said. "Hey," Leiber said, "I stand in line—the Orioles were one of the *great* groups. But Deborah Chessler?" "She wrote 'It's Too Soon to Know,'" I offered, and immediately, over the phone, Jerry Leiber sang the entire song. He didn't sing it the way Sonny Til sang it, despairing and uncertain, as if from some foreign land. Leiber sang with his voice sparkling with energy, with long-gone good times, even bad times, pumping his heart.

> Does she love me
> It's too soon to know
> Can I believe her
> When she tells me so
> Is she fooling
> Is it all a game
> Am I the fire
> Or just another flame

"Am I the *fire*," Leiber said with professional admiration. "Did she write the words *and* the music?" "She did," I said. "She was one *bitch* of a songwriter!" he said. "I'm *surprised*. I thought I knew pretty much everything about this. I always assumed the songwriter for the Orioles was black—just like people thought Mike and I were black. But this is funny, it's ironic, it's weird. I always thought Deborah Chessler was a black *dude*."

The record, a friend of mine said not long ago, "was like a cloud passing." The Orioles didn't soar, they hovered. Sonny Til's keening tenor moved so slowly, with such caution, desire, and dread, that it was as if you could hear him shaping every word. Alexander Sharp and Johnny Reed moaned wordlessly, humming like ghosts in the background. There was a certain gentle fatalism in Tommy Gaither's few guitar notes. The ordinariness of George Nelson's brief second lead only dramatized the strangeness of Til's. Til went up high at the end; the rest draped their voices around his like a shroud. The parts of the performance didn't exactly fit and the whole was a secret language the heart translated as the mind asked what was going on.

> Though I'll cry when she's gone
> I won't die
> I'll live on
> If it's so, it's too soon
> Way too soon
> To know

If this was the first rock 'n' roll record, it wasn't only that it came out of nowhere, that it married black and white ("The giant wedding ceremony," as Sun Records co-manager Marion Keisker said of Elvis's first record), that it was urban, that it was primitive-modernist. By its very nature, it didn't fit. Suddenly, everything around it, on the radio, on the jukeboxes, sounded stale. In the voices you could hear—and you can hear today—a quality of contingency, a setting of everything in doubt, the echo of an event, happening now. The feeling is, had things been just slightly different—the weather, the circumstances of the singer's birth, the news—this event could have turned out differently, or never happened at all. It's a sense of open possibilities; it is also a sense of danger, a fear of everything closing up.

For as long as the record keeps its life, the singer escapes genre and the music has no style. The event happened once, and even though you can play the record over and over and always make it new, the event itself will never happen again. In Sonny Til's "It's Too Soon to Know" you can hear the heroine of Jill McCorkle's novel *Ferris Beach* just before she takes the leap: "I knew that I was going to follow him inside without even turning to see if a familiar car was passing or if someone we knew was walking past or spying from some window. I knew I was going to lie there with him on that sleeping bag and I was going to look through the slit in the drapes to that empty room, the windows there, beyond which the trees were lush and green. I was going to pretend that there was no day other than this one, no world beyond those trees; there was no future, no guarantee that I would turn sixteen, this was it."

The Orioles would have many more hits, on into 1953, when "Crying in the Chapel" crossed over from the black charts into pop. There was "Tell Me So," Chessler's "Forgive and Forget," the stunning "Kiss and a Rose," but there would never be anything like "It's Too Soon to Know," not as money and not as love. With instant cover versions from Ella Fitzgerald, Dinah Washington, the Ravens, a dozen others, some of them hits too, but falling short of the Orioles' Number One, the song drew a line. Nothing would ever be the same again. From this point on, in fits and starts, but with a new standard of value—the sincerity of marginalized, ghettoized voices from blues and country now confronting the entire nation, Hank Williams and Howlin' Wolf demanding that the nation respond in kind—people would seek what the Orioles had found. In their best moments they would refuse to settle for anything less.

"I sang it," Deborah Chessler says of the day she brought the group the song. "The boys backed me up. They got the harmony behind me. I was singing lead. I gave the lead sheet to Sonny. We went over it a couple of times." She pauses—so simple. No, it wasn't simple. "Do you want me to tell you how I wrote it—*why* I wrote it? Remember me saying there were times when I was unhappy?"

"A fellow told me that he loved me, that he wanted me to marry him." She was still married; the man knew it; he knew her husband and thought he could get him out of the picture. "I didn't feel I knew him so long. My mother and I had come to New York, and he had taken us both out to dinner, and then, after we'd brought my mother back, we could take a ride, and he'd show me around. And during that ride, he told me that he cared for me so much, and I came back, and I told this to my mother. So she said, 'Why not? You're blind, you don't see.' And I said to her, 'How can you be sure that he loves me? [Disdainfully] Why should he even *say* he loves me? He don't know me that well.' She says, 'You happen to be a very wonderful girl, so he *knows*.' I said, 'Aw, Mom, it's too soon to know.'"

"Then I had to go to the bathroom. We were in the Forrest Hotel. While I was in the bathroom, I said to my mother, 'Mom, get me a piece of paper!' She looked, and there was no paper.

She said, 'Here's a pencil'—I tore the toilet paper. And I wrote: 'Does he love me? It's too soon to know.'" She's matter of fact: "Can I believe him—when he tells me so?" Suddenly she's more urgent: "Is he fooling, is it all a game, am I the fire, or"—and with a verbal shrug of the shoulders, the melodrama fades and ordinary life returns—"just another flame?" "It just *came* out. Everything."

She signed a publishing contract with Edwin H. Morris, a concern now owned by Paul McCartney: a $5000 advance and a $5000 bonus. It was more than four times what she'd earned in a year as a saleswoman; in 1948 it was enough to buy a house and a new car for cash and then wonder what to do with the rest of the money. But she knew right away it wasn't just another song.

After "It's Too Soon to Know" the Orioles' career was a career. Over the years their impeccable uniforms, their immaculate grooming, their teasing, quick-step choreography, and the ecstasy they provoked in their fans—the way they proved that the slightest movement could drive a thousand people wild—would be imitated everywhere, and today it is all familiar. Their business arrangements were not imitated. Told a manager took twenty-five percent, Chessler started out at twenty, then cut it to fifteen. After a year, when she saw what was left for the Orioles after the booking agent took his ten percent off the top, after expenses for clothes, laundry, transportation, hotels, meals, valet, road manager, she called a meeting. "I said, 'I can't take more than what you're getting. So instead of five Orioles, there's going to be six.' And they said, 'We are six.'"

"They were all clean-cut, clean-living guys," Chessler says. "The best." She learned club owners' tricks and how to beat them, how to count the house, how to look for tickets shoved in after a show had started, how to fight phony expenses, how to make trouble: "'That girl's a bitch, you can't work with her!' 'Don't cheat my group and I'll be *wonderful* to work with.'" She learned how to handle Southern cops and judges who were sure a white woman traveling with black men meant one thing.

By car, station wagon, and bus, driving all night, they played countless one-nighters throughout the South, the East Coast, the Midwest, finally, near the end, making it as far as Los Angeles and San Francisco. They headlined weeks at the Apollo, toured with Fats Domino, starred in Duke Ellington's revue. In 1950, on the way home from a show in Massachusetts, Tommy Gaither fell asleep at the wheel and was killed; it wasn't the only such accident, just the worst. Chessler's mother died as the group played Detroit; she was only forty-eight.

Chessler began to leave more to the road manager. George Nelson left, replaced by Gregory Carroll of the Four Buddies, and there was a new guitarist, and a pianist, all paid show by show: now, really, there were four Orioles. "Crying in the Chapel" was a big hit, but it was a fluke, and there was no longer any fellowship in the sound. In a way, now, there were no Orioles at all.

Chessler felt the pull toward a regular life. It had been six years. There was a man she wanted to see more than once a week, or once a month. "They won't last eight months without you," her agent said. "They know you were the nucleus." He was right. The Orioles scattered. Sonny Til found a new backing group, kept the Orioles name, and went on, releasing his last album in 1981, the year he died; Alexander Sharp and George Nelson had died long before. Johnny Reed was out of the music business. It was over when it was over.

As for Deborah Chessler, in that epochal year of 1954—the year of Brown v. Board of Education, the Supreme Court decision ruling school segregation unconstitutional, and of Elvis Presley's first record, ruling musical segregation a fraud, the year historians would look back to as the mark of a new era—she went back to Kitty Kelly Shoes. "They'd said I'd always have a job waiting for me; I was put in charge of the counter, selling stockings. It was like I had never left."

Today Deborah Chessler and her husband sometimes have fun working as extras in the movies and TV shows shot around Miami Beach. On the set for NBC's *South Beach*, Chessler got her latest tune, "South Beach," to producer Brooke Kennedy ("It's the playground where people play hide and seek"); she's not expecting anything.

Deborah Chessler is a woman who slipped in and out of history—making some, leaving the world slightly changed, then disappearing into it. All she and the Orioles left behind was the expressive power of a new, as-yet-unnamed music—a power they were perhaps the first to define, and that in their own way they defined to the full.

"It was what we did," Chessler says bluntly. Ask her if she was a pioneer, and she'll tell you no. Ask her if she thinks of herself as someone who crossed racial boundaries, who challenged gender roles, who broke rules, and she'll hoot at you.

But she will tell you about a day in 1948, in New York City, when she found herself walking down Broadway, hearing "It's Too Soon to Know" booming out of every music store, hearing people all around her singing it on the street, and admit that for a moment she felt part of a world she helped make. "Yes," she says. "Sure I did."

Rolling Stone, 24 June 1993

Think We Might Get Some Rain?

I f an artist's work doesn't end, doesn't decay in the making, it can sustain a sense of history—of time and its affairs passing, accumulating, building up, and in moments clearing like a storm breaking. "There is no such thing as art history," Walter Benjamin wrote to his friend Florens Christian Rang in 1923. "The same forces which become explosive and temporally extensive in the revealed world (that is, history), emerge intensively in the taciturn world (that is, the world of nature and art)"; the key word is perhaps "emerge." Bruce Conner the sculptor, filmmaker, photographer, graphic artist, etc., has been making engraving collages off and on for more than thirty years, since the early 1960s; lately their intensity has increased. There's less of the easy humor of juxtaposition: an eagle's head on Jesus' body. There's more of a hovering threat delivered by whole and unified fields.

These are "paper collages made up of images from steel and wood engravings" (Conner), images taken from around the turn of the century. The stylistic link to Max Ernst's collages is as self-conscious as it ever was (Conner once thought of mounting a show of his own pieces as the work of an artist contemporary with Ernst, or even as the work of a precursor), but that link is far less controlling than it used to be. Parody is gone; these days, Ernst and Conner share little more than the look of their means. Ernst's collages, crowded with furniture and decorations, are nearly all set indoors. They're social critiques of the suffocating manners of the nineteenth-century bourgeoisie. Conner's collages are mostly set in open spaces, even in the wilds, on jagged mountains. At their strongest they are pristine and unbroken apprehensions of a dislocation that has little if anything to do with human agency. They are dramatizations of an uncanny force— or the force of the uncanny—that preexisted and will outlast any social construction. Often there are pyramidal shapes, or open eyes embedded in the landscape, eyes fixing whoever might be casually glancing at the picture—whoever has yet to notice that he or she is being watched in turn. Eyes that see but don't care.

In the 1990 *Fear of Liberty,* three geysers erupt in a clearing. One of them is enormous, like the confirmation of some biblical curse; still, the rendering of natural movement in the section of old engraving that Conner has scavenged is so precise the scene seems almost from a photograph. Your first impression is of event, of the real. That impression is then sent to war against the fantastic. Beneath the huge geyser there is only fairy tale and panic.

At the foot of the geysers is a swamp, and from the muck emerges the raised arm of the Statue of Liberty, torch aflame, with a giant butterfly's wing fluttering from its back like a flag. It's the Statue of Liberty as the Creature from the Black Lagoon, the confirmation of a curse now from some other bible. Dwarfed by the geyser, the butterfly arm itself dwarfs the figures below it: on the ground everything is fright. Well-dressed tourists flee. A man on horseback, a person fallen into the mud, men with their arms waving: *RUN! RUN!* There is an eye in the largest geyser, but it isn't looking down; it doesn't have to. The eye saw this scene before it happened. It saw you before you saw it.

Incidents

> Communion of bum magicians
> > congress of failures from Kansas & Missouri
> working with the wrong equations
> Sorcerer's Apprentices who lost control
> > of the simplest broomstick in the world:
> > > Language
>
> —Allen Ginsberg, "Wichita Vortex Sutra," 1966

I went to Bruce Conner's house in San Francisco to ask him about the gnostic, even Masonic symbolism that seemed to be at work in his collages, and about Rebecca Solnit's comment, in her book *Secret Exhibition: Six California Artists of the Cold War Era*—a study of the late Wallace Berman, Jess, the late Jay DeFeo, Wally Hedrick, George Herms, and Conner—that when Conner graduated from the University of Nebraska, in 1956, and moved on to the Brooklyn Museum Art School, "he met people involved with esoteric traditions." In two long conversations Conner responded in many different ways.

First he told a story about the persistence of the hidden and the impulse of the hidden to reveal itself. Conner and his wife, Jean Conner, have lived in San Francisco since 1965; they first arrived in 1957. In 1961 they were about to leave for Mexico out of fear of nuclear holocaust. They'd sold almost all their possessions. While Conner was packing up what was left, he looked out his window onto Oak Street, a commuter artery, and noticed how the words painted on the pavement outside—

SLOW
FIRE
HOUSE
AHEAD

—had changed. The firehouse was long closed, the warning had been allowed to fade, and the first word now read

LOV

So Conner conceived a parting gesture. He cut out stencils, went down to the street, and in white painted

LOVE

on the asphalt. It took longer to get away than he'd planned, though, and even before the Conners could leave someone had called the police, who had called a street crew, which had painted out the offending word—but too carefully. The crew painted the word over in black, letter by letter: not the original SLOW but Conner's LOVE, which thus remained as a negative image. Not only that: the city was forced by its own means to keep the image intact. The heavy traffic on Oak Street continually eroded the black cover layer, bringing up Conner's white LOVE; again and again workers were called back to apply the black paint. When the Conners finally returned to San Francisco the image was still waiting for them.

The occult, in other words, was part of everyday life; as for "esoteric traditions," Conner said, "I knew about all that from Wichita." Conner grew up there from the mid-thirties on, and then attended Wichita State University. As a boy he was involved with the local magicians' society, and learned the techniques of illusion; from the early 1950s he remembers an ecstatic mystical lecture by L. Ron Hubbard, who for a time based the nascent Church of Scientology in the town. More to the point, Conner's grandfather was a thirty-third–degree Mason, privy to anagogic ceremonies and cryptic handshakes. A sense of great and ancient secrets was part of Conner's family life; as we talked, he brought out his grandfather's copy of the classic Manly P. Hall compendium *The Secret Teachings of All Ages—An Encyclopedic Outline of Masonic, Hermetic, Qabbalistic, and Rosicrucian Symbolical*

Philosophy: Being an Interpretation of the Secret Teachings Concealed within the Rituals, Allegories and Mysteries of All Ages. Throughout the book are crude illustrations of mythological and fantastic figures—illustrations that, as revisioned with infinite care and patience by a boy grown up, changed into Conner's engraving collages as surely as did any by Max Ernst. Conner's pieces can cast spells; the pictures in the big mystical book merely pretend to, but you can imagine that this is where the primeval urge to cast a spell became Conner's own.

There was as well the conviction that spells had already been cast. When Conner was growing up in Wichita, he says, it seemed to him apparent that "in the adult world, and in school, words were weapons. I learned to distrust words. I placed my bet on vision." There is a signal memory from early childhood: Conner's father is out in the front yard. A neighbor comes by. Conner tells the story as if it unfolded the hour before, the dialogue seamless: "Hi, Joe." "Hi, Nick." "How're you doing." "I'm doing fine." "Great day, isn't it." "Sure is." "Think we might get some rain?" "Could be." "How's the wife?" "Real good." "Well, gotta go now." "Well, see you." "See you."

"I was amazed," Conner says, grinning. "I was *suspicious*. I thought, kids don't talk like this! They've got to be hiding things from us! Conversations like this have got to be a *code*."

Secrets

> Turn right next corner
> > *The Biggest Little Town in Kansas*
> > *Macpherson*
> —Allen Ginsberg, "Wichita Vortex Sutra"

When Conner was born, in McPherson, Kansas, in 1933, the world might have thought it knew the likes of Kansas best through the persona of Midwestern booster George F. Babbitt, the antihero of Sinclair Lewis's 1922 satirical novel. But less than sixty years had passed since the last Indian raids—or the heyday of Dodge City, with Wyatt Earp, formerly sheriff in Wichita, Bat Masterson, Luke Short, and Doc Holliday striding cool in the shadow of Boot Hill. Earp died only four years before Conner was born; in 1933 there were still people who remembered "Bleeding Kansas," the years when the territory was torn apart by pro- and antislavery guerrillas—from the would-be prophet John Brown, who killed five in the Pottawatomie Creek Massacre in 1856, to the fiend William Quantrill, whose attack on Lawrence in 1863 left the town burning and 180 men dead in the streets. If Kansas historian Kenneth S. Davis is right when he says that "the most interesting and significant fact" about this legacy is that it "had so little penetrative or shaping impact upon the essential, the permanent Kansas mind or character," he can be right only on the surface. One perhaps thinks less of Babbitt than of all that had to be repressed for him to come to life, or of the shapes an "essential, permanent" Kansas culture forced—or sparked—some inner lives to take. Reading Davis, I thought of Babbitt, but also for the first time in twenty years of *The Adventures of Phoebe Zeit-geist*—a 1968 comic serial by Michael O'Donoghue and Frank Springer—and of the cabal of Plains States satanists loose in its panels.

Beneath an ordinary-looking bank is their "dread Temple of Necrophilia," entered only by means of awful incantations and strange hand gestures, where "torchlit grottos" hold "preserved corpses . . . caught at the peak of erotic frenzy," one of them with an "electric motor designed to simulate the throes of ecstasy installed in her pelvis. Known as 'Our Lady of Perpetual Orgasm,' she has not ceased gyrating since she was turned on in 1911 . . ." Or, as Conner put it in college, when in 1955 he recast a Les Baxter pop hit called "Wake the Town and Tell the People" into an incantation of his own, a song he still sings happily:

> Burn the town and kill the people
> Disembowel Parson Brown
> Hang the mayor from the steeple
> Tear the jailhouse down
> Rape the nuns at old St. Mary's
> Crucify the PTA
> We'll get stinking drunk at Harry's
> And kill ourselves on Christmas Day

A morbid fantasy, sophomoric humor—and for anyone attuned to what was hidden, real enough. When Conner began working in San Francisco in the late fifties, humor and morbidity found a field in assemblage, in the fluid sculptures that, along with George Herms and Wallace Berman in Los Angeles, he made out of found objects (or "lost objects"), anything from junk picked up on the street to nylon stockings a friend might be ready to throw out. Humor, morbidity—the mix was never stable.

The pieces weren't meant to be stable. Conner saw them not as finished objects but as process, as events that could be added to, altered, that were in some sense alive, and often they looked it, even though they also often looked like dead animals. When his assemblages began to be bought and, so to speak, killed—hidden away in the bowels of museums or archives—Conner lost heart for them. He took his photos of the works—the only proof he had, in some cases, that they had ever existed—tore the photos into pieces, and returned the pieces to the streets where the works had come from in the first place.

One of the assemblages that went missing was the 1960 *Black Dahlia*. When in 1961 Conner sent it on consignment to Walter Hopps at the Ferus Gallery in Los Angeles, he announced its imminent arrival with a postcard addressed to "Mr. Necro-Phil." "I remembered the winter of '47," Hopps says today, "when the whole Elizabeth Short thing hit the papers." He bought the piece, and it has not been seen in public since.

Elizabeth Short, "The Black Dahlia," was a movie hopeful who had turned to prostitution. Her body was found in Los Angeles in a vacant lot, burned and slashed and mutilated, cut in two at the waist, eviscerated and drained of blood. The city put 250 cops on the case, which was never solved. Conner's version is a dream of the event, as if just before the fact—all motive and portent, no act.

The guts of the assemblage are crammed inside a stocking. The scene that is made seems set under water, as if this were not only the Black Dahlia but the first corpse in Raymond Chandler's *The Lady in the Lake*. The elongated shape of the piece can give it a phallic cast; if you see it that way, what otherwise might look like seaweed looks like scrofula or the leavings of syphilis. The whole bottom two-thirds of the thing is dank, seemingly in motion, decomposing, with every recognizable part-object a surprise: bits of a Sunday comic strip, feathers for evening wear, the edge of a razor blade, an old, Oriental-looking death's-head tattoo. At the top, with black and silver sequins along one side and a nail through her back, is the woman, naked. Her buttocks are pocked by pin marks; there is a strip of black cloth around her waist, as if to mark the spot where her body will be severed. But such language gets nowhere with the aura that rises from the work like perfume.

What is most shocking about *Black Dahlia* is not its horror, which is clear and irreducible, but its stillness, its peacefulness. The woman—an image from a sex magazine—is waiting. As she lies on her stomach, the expression on her face, turned to one side, is unreadable: patient, accepting, doped, perhaps just thoughtful. She seems close enough to touch and a million miles away. There are secrets here; it isn't clear that they are hers, or even the artist's, or the killer's. *Black Dahlia* hangs from its fraying cord; what is heaviest is its quality of suspension, of morals or limits.

Elegy

Conner's 1992 engraving collage *Picture Window* has no Masonic eye winking in its shadows. Instead, echoing the outlines of a one-inch square and of two Giza pyramids, one large, one small, along the right side of its base, the modest, almost perfectly square piece has one big eye, right at its heart: the recessed square that is also a door.

"We're on the *surface* of a field of consciousness that pops up and looks at itself," Conner says. "From a human point of view, that consciousness is being entertained. . . . When I do these collages, and those little eyes appear, they're like this field, this undifferentiated field that has imposed itself on us. It pops up and looks around. You don't know what it's thinking—you don't know," Conner laughs, "what *other people* are thinking!"

"So the eyes for me represent," Conner said finally, "the eyes that are traveling through the environment, looking at it, that happen to just settle down—it's almost as if they were my eyes, sometimes."

The modesty, or self-effacement, of those last words is striking, but so is the self-effacement of *Picture Window,* or the artist's disappearance into it. Unlike Conner's other collages, *Picture Window* has no plainly defined objects in it; it is not a seamless field, but scored with borders, which make shapes that hold discrete wisps of imagery not precisely congruent with those around them. It's a picture of drift, a collage of air, though sometimes what first are clouds settle in as earth and trees, then lift off again.

Looking, you might think of Seurat, Monet—a severe yet ethereal Impressionism. But the work is also coming toward you from the edges of a Turner, and from the distances in Caspar David Friedrich's *Wanderer above the Mists*—without the intellectual in that painting, his mountaintop contemplation. His presence is somehow absorbed but not dissolved by the natural features in *Picture Window,* so that those features as such now contain his consciousness, or intent, or will—it's impossible to say.

The longer you look at *Picture Window,* the more you have the feeling you are being looked at. This is a power piece: by the act of watching you set its component parts in motion, but the recessed door at its center, the picture window, doesn't move. The work is a magic lamp, spectral and absorbing: I mean that it can make the viewer feel like a specter, and that it can absorb the viewer. Scribbled in my notes: "This piece is evil."

What I remember in my chest, though, is a swirling sensation, a flood of pleasure, the smile of oblivion. After a time, the aura fades, of course; you might feel that what you see is only a veneer, a mask, almost literally a smokescreen over whatever it is that's truly there. And part of what is there is no more than the momentary perfection of a chosen medium, a perfection that now leaves the form itself open and unsatisfied, ready for the next act, the ground now cleared, its harvest proof that no histories are ever finished. As in three more lines from Allen Ginsberg's Kansas poem: "I here declare the end of the War! Ancient day's Illusion!— / and pronounce words beginning my own millennium."

Sources

Films are listed by title. Recordings by one artist or group are listed by performer; recordings by various artists are listed by title.

Agee, James, and Walker Evans. *Let Us Now Praise Famous Men: Three Tenant Families* (1941). New York: Ballantine, 1966. In 1989, to coincide with the publication of Dale Maharidge and Michael Williamson's *And Their Children after Them,* Houghton Mifflin reissued *Let Us Now Praise Famous Men* as a trade paperback. Despite a good new introduction by John Hersey, it was like a bad CD reissue of a classic LP that didn't need to be remixed, with Evans's photographs printed as high-toned glossies—much too dark and with a noticeable lack of focus.

All You Need Is Cash. Directed by Gary Weis; written by Eric Idle. 1978. Released 1980 as *The Rutles: All You Need Is Cash* (Pacific Arts Video).

Ambler, Eric. *Background to Danger.* London: Hodder & Stoughton (as *Uncommon Danger*) and New York: Knopf, 1937.

——— *Cause for Alarm.* London: Hodder & Stoughton and New York: Knopf, 1938.

——— *A Coffin for Dimitrios.* London: Hodder & Stoughton (as *The Mask of Dimitrios*) and New York: Knopf, 1939. My piece "The Mask of Dimitrios" appears, in somewhat different form, as the introduction to the 1990 Carroll & Graf edition.

———— *The Dark Frontier.* London: Hodder & Stoughton, 1936.

———— *Epitaph for a Spy.* London: Hodder & Stoughton, 1938, and New York: Knopf (rev. version), 1952.

———— *Here Lies: An Autobiography.* London: Weidenfeld & Nicolson and New York: Farrar Straus Giroux, 1985.

———— *Journey into Fear.* London: Hodder & Stoughton and New York: Knopf, 1940.

———— *Judgment on Deltchev.* London: Hodder & Stoughton and New York: Knopf, 1951.

American Hot Wax. Directed by Floyd Mutrux; written by John Kaye. Paramount, 1978.

Amnesty International. *Report on Torture.* New York: Farrar Straus & Giroux, 1975.

Arendt, Hannah. *Eichmann in Jerusalem: A Report on the Banality of Evil* (1963). Rev. ed. New York: Viking, 1965.

———— *On Revolution.* New York: Viking, 1963.

Beat Generation, The. Produced by James Austin with Stephen Ronan and Gordon Skene (Rhino Word Beat, 1992).

Benjamin, Walter. *Briefe, Vol. 1, 1910–1928.* Frankfurt am Main: Suhrkamp Verlag, 1966. The letter of 9 December 1923 quoted on p. 241 was translated by Rodney Livingstone.

———— "The Work of Art in the Age of Mechanical Reproduction" (1936), in *Reflections,* ed. Peter Demetz. Translated from the German by Edmund Jephcott. New York: Harcourt Brace Jovanovich, 1971.

Berger, John. *The Success and Failure of Picasso.* Harmondsworth, Eng: Penguin, 1965, and New York: Penguin, 1980.

Bland, Bobby "Blue." "St. James Infirmary," on *Two Steps from the Blues* (Duke, 1960). Reissued on *Turn on Your Love Light: The Duke Recordings, Vol. 2* (Duke/MCA, 1994).

Bloom, Harold. *The Book of J.* Translated from the Hebrew by David Rosenberg, interpreted by Bloom. New York: Grove Weidenfeld, 1990.

Blum, Howard. *Wanted! The Search for Nazis in America.* New York: Quadrangle, 1977.

Booth, Stanley. *Dance with the Devil: The Rolling Stones and Their Times.* New York: Random House, 1984, and London: Heinemann, 1985, as *The True Adventures of the Rolling Stones.*

Brown, Norman O. "Dionysus in 1990," in *Apocalypse and/or Meta-morphosis*. Berkeley: University of California Press, 1991. See also "Apocalypse: The Place of Mystery in the Life of the Mind," *Harper's*, May 1961, collected in Loren Baritz, ed., *Sources of the American Mind*, vol. 1 (New York: John Wiley, 1966).

Brown, Richard "Rabbit." "James Alley Blues" (1927). Collected on Harry Smith, comp., *Anthology of American Folk Music, Volume Three: Songs* (Folkways, 1952) and on *Country Blues: The First Generation: Papa Harvey Hull and Long Cleve Reed, Richard "Rabbit" Brown, Complete Recordings* (Matchbox, U.K.).

Calasso, Roberto. *The Ruin of Kasch*. Translation by William Weaver and Stephen Sartarelli of *La rovina di Kasch* (1983). Cambridge: Harvard University Press, 1994.

Camus, Albert. *The Rebel*. Translation by Anthony Bower of *L'homme révolté* (1951). New York: Vintage, 1959. Cover design by Leo Lionni.

Cantwell, Robert. *Ethnomimesis: Folklife and the Representation of Culture*. Chapel Hill: University of North Carolina Press, 1993.

Cast a Deadly Spell. Directed by Martin Campbell; written by Joseph Doughtery. HBO, 1991. HBO Home Video, 1992.

Castoriadis, Cornelius. "The Movements of the Sixties," *Thesis Eleven*, 18/19 (1987).

Chipp, Herschel B. *Picasso's "Guernica": History, Transformations, Meanings*. Berkeley: University of California Press, 1988.

Clark, T. J. *Image of the People: Gustave Courbet and the 1848 Revolution* (1973). Princeton: Princeton University Press, 1982.

——— *The Painting of Modern Life: Paris in the Art of Manet and His Followers*. New York: Knopf, 1984.

——— "Reading 'On the Social History of Art,'" as "'On the Social History of Art' wiedergelesen." *Texte zur Kunst* (Cologne), 2 (Spring 1991).

Condon, Richard. *The Manchurian Candidate*. New York: McGraw-Hill, 1959.

Cooke, Sam. "Wonderful World" (Keen, 1960). Paul Simon and James Taylor added the "Middle Ages" verse for the version of the song included on Art Garfunkle's *Watermark* (Columbia, 1978) under the title "(What a) Wonderful World," though this rewrite is best heard in Terrence Trent D'Arby's 1987 performance, the B-side of his 12″ single "Wishing Well—A Tone Poem (The Cool in the Shade Mix)" (Columbia).

Cranston, Alan. "The World according to Gorby" (interview with Mikhail Gorbachev). *Rolling Stone,* 25 August 1990.

Davis, Mike. *City of Quartz: Excavating the Future in Los Angeles.* London and New York: Verso, 1990.

Dawidowicz, Lucy S. *The War against the Jews, 1933–1945.* New York: Bantam, 1976.

Dead Man's Curve: The Story of Jan and Dean. Directed by Richard Compton; written by Dalene Young. CBS-TV, 3 February 1978.

Debord, Guy. *Mémoires* (1958). Paris: Jean-Jacques Pauvert aux Belles Lettres, 1993.

——— *Panegyric.* Translation by James Brook of *Panégyrique* (1989). London and New York: Verso, 1993.

——— *The Society of the Spectacle.* Translation by Donald Nicholson-Smith of *La société du spectacle* (1967). New York: Zone, 1994.

Doctorow, E. L. *Ragtime.* New York: Random House, 1975.

Dylan, Bob. "Blind Willie McTell" (1983), on *the bootleg series [rare & unreleased], 1961–1991* (Columbia, 1991).

——— Press conference, San Francisco, 3 December 1965. Published as "The Rolling Stone Interview," *Rolling Stone,* 14 December 1967.

Eco, Umberto. *Foucault's Pendulum.* Translation by William Weaver of *Il pendolo di Foucault* (1988). New York: Harcourt Brace Jovanovich, 1989. Interviewed in 1986 in *Newsweek* for a piece titled "Master of the Signs," Eco said: "Even though all visible traces of 1968 are gone, it profoundly changed the way all of us, at least in Europe, behave and relate to each other. Relations between bosses and workers, students and teachers, even children and parents, have opened up. They'll never be the same again." Quoted in Eco, *Apocalypse Postponed,* ed. Robert Lumley (Bloomington: Indiana University Press and British Film Institute, 1994).

Eliade, Mircea. *The Myth of the Eternal Return; or, Cosmos and History.* Translation by Willard R. Trask of *Le mythe de l'eternel retour: archetypes et repetition* (1949). Princeton: Princeton University Press, 1974.

Ernaux, Annie. *Simple Passion.* Translation by Tanya Leslie of *Passion Simple* (1991). New York: Four Walls Eight Windows, 1993.

Fraser, Donald, ed. *1968: A Student Generation in Revolt.* New York: Pantheon, 1988.

Fuentes, Carlos. "Central and Eccentric Writing," *American Review,* no. 21 (New York: Bantam, 1974).

Gifford, Thomas. *The Wind Chill Factor.* New York: Ballantine, 1975.

Ginsberg, Allen. "America" (recorded 1959); included on *The Beat Generation.* For an earlier, public reading of the poem—an uproarious, stand-up comedy version, taped 18 March 1956 at Town Hall Theatre in Berkeley, California, see Ginsberg's *Holy Soul Jelly Roll: Poems and Songs, 1949–1994* (Rhino Word Beat, 1994). Ginsberg: "I didn't think 'America' was much of a poem, nor did Kerouac. It's one-liners in different voices, sardonic schizophrenia, the tone influenced by Tzara's Dada manifestos."

—— "Wichita Vortex Sutra," in *Planet News.* San Francisco: City Lights, 1968. See also *Collected Poems, 1947–1980* (New York: HarperCollins, 1984).

Goodall, H. L., Jr. *Living in the Rock N Roll Mystery: Reading Context, Self, and Others as Clues.* Carbondale: Southern Illinois University Press, 1991.

Goines, David Lance. *The Free Speech Movement.* Berkeley: Ten Speed Press, 1993.

Handke, Peter. *Short Letter, Long Farewell.* Translation by Ralph Manheim of *Der kurze Brief zum langen Abschied* (1972). New York: Farrar Straus & Giroux, 1974.

Harel, Isser. *The House on Garibaldi Street.* New York: Bantam, 1976.

Hobsbawm, Eric. "The New Threat to History." *New York Review,* 16 December 1993.

Johnson, Robert. *King of the Delta Blues Singers* (Columbia, 1961). Superseded in 1990 by *Robert Johnson: The Complete Recordings* (Columbia), a two-CD box, and reissued in 1994 in Super Bit Mapping format CD with the original liner notes by Frank Driggs.

Jolis, Alan. "Coup de Grace." *Vogue,* November 1991.

Kuhn, Thomas. *The Structure of Scientific Revolutions.* Chicago: University of Chicago Press, 1962.

Leroi-Gourhan, André. *Treasures of Prehistoric Art.* Translated from the French by Norbert Guterman. New York: Abrams, 1967.

Lukacs, John. *The Last European War, 1939–1941.* New York: Anchor, 1976.

Maharidge, Dale, and Michael Williamson. *And Their Children after Them.* New York: Pantheon, 1989.

Manchurian Candidate, The. Directed by John Frankenheimer; written by George Axelrod. United Artists, 1962. MGM-UA Home Video, 1988.

Marshack, Alexander. *The Roots of Civilization: The Cognitive Beginnings of Man's First Art, Symbol and Notation.* New York: McGraw-Hill, 1972. Rev. ed. Mt. Kisco, N.Y.: Moyer Bell, 1991.

Maynard, John Arthur. *Venice West: The Beat Generation in Southern California.* New Brunswick: Rutgers University Press, 1991.

McCorkle, Jill. *Ferris Beach.* Chapel Hill, N.C.: Algonquin, 1990.

McTell, Blind Willie. *The Early Years, 1927–1933* (Yazoo).

—— *Last Session* (1956) (Prestige-Bluesville).

Morantz, Paul. "The Road Back from Dead Man's Curve." *Rolling Stone,* 21 September 1974.

Murray, Albert. *The Omni-Americans: New Perspectives on Black Experience and American Culture.* New York: Avon, 1971.

Nashville. Directed by Robert Altman; written by Joan Tewkesbury. Paramount, 1975.

O'Donoghue, Michael, and Frank Springer. "Episode IV: 'Liquidated Assets,'" in *The Adventures of Phoebe Zeit-geist.* New York: Grove Press, 1968.

Orioles. "It's Too Soon to Know" (It's a Natural, 1948).

Paglia, Camille. *Sexual Personae: Art and Decadence from Nefertiti to Emily Dickinson.* New Haven: Yale University Press, 1990.

Pales, Léon. *Les gravures de La Marche: II, Les humaines.* Paris: Ophrys, 1976.

Plant, Sadie. *The Most Radical Gesture: The Situationist International in a Postmodern Age.* London and New York: Routledge, 1992.

Red River. Directed by Howard Hawks; written by Borden Chase and Charles Schnee, from a story by Chase. United Artists, 1948.

Savio, Mario. Speech during Free Speech Movement, 2 December 1964. An audio recording appears on *Is Freedom Academic? A Documentary of the Free Speech Movement at the University of California, Berkeley, Fall 1964* (KPFA-Pacifica Radio LP, 1964). The speech is correctly quoted in Seymour Martin Lipset and Sheldon Wolin, ed., *The Berkeley Student Revolt: Facts and Interpretations* (Garden City, N.Y.: Anchor, 1965).

Schneider, Peter. *The German Comedy: Scenes of Life after the Wall*. Translation by Philip Boehm and Leigh Hafrey of *Extreme Mittelage: Eine Reise durch das deutsche Nationalgefühl* (1990). New York: Farrar Straus & Giroux, 1991.

——— *The Wall Jumper*. Translation by Leigh Hafrey of *Der Mauerspringer* (1982). New York: Pantheon, 1983.

Searchers, The. Directed by John Ford; written by Alan LeMay, from a novel by Frank Nugent. Warner Bros., 1956.

Seventh Seal, The. Directed by Ingmar Bergman. Svensk Filmindustri / Janus Films, 1956.

Solnit, Rebecca. *Secret Exhibition: Six California Artists of the Cold War Era*. San Francisco: City Lights, 1990.

Sontag, Susan. *A Susan Sontag Reader*. New York: Farrar Straus & Giroux, 1982.

Stevenson, William. *The Bormann Brotherhood*. New York: Harcourt Brace Jovanovich, 1973.

Symons, Julian. "Touching Eighty But Not Speeding" (interview with Eric Ambler). *Times* (London), 23 June 1989.

Thompson, William Irwin. *At the Edge of History*. New York: Harper & Row, 1971.

Toole, John Kennedy. *A Confederacy of Dunces*. Baton Rouge: Louisiana State University Press, 1980.

Trocchi. Alexander. *Cain's Book* (1960). New York: Grove, 1992.

——— *Sigma Portfolio*. London: Sigma, 1965. Twenty-six items by various authors assembled by Trocchi, including his "Potlatch—An Interpersonal Log."

Trotsky, Leon. *Istoriia russkoi revoliutsii (The History of the Russian Revolution)*. Berlin: Granit, 1931.

Wark, McKenzie. "Vectors of Memory . . . Seeds of Fire: The Western Media and the Beijing Demonstrations." *New Formations*, 10 (1990). Adapted and retitled "Site #3: Tiananmen Square, Beijing—Seeds of Fire," for Wark's *Virtual Geography: Living with Global Media Events*. Bloomington: Indiana University Press, 1994.

Wenders, Wim. *Emotion Pictures: Reflections on the Cinema*. Translated from the German by Jean Whiteside in association with Michael Hoffmann. New York: Faber and Faber, 1990.

Wright, Lawrence. *In the New World: Growing up with America from the Sixties to the Eighties*. New York: Random House, 1989.

Acknowledgments

Lindsay Waters, my editor at Harvard for over ten years, had the most to do with making this book happen, in a dozen ways. Earlier he rescued me; this time he drew maps. At Harvard I am grateful as well for the counsel and support of Nancy Clemente, Gwen Frankfeldt, Claire Silvers, Paul Adams, Alison Kent, and Chris Palma. Jon Riley, my editor at Picador, was also the co-editor of this book, and I relied on his judgment and enthusiasm. My agent, Wendy Weil, with her assistant, Claire Needell, and her representative in London, Anthony Goff, would have been ready to solve any publishing problems, had any come up. I thank Lionel Dean for his fine index.

Since this is a collection—where I have rewritten most of the pieces included here to various degrees, and changed most of the original titles—my most direct debts are to those who helped get my writing into print in the first place. I began writing in 1968, for *Rolling Stone,* and still write there; as they have across four decades now, my thanks go to Jann Wenner, and also to David Young, Barbara Downey Landau, and especially Anthony DeCurtis. At the *Village Voice,* Richard Goldstein offered to run a piece on *Nashville* and *Ragtime* on the basis of my wasting his time complaining about them over the phone; Doug Simmons responded similarly to a report of a talk on Robert Johnson I'd given for Leon Litwack's course in African American history at the University of California at Berkeley; Leon later passed on the invitation of the graduating students of the Department of History to speak at their ceremonies. Since its founding in 1990, *Common Knowledge* has been reinventing the academic or intellectual journal, and I've been privileged to be part of that, and to work with Jeffrey Perl, Robert Nelsen, JoAnn Corrigan, and Jeanine Bartolo. I have been working with *Artforum* since 1983, always with David Frankel; though Ingrid Sischy always found room for whatever I had in mind, since Jack Bankowsky became editor he has come up with ideas I would never have thought of, notably a piece on Bruce Conner, and I thank him along with Sydney Pokorny, who never forgets anything. My friend Wendy Lesser, whose *Threepenny Review* rests entirely upon her personality and anonymity, always keeps the editorial light on; I've knocked late more than once. I thank as well Andrew O'Hagan at the *London Review of Books;* Steve Wasserman, my student in 1971 and a friend since, for the John Wayne assignment at the *Los Angeles Times;* Tom Morgan and Greg Mitchell at *Politicks;* Cynthia Rose at *The Wire;* Heidi Benson at *San Francisco Focus;* Katherine Spielmann at *Puncture;* Isabelle Graw at *Texte zur Kunst;* Ilena Silverman at *Harper's;* and at *New West* and its later incarnation, *California,* where the editing was such that one could write about anything and then rewrite until one was writing about something, Jon Carroll, Nancy Friedman, Janet Duckworth, Bill Broyles, and especially B. K. Moran.

Many other friends, acquaintances, and people I barely knew helped with suggestions, reproval, advice, information, by providing hard-to-find books, movies, and other documents, and some aided me more than I can tell by example, as inspiration: my brother-in-law William E. Bernstein, who luckily for me one day expressed shock that I'd never read Eric Ambler; Sara Bershtel; Stanley Booth; the staff of Canyon Cinema in San Francisco; Kent Carroll of Carroll & Graf, who printed my "Mask of Dimitrios" as the introduction to his edition of *A Coffin for Dimitrios;* Bruce Conner and Jean Conner; Barry Franklin; Walter Hopps and Alberta Mayo of the Menil Collection in Houston; Pauline Kael; the late Walter Karp, a great critic and a great patriot; Paula Kirkeby of the Smith-Andersen Gallery in Palo Alto; Peter Kirkeby; Edith Kramer and Nancy Goldman of the Pacific Film Archive in Berkeley; Tom Laqueur; Tom Luddy; Alexander Marshack; Léon Pales; Shirley Reingold and Paul Reingold; Alvin Rockwell; Ruth and Marvin Sackner of the Sackner Archive of Visual Poetry in Miami Beach; Tim Savinar; and the late Steven Star.

More than anything, though, this book comes out of an ongoing conversation, ranging from exultation to gossip to despair, with politics all mixed up with art. As they have been for a long time, most often part of it were Robert Christgau, Dave Marsh, John Rockwell, Howard Hampton, Jon Savage, Simon Frith, Kit Rachlis, Peter Guralnick, Jim Miller, and Jenny Marcus; more a part of it than they were for other books were Emily and Cessie. See you around the next turn.

Credits

Index